f
14.10.05

Achieving Success in Second Language Acquisition

This clear and informative textbook is designed to help the student achieve optimal success as a language learner and user. Aimed at beginning to intermediate undergraduates and above, it teaches students to understand their own preferences in learning, to develop individual learning plans and approaches, and to select appropriate learning strategies. The authors – all leading experts in language teaching – base their advice on theories of learning, cognition, and memory, concepts which they explain in simple and accessible terms. The book is divided into three parts, on learning, language, and communication, and provides students with communicative strategies for use in real-life interaction with native speakers. Each chapter contains an overview and review section, with learning activities that students can carry out by themselves, in groups, or in the classroom. Equally suitable for use both by individuals and as a class text, this book will become an invaluable resource for all language learners.

A learning styles test to accompany this book can be found at
http://www.cambridge.org/052154663X

Achieving Success in Second Language Acquisition

BETTY LOU LEAVER,
MADELINE EHRMAN, AND
BORIS SHEKHTMAN

CAMBRIDGE
UNIVERSITY PRESS

CAMBRIDGE UNIVERSITY PRESS
Cambridge, New York, Melbourne, Madrid, Cape Town, Singapore, São Paulo

CAMBRIDGE UNIVERSITY PRESS
The Edinburgh Building, Cambridge CB2 2RU, UK

Published in the United States of America by Cambridge University Press, New York

www.cambridge.org
Information on this title:www.cambridge.org/9780521837510

First published 2005

Printed in the United Kingdom at the University Press, Cambridge

A catalogue record for this book is available from the British Library

Library of Congress cataloguing in publication data
Leaver, Betty Lou.
Achieving success in second language acquisition / Betty Lou Leaver, Madeline Ehrman, and
Boris Shekhtman.
     p.   cm.
Includes bibliographical references and index.
ISBN 0 521 83751 0 – ISBN 0 521 54663 X (paperback)
1. Second language acquisition.   I. Ehrman, Madeline Elizabeth.   II. Shekhtman, Boris.   III. Title.
P118.2.L43   2004   418 – dc22   2004056142

ISBN-13 978-0-521-83751-4 hardback
ISBN-10 0-521-83751-0 hardback
ISBN-13 978-0-521-54663-8 paperback
ISBN-10 0-521-54663-X paperback

Contents

Notes on authors

BETTY LOU LEAVER (PhD, Pushkin Institute, Moscow) is Dean of the Amman Campuses of New York Institute of Technology at Jordan University for Science and Technology in America, Jordan and NYIT Associate Dean of Global and International Education. She has directed language programs at the Foreign Service Institute, the Defense Language Institute, the American Global Studies Institute, and NASA, and has provided consultation on language learning to ministries of education in nearly twenty countries. She is the author and/or editor of more than 150 publications, including *Content-Based Instruction: Models and Methods* (Georgetown University Press, 1997); *Teaching the Whole Class* (Corwin Press, 1997; Kendall Hunt, 1998); *Passport to the World: Learning to Communicate in a Foreign Language* (1999); *Twelve Years of Dialogue on Teaching Russian* (1999); *Developing Professional-Level Language Proficiency* (Cambridge University Press, 2002); *Individualized Study Plans for Very Advanced Students of Foreign Languages* (MSI Press, 2003); *Achieving Native-like Second Language Proficiency: A Catalogue of Critical Factors: Volume 1: Speaking*; and *Task-Based Instruction: Programs and Practices* (Georgetown University Press, 2004).

MADELINE EHRMAN (PhD, The Union Institute) is Director of Research, Evaluation, and Development at the Foreign Service Institute, where she founded and heads the Learning Consultation Service in the School of Language Studies. She is concurrently a Senior Researcher at the Center for the Advanced Study of Language at the University of Maryland, where her focus is the role of language learning aptitude and individual differences in reaching very high levels of proficiency. Also a trained psychotherapist, Dr. Ehrman has written and presented extensively on the psychology and psychodynamics of language learning and teaching; she has contributed extensively to the literature on individual differences, especially learning styles. Her large number of publications, using her background in both psychology and linguistics, includes *Understanding Second Language Learner Difficulties* (Sage, 1996); and *Interpersonal Dynamics in Second Language Education: The Visible and Invisible Classroom* (Sage, 1998). Dr. Ehrman has provided consultation to a number of programs nationally and internationally.

BORIS SHEKHTMAN (MA, Grozny Pedagogical Institute, Russia) is President, Specialized Language Training Center in Rockville, Maryland and Operational Director of the Coalition of Distinguished Language Centers. He has taught Russian at Howard University and at the Foreign Service Institute, where he earned the Una Cox Chapman Award for teaching excellence. He has provided consultation to government and private language programs in the USA and England. His publications include *Mark Smith's Diary: Cross-Cultural Lessons in Russian–American Mentality* (Foreign Service Institute and ERIC, 1986); *How to Improve Your Foreign Language Immediately* (SLTC, 1990; MSI Press, 2003); *Developing Professional-Level Language Proficiency* (Cambridge University Press, 2002); and *Working with Advanced Foreign-Language Students* (MSI Press, 2003). He has lectured extensively in the USA and England.

Acknowledgments

We would like to thank, first and foremost, Dr. Katharina Brett of Cambridge University Press for developing a keen interest in this project and pushing for its being undertaken and completed in a relatively short time frame. Originally, the book was to have been Volume II of *Passport to the World: Learning to Communicate in a Foreign Language* (edited by Leaver, Dubinsky, and Champine), a book that introduces language-learning precepts to high school and college students with no previous language-learning experience. However, Kate convinced us to write a very different book for a rather different audience (university students who perhaps have had a little or a moderate amount of language-learning experience), and that has proved to be a good and interesting suggestion. We would also like to thank Helen Barton for stepping in mid-stream to shepherd the book to completion and for all the support she has given to this project since taking it on.

We would also like to thank the Cambridge University Press readers who twice assessed the book's marketability and contents for us, first as a second volume, then as a different kind of book. The first round of comments very strongly influenced the proposed redesign, and the second set influenced the contents.

Few authors are talented enough to write, revise, and refine books entirely on their own. Other eyes and other minds always help. For that reason, we would like to thank the following individuals who read the manuscript version of this book: Nawal Alkhaja, Debra Blake, Tarek Elgendy, Aziza El-Youssoufi-Ghanim, Douglas Gilzow, Sharon Flank, Carl Friborg, Anna Jacobson, Eileen Kaht, Hanan Khaled, Sam Lee, Suzan Melahani, Roxana Ma Newman, Benjamin Rifkin, Richard Robin, Jane Shuffelton, and Melissa T. Smith. Their insights and comments served to make this a better book. Foremost among these individuals has been Dr. Melissa Trimble Smith (Youngstown State University), who has been extremely helpful in the development of this version of the book. Since she has used *Passport to the World* with her students for several years, she had some very good insights into how the book could be changed to meet the needs of the kinds of students she was working with at the university more precisely. She also shared her suggestions on various sections of the final draft. Her feedback has been very helpful and much appreciated. We would especially like to thank Dr. Roxana Ma Newman, as well, for a very careful look at part I with the eye of a linguist and for providing many suggestions for improvement. We would also like to thank Mahdi Alosh, Tarek Elgendy, and Elizabeth Knutson for answering specific questions that arose during the writing of this book and Patricia Boylan for facilitating the reading of this manuscript by a team of experienced foreign-language teachers and course developers, as well as Carl Friborg, Sharon Flank, Anna Jacobson, Hanan Khaled, Cornelius Kubler, Sam Lee, John Lett, Roxana Ma Newman, Benjamin Rifkin, and John Thain for information, citations, and examples that we have included in the book.

Any errors or omissions are, of course, those of the authors alone. In the case of one of the authors, who works for the US Department of State, the material in this book represents the opinions of the author and not the US government.

Note to the reader

For whom is this book intended?

This book was prepared especially for the undergraduate university *student* with some experience in language learning. If you are such a student, then this book is for you. The goal of the book is to help you improve learning strategies and maximize your strategic competence in ways that will allow you not only to improve your language-learning efficiency but also to interact with native speakers in communicative ways, using what you already know to its fullest advantage.

This book is additionally recommended to current and future foreign language *teachers* to help them take into consideration their current uses of language-teaching methodology from the viewpoint of their student-learners and to assist them in enhancing/developing reflective practice in teaching that takes into consideration the specific nature of their educational setting and its individual learners.

How did this book come into being?

This book has come into being through two evolutions. It is the third revision and expansion of the research compiled for (and used in) a previous government multimedia program on learner success and, later, in a book for beginning-level high school and college students. The information has been adapted in this book for the university student who already has some experience in language learning; in addition, much new information has been added.

In the mid-1990s, the first author of this book collaborated with a team of course developers in the preparation of a multimedia course intended to increase student success at US government language schools. The course was prepared by the American Global Studies Institute in cooperation with Litton/PRC and under the direction of the Defense Language Institute.

Following the completion of the multimedia materials, many of the authors of those materials developed a book that could be used by a wider audience, including their own students. That book was called *Passport to the World: Learning to Communicate in a Foreign Language* (Leaver, Dubinsky, and Champine, 1999). *Passport to the World* was intended as a general book for those just starting out in language study, regardless of age and school grade, and, indeed, it has been used by high-school and college students and teachers. That book has also been widely shared with language learners around the world through three guest appearances by one or more of its editors on the "Talk to America Show," hosted by the Voice of America.

It was the suggestion of Katharina Brett of Cambridge University Press that this book be transformed (with a great many changes – additions and adaptations) into the current volume. She saw the potential of *Passport to the World* to become applicable to the university and experienced learner. As a result of her vision and that of unidentified readers of the proposal to revise *Passport to the World* for a different audience, many new topics have been included. Further, since the audience is intended to be learners who already have some experience in language learning, all topics are explored in significantly greater depth than the topics were treated in the earlier versions.

How to use this book

This book may be used in a number of ways. Some teachers might want to use it as a textbook in a course about language learning or as a supplemental textbook in a foreign language classroom. Other teachers might want to assign some chapters as homework or recommend it for additional reading. Still others might like to use it as a framework for building their own courses or materials designed to help students become better language learners. As a student, you might find yourself using this book in any one of these situations. If you have just found this book on your own, you might like to read it as a guide to becoming more effective in your language-learning work. For those using the book in class, the preview, summary, and activities built into each chapter can guide teachers and their students in the most efficient use of the book.

Each chapter also includes several topics. These topics are interrelated, but teachers and/or their students could easily select some, and not necessarily all, topics. Each topic is described in some detail, followed by the presentation of a concrete application (sample problem and solution). Additional reading suggestions for the topic can be found at the end of the chapter. Also at the end of each chapter, there is a review, pulling together all the information into a "big picture."

Following the summary, you can find a set of activities intended to give you practice in the concepts presented in the chapter. Your teacher might have you work these activities out in class, or he or she may assign them as homework. Some of them can engender much discussion. Others are simple exercises meant to develop habits. Answers, where they are obvious and specific, are provided at the back of the book.

At the very end of each chapter is a list of further readings. These are books and articles on the various topics presented in the chapter. They are not the reference list of citations used in the chapter; that reference list is at the end of the book.

Appendices include a glossary of terms, self-evaluations, and other optional forms of assistance for students who wish to improve their language learning efficiency and increase their success. Additional help is also available on the Internet.

Description of contents

Part 1 Learning

Chapter 1. Planning foreign-language study

This chapter explores the many reasons for studying a foreign language. It can help teachers and students understand the scope and requirements of language acquisition and guide readers in planning both short-term language learning goals, as well as lifelong language learning activities. Among the factors discussed are various options (including Internet assists, independent learning, use of a native speaker, classroom study, study abroad, etc.), anticipated difficulties, time factors, and other elements that typically appear over the life of a learner who stage by stage improves his or her language ability.

Chapter 2. Understanding the role of cognition in the learning process

Your language-learning experience will differ, depending on whether this is your first, second, or third language. (By the time you are into a third language, cognitive processes used for language learning will be much closer to instinctive.) Regardless, though, of how many languages you have studied, you will fare better in language learning activities if you understand such concepts as decoding and encoding and the difference between knowledge and proficiency if you do not already. Topics covered in this chapter include cognition (thinking processes), memory (storing and recalling what has been studied), aptitude (ability to learn languages), and metacognition (thinking about thinking).

Chapter 3. Learning styles and learning strategies

This chapter helps you understand your own learning styles. The scales used are sensory preferences (kinesthetic-visual-auditory) and cognitive styles (the E&L Construct). The E&L subscales are introduced and used throughout the chapter and the remainder of the book. This chapter also discusses the relationship between learning styles and learning strategies, as well as presenting some common taxonomies of learning strategies.

Chapter 4. Understanding feelings and personality in language learning

A variety of affective (emotional) variables are presented in this chapter, including foreign-language anxiety, test anxiety, motivation, self-efficacy, personality, ego boundaries, and defense mechanisms. In this chapter, you will find strategies for better managing the emotional aspects of foreign-language learning.

Chapter 5. Interpersonal dynamics in the learning process

This chapter considers student–student relationships, teacher–student relationships, and student–group relationships. Topics include levels of interaction, the importance of group cohesion, individual differences and group dynamics, teachers, teacher–student relations, and student–student relations.

Part 2 Language

Chapter 6. Verbal language

This chapter has three sections. The first addresses the nature of linguistic structure. Examples are given from languages belonging to a variety of linguistic categories and comparisons are made with English. Exercises are based on an artificial language, providing an opportunity to practice learning aspects of morphology, syntax, and other linguistic characteristics that differ from English. Next, this chapter examines pronunciation, including individual pronunciation, elision, and accent reduction, and other aspects of oral language production are also discussed. Finally, this chapter looks at strategies that help students develop their vocabulary reserve.

Chapter 7. Sociolinguistics: the right expression

This chapter introduces students to concepts of sociolinguistic competence. It provides specific examples of tailoring language, understanding register (style level), knowing the rules of turn-taking, and strategies for acquiring this kind of competence.

Chapter 8. Unspoken communication

This chapter looks at the kinds of communication that occur without words. Topics include gestures, cultural behaviors, taboos, personal space, and body language.

Part 3 Independence

Chapter 9. Self-regulation and learner autonomy

This chapter discusses the student's role in the learning process and how students can take control of their own learning. Topics include cognition in self-regulation, affect in self-regulation, interpersonal dimensions of learner autonomy, and the teacher's role in self-regulated learning. In addition, the chapter discusses – and dispels – some common myths about independent learning.

Chapter 10. Controlling spoken and written communication

This chapter addresses topics that are more common outside the classroom than inside. It explains the linguistic interrelationship between participants in a conversation and provides suggestions on how to handle the unevenness in linguistic ability in these situations successfully through tactics for managing speech. This can immensely benefit continuing students who have already developed some language ability but do not necessarily know how to use that ability to greatest advantage.

Epilogue: from here to there: attaining near-native proficiency

Most students will be taking a language for university requirements or general interest. Few are likely to make a career based exclusively on language skill. For those of you who do, however, the typical level of language proficiency attained in a university foreign-language program is insufficient for professional use of the foreign language. This chapter describes what you will need to do to bridge the gap from very good proficiency to near-native proficiency, based on the limited current research and teaching programs available at this level.

Appendix A. Answers to "practicing what you have learned"

Appendix A contains suggested responses to the practical exercises. In cases where there are no concrete answers, discussions are included.

Appendix B. Learning strategies taxonomies

Appendix B provides a listing of the more common learning strategies taxonomies. Students and teachers interested in these taxonomies can explore them further if they so desire.

Reference list

The reference list contains all the works cited in this book. In addition, each chapter contains a list of pertinent books, articles, and websites for readers who would like to explore the chapter topics in greater depth.

Part I

Learning

1 Planning foreign-language study

Preview

This chapter will ask you to think about a number of things that we associate with language study. With the exception of some "natural language learners," students who succeed at language study usually plan their study in advance and check their progress along the way, fine-tuning as they go. They look at language learning not only as something that is accomplished in the classroom during a particular course, but as a lifelong activity, if not commitment, and as learning that they can work on in many places, even on their own. Some of the questions you will be asked to consider in this chapter are:

- **Why am I studying this foreign language?** You will benefit most from language study if you orient your learning activities around your reason for studying the language. You may, of course, over time discover other reasons for continuing to study.
- **What is foreign language study?** You probably know what a foreign language course is, in general, but have you thought of foreign language study in terms that go beyond the classroom and the textbook?
- **How is studying a language as an adult different from studying it as a child?** You may find that your experiences in your school classes differ quite radically from your university experiences. Some of that is because of educational level. There are other reasons, too, including, for example, the fact that in many ways adults learn differently from children.
- **How should I plan my language study for this course?** This is a very important question, because planning is often at the root of your success. Poor planning results in efforts that – while not wasted – could have been put to better use.
- **How long should I study a foreign language?** The answer to this question depends on your answers to many of the previous questions. The better you need or want to know a foreign language, the longer you will need to study it. There are some statistics that show how long it takes a speaker of English to reach various levels of skill (we call that *proficiency*) in various languages. You can use those statistics as a yardstick, or you can make a decision based on some other criterion more closely related to your plans for future language use.
- **How do I make language learning a part of my life in the future?** One language course is not, unsurprisingly, sufficient for language learning, but even a collection of courses is less helpful, in general, than a fully thought-out

and cohesive program that includes such varied components as coursework, study abroad, independent study, outside reading, Internet support, use of a native speaker, practica, foreign work assignments, internships, and a range of other opportunities and activities designed to improve your language proficiency.

The purpose of language study

Why are you studying a foreign language? There are probably nearly as many answers to that question as there are students in your classroom. Take a look at some of the reasons other students have given for studying a foreign language. Very likely, your reason(s) can be found among them.

- Gaining skills for a job
- Gaining access to foreign bodies of knowledge
- Traveling abroad
- Studying abroad
- Working abroad
- School requirement
- Personal edification
- Interest in linguistics
- Parental influence
- Becoming familiar with your heritage
- Understanding people in your neighborhood
- Maintaining knowledge

Gaining job skills

There are many different kinds of jobs that require foreign-language skills. The number of jobs that require language skills is growing as the world becomes smaller. Moreover, many jobs that do not require language skills do benefit from workers who have them. In other words, having a high level of foreign-language proficiency can sometimes help you get the job you want over other highly qualified candidates. Some of these jobs are in your own country; others are abroad.

Jobs in your own country

Some jobs in your own country require a low level of language skills. These might be jobs that require you to ask repetitive questions and understand a range of standard answers in a second language. One example would be the position of security guard in a setting with a diverse language population.

Other jobs require a very high level of language skills. These might be jobs that ask you to interpret what someone from another culture really means or interact with native speakers in constantly changing situations. An example of the former would be an interpreter at an intergovernmental negotiations table; an example of the latter would be a secretary in the headquarters of an international company.

Some positions do not require foreign-language skills, but the employers consider the skills to be of value to the company or organization. In these cases, the employee with language skills is more likely to be promoted or given coveted assignments. Sometimes, too, the employer considers language skills important enough to pay a bonus of some sort to employees who reach specified levels of language proficiency.

Jobs abroad

While some students decide to take foreign-language courses because they want to study abroad, others learn of work-abroad opportunities once they are in foreign-language classes. Historically, a number of companies based in English-speaking countries have offered internships abroad, and a number of foreign companies have opened their doors to interns who speak their language sufficiently well to assist with various business activities.

More and more businesses with foreign offices are requiring that an increasing portion of their personnel be fluent in the local language. General Electric, for example, considers foreign-language skills to be very important for its employees and language proficiency can often be the key ingredient as to why one employee gets hired over another (Mears, 1997).

Learning a language to enhance performance on a job means that the language will be a tool for you to use at work. Such a reason for language study is one example of "instrumental motivation" (see chapter 3 for more information about motivation in general).

Gaining access to foreign bodies of knowledge

Traditional foreign-language majors often end up in literature or linguistic tracks. For both of these areas of study, language skills are needed. If you really like foreign literature, you will find your enjoyment much enhanced and your understanding greatly refined if you can read the literature in its original language without impediment. If you enjoy linguistics and the science of how languages are constructed and evolve, you will find greater understanding and a stronger base for generalizations if you have a very good understanding of the structure and evolution of at least one language other than your own. If you can also speak that language, you will gain insights into linguistics that theory alone will not give you.

Non-majors who have studied a foreign language in depth are students who want greater insights into foreign research, theory, and contributions in any number of disciplines. Future scientists like to know what their counterparts in other countries are doing without having to wait for articles and books to be translated or cited. History, political science, and art are fields that overlap very closely with foreign-language study. Being able to read about these areas in original works, talk to foreign practitioners, and/or publish your own views either at home or abroad have been motivating goals and experiences for many foreign-language students.

Traveling abroad

While many people do travel abroad without knowing the language of the countries that they will be visiting, most will tell you that they wished they had learned some of the language before going there. If you are simply a tourist abroad, it is often possible to get by with English alone, given that English is typically the language used for international business and tourism. However, under such circumstances, you will see mostly the surface phenomena of a land – its architecture, its museums, and perhaps some of its customs. Needing an interpreter to communicate with citizens significantly reduces the amount of communication and kind of relationship that is possible. It is having a shared language that leads to a true understanding of a country by a foreigner. Further, even the person who is only interested in tourism may still find the need for access to the local language from time to time. After all, not everyone everywhere speaks English, and unforeseen circumstances do swallow up a tongue-tied tourist from time to time.

Studying abroad

Anyone who is planning to study abroad in a non-English-speaking country is very likely to be a student of foreign languages already, although there are cases in which students go abroad to institutions and programs where they can "squeak by" without the local language. This latter group is missing out on tremendous opportunities. They will not have access to the local culture. They will spend much time in a place and come back knowing little about it.

Students with lower levels of foreign-language proficiency do not make as many relative gains in proficiency from study abroad experiences as do students with higher levels. Up to a point, the higher the language proficiency when one goes abroad, the more one can learn about the culture and achieve in improved language skills in the same amount of time – up to a professional level of proficiency (Brecht, Davidson, and Ginsburg, 1993). At the highest levels of proficiency, however – those associated with professional-level ability – additional study abroad carried out in the typical fashion of being in a classroom with other foreigners does not seem to make a significant difference in regard to measurable proficiency gain and the sociocultural value can be obtained through immersion work with immigrant communities at home (Bernhardt, cited in Ehrman, 2002). Rather, study abroad needs to take the form of foreign-degree work

(Leaver, 2003a) or instructed study at home with targeted, short-term assignments abroad (Shekhtman, 2003b). (More information on issues of the nature and value of study abroad for high-level learners can be found in the epilogue to this volume.)

School requirements or recommendations

Some programs, for obvious reasons, require students to study a foreign language. One example might be a degree in international relations. Perhaps this is the reason that you are studying one. What proficiency you will acquire in the language, in this case, will depend on how many semesters your institution requires, how well you succeed in the courses, and how interested you are in exploring the use of the language outside the classroom. Even if you did not want to take a foreign language and feel that you are being forced into it by your institution, advice on language learning provided in this book can help you be successful and gain some enjoyment from your classes.

Personal edification

Some students are very interested in foreign cultures. The more they study these cultures, the more they realize that in order to understand them, they need to have access to their literature, art, music, and other cultural mentifacts and sociofacts (and maybe even to plan one or more trips there). The deeper you go, the more you will need foreign language skills.

Knowing about the world and the people in it can be fascinating in and of itself. In this case, it is difficult to say whether the language is a tool (instrumental motivation) or a mechanism for understanding and being accepted by natives of the foreign culture (integrative motivation). Integrative motivation pushes students to bond with members of the foreign culture; it is, in many cases, a desire to act like and be accepted as a member of the culture.

Interest in linguistics

Some students are fascinated by linguistics and languages. They study one language after another, develop really good language learning skills, and with time become polyglots. Of course, some languages of polyglots will be strong, and other languages will be weak. Two of the authors of this volume are polyglots. One has studied seventeen languages, has been tested at professional fluency (and higher) in five of them; the other languages range from nascent to limited working knowledge – as is typical of a polyglot. She does much work overseas; her knowledge of many languages opens doors of all sorts. The other has worked with languages from all over the world both as a linguist and in helping others learn them. Her understanding of how languages are learned is enhanced by her experience with a wide range of language types.

Parental interest

Some students study a particular foreign language "because my parents made me do it." Parents have a number of reasons for wanting their children to study a foreign language. These include the enhancement of career options that comes with foreign language skills, the parents' own enjoyable experiences in foreign-language learning, and family heritage, among many other reasons. Even if you feel that you are being "forced" to study a language that was "picked out" for you by your parents, this book can help you be a successful language learner. In the process, you might even find that you really do like the language you are studying. (After all, you do have some of your parents' genes in you!)

Familiarity with heritage

Students whose heritage is other than that of the country in which they are living are often interested in learning about their relatives and ancestors. While one can learn much from the study of culture alone, acquiring high-level language proficiency can help tremendously in understanding one's heritage. These skills open doors to the literature and the people of the parent nation. They also provide a conduit to a culture that, if you are a heritage learner, belongs to you and has shaped who you are today whether you are aware of it or not. Studying the language provides insights not only into the foreign culture but into your own kin culture, as well. The history of your relatives and the culture from which they emanated becomes more alive, understandable, and rich when you can access it, using the foreign language.

Understanding the neighbors

Some students live in neighborhoods where a foreign language dominates. For example, in Salinas, California, Spanish can be heard in as many establishments as English, and on the east side of town English is sometimes hardly useful at all for communication. A great many students study Spanish, then, to understand their neighbors. Another example is Secretary of State Colin Powell, who learned to speak Yiddish while working in a Jewish-owned baby-equipment store in New York City.

Being in a two-language community often dictates what a student's second language will be. (Additionally, there are lots of opportunities to practice the language outside of class.) This is equally true for students who live in border towns in Europe. Frequently, borders and languages are permeable. Without the

---

CASE STUDY

Problem

Sharon has just learned that she must take a foreign language in order to complete her university requirements. She had two years of Spanish in secondary school and absolutely hated it – and she barely passed. What is she to do?

Possible solutions

(1) It could be that Sharon and Spanish just did not get along. In that case, it might be better to start over with a new language and a new attitude. She could choose French, Italian, or Portuguese, if she thinks part of the problem was her aptitude for languages. In this way, she will be able to make use of some of the common elements between these languages and Spanish: the general grammatical structure, some cognate words, and the like. This will give her a little bit of a head start and may be just what she needs to succeed this time.

(2) Sharon can decide to continue with Spanish. There are some good reasons for this. If she can remember some of her Spanish, she will already have a basis for continuing, and if she remembers enough to skip a course or two, it will take her less time to get through the requirement than if she starts over with a new language. Sharon should analyze what happened in high school. Perhaps her problem was a learning style incompatibility with the teacher; this may not be the case with her university teacher(s). Maybe the problem was lack of learning strategies; she can then learn some learning strategies (like the ones presented in this volume) and set herself up for success this time around.

Figure 1.1

second language, everyday living becomes more complicated. In some cases, some of the second language is acquired through osmosis-like processes (see also chapter 4, ego boundaries); in others, either it is not learned, or learning must be done the hard way, by classroom.

Maintaining knowledge

Anyone who studies a language has invested much time and effort into acquiring knowledge and proficiency. This is even more the case for those who begin studying foreign languages when they are young children. One reason to continue studying a foreign language is to protect this investment. It is far too easy to forget a foreign language and re-learning does not always come as easily as re-learning some other subjects.

The nature of language study

The second question that you can ask is: what is foreign language study? Some experts consider that language learning consists of acquiring four skills – reading, writing, listening, and speaking – and four sets of enabling knowledge – grammar, vocabulary, pronunciation, and cultural understanding. The former are the means for developing communicative competence, or the ability to use the language for communication with native speakers in authentic situations. The latter are the building blocks that you will need in order to acquire any one of the four language skills. Some learning strategies will work for all seven of these objectives. Others will be pertinent to only specific skills or enabling knowledge. So, let us look at each of the skills from the point of view of what it is, what the sets of enabling knowledge are, and what kinds of strategies can be best used to become proficient at that skill. (Specific strategies are discussed in chapter 3.)

Reading

Reading is termed a receptive skill; the other receptive skill is listening. (You might have heard reading and listening referred to as "passive" skills. That is a misnomer. There is nothing passive at all about learning to read and listen well: both require *active* processing skills.) What "receptive" means is that the reader receives input from a writer. Rarely does the reader have the opportunity to question the author about what he or she really had in mind when writing a text. However, in reading, a reader can, at least, read the text multiple times in order to make sense of it.

Reading consists essentially of decoding and interpretive skills. Decoding at a simple level is a matter of matching symbols (letters, characters) to sounds and/or words. At a very high level, decoding is a matter of interpreting social consciousness from words.

In order to read any kind of text, readers must decipher symbols. English speakers generally have an easier time decoding Latinate alphabets (even though some letters may look a little different) than non-roman alphabets, such as Arabic, Georgian, Cyrillic, or Chinese. There are about three dozen different writing systems in the world, including alphabets, syllabaries (a set of graphic symbols, each of which represents a syllable in the language), and other kinds of writing systems. Some writing systems encode from left to right, others from right to left, and yet others from top to bottom. Each new script can pose a challenge to a brain already habituated in one or another type.

Decoding takes many forms. One decodes letters into meaningful sounds. One decodes foreign-language words into the things and actions they describe. One decodes full sentences and texts into interrelated units of meaning. How difficult message decoding is depends on how saturated the message is with sociocultural schemata, how sophisticated the writing of the author is, how much the author implies rather than states directly, and how differently text organization differs from one's native language text structure (i.e. where the ideas come in the text – in the beginning or later, a highly convoluted and circuitous structure or one that is linear and stated up front, one with conclusions or without, with repetition of ideas or without, with introductions or without).

To be able to read well, you will need to know a lot of words, and you will need to know the grammar rules. That is the minimum enabling knowledge. You will also need to know the scripts of the language (i.e. formulaic exchanges, such as the way people interact in a telephone call or what goes on and gets said at a grocery store – while oral in nature, they are reflected in texts written in an informal style about everyday life), the way native texts are organized (something linguists call discourse competence), and how texts differ according to genre-specific ways of writing. For example, newspaper articles are written very differently from science fiction, and so on.

The list below contains a few tips for becoming good at reading. Following the list is an explanation of how to put these tips into action.

- Read a lot.
- Learn about text organization.
- Learn writing conventions.
- Explore genre differences.
- Develop knowledge about the target culture (and the world, in general).

Extensive reading

To become a proficient reader, you will need to spend a lot of time reading. One of the most important findings about acquiring good reading proficiency is that time on task is very important. In short, the more you read, the better you will read.

In extensive reading, however, you will probably make the most progress if you carefully choose the level of text you are reading. If the text is too simple, you may learn some new factual information and gain some reading speed, but you will not increase your knowledge of vocabulary and structure and, therefore, will make limited progress in gaining proficiency in reading. Likewise, if you choose a text that is too far above your level, you will also impede your progress in gaining proficiency because you will be spending too much time trying to figure out what the text means. The best text is the one that is just a little beyond your comfort range. Then you will be able to use the text effectively to take the next step in proficiency development.

Text organization

You can improve your reading significantly by learning all you can about how various kinds of written materials in your foreign language are organized. Are they organized similarly to American English, where one starts with a topic paragraph and topic sentence that gets developed by adding details? Or are they organized like texts in Persian, in which a topic is repeated several times in circular fashion, with each iteration adding new information? Or is the text organization unique in some other way? As new language learners, we often approach a foreign text with the same expectations we have for texts in our own language, and it can be very confusing for us when there are significant differences in the ways in which thought is encoded between languages.

Writing conventions

Punctuation is one writing convention, and while it seems like a simple thing, habits are hard to break. Even very advanced students often make mistakes in punctuation. Just as learning to punctuate in your own language meant learning to pay attention to details that perhaps did not seem entirely meaningful, so learning to punctuate in a foreign language means learning to pay attention to language-specific details – and to notice and remember where punctuation rules differ. For example, in American English, when making a citation, the final period goes inside the close-quotation mark. In most European languages, including British English, it goes outside the close-quotation mark. There are similar differences in the use of footnotes, dashes, placement of commas, and capitalization.

There are other kinds of writing conventions, some formal, some very informal. These can be marks, omitted letters, or ways to indicate an obscenity. For example, in American personal letters and notes, the marks xxxooo mean hugs and kisses. Omitted letters often occur in words that we might not want to say aloud, e.g. d—n and f—k. Another way of expressing the latter obscenity is by use of a combination of marks such as !*#!!. Similar marks can also be used to express surprise or hitting. The interpretation is situational. Other languages also have these kinds of writing conventions, and you will get to know them as you read more.

Yet other kinds of writing conventions have to do with the way text is organized. For example, English is written from left to right, Arabic from right to left, and Chinese from top to bottom.

Genre differences

You will become a competent reader, indeed, if you explore the various genres and how they differ in specific ways from the general text organization patterns. For example, literary texts are typically structured differently and use different grammar and vocabulary than do newspaper texts. Even within a newspaper, there are different genres: sports reports, weather forecasts, political commentaries, and so on and so forth.

Cultural and world knowledge

We call cultural and world knowledge background *schemata* (pieces of information that you know that you can use in learning new information). This is particularly important for developing reading skills. The more you know about the world, the better you will be able to understand factual information written about it, as well as authors' opinions about it. The same is true for the target culture.

The more you know about the culture, the better you will be able to understand texts that are highly imbued with cultural values, ideas, and ways of doing things.

Writing

Writing is the opposite of reading. Instead of interpreting authors' meanings, you become the author and need to express your ideas in ways such that others can interpret your meanings accurately. This means that writing is a *productive* skill, whereas reading is a *receptive* skill. In writing, unlike in reading, one does have control over the speed of production and the content of the message. Of course, where the alphabet is different from that of your native language, you will need a lot of practice writing in the foreign alphabet before you can expect to have any kind of speed in writing.

Writing is the opposite of reading in another way, too, in that good writing is a matter of *encoding* your thoughts into symbols, words, and texts that communicate what you want to say, whereas reading required *decoding*. As with reading, the enabling knowledge for being able to write in a foreign language consists of knowing a lot of words and having a good command of grammar. It is also important to know what the scripts (formulas) of the language are so you can decide whether or not or how to use them. Keep in mind the following:

- One learns to write by writing.
- Writing alone is generally not enough. You will need to learn writing conventions, style requirements, and genre differences for your language.
- One learns to write by reading.
- Good reading strategies can be good writing strategies.

Writing by writing

Writing in any language – your own or a foreign one – is a skill. As with any skill, proficiency requires knowledge and practice – much practice. Use every opportunity you can to write, whether it is in taking notes in class, leaving a note for a friend, or writing to a pen-pal. Perhaps your course work will include composition, a task that is not as often required in foreign-language courses as perhaps it should be. You certainly do not have to wait for your teacher to assign you a writing task. Write compositions of all sorts, even short stories and poetry, if you are so inclined and so talented, and ask your teacher or a native speaker to correct them for you. In learning to write by writing, much of the initiative is yours.

More than writing alone

Just as simply writing notes to your friends probably did not make you a good writer in your native language, so, too, simply writing by itself will not make you a proficient writer in the foreign language. Writing, in fact, has

been reported by many high-level language users as being one of the most difficult skills to acquire. You will need to learn writing conventions (see the earlier
section on writing conventions for your language), and you will need to learn the
requirements of various styles and genres. Different genres (newspaper articles,
journal publications, fiction) require differing kinds of annotation, as well as different choices in words and text organization. In English, there are some helps:
the *APA Style Manual* (American Psychological Association, 2001); the *Chicago
Manual of Style* (University of Chicago Press staff, 2003); and *Elements of Style*
(Strunk, White, and Angell, 2000) are just a few. For most of the languages you
will be studying, there may be style manuals for native speakers; some of these
may be adaptable for your use as a student of foreign languages. You may have
noticed (or been taught) genre differences in reading. However, being able to
recognize them is not the same as being able to produce them. For production,
one needs much practice, which takes you back to the earlier strategy: learn to
write by writing.

Writing strategies

The things that you learned in the previous section about how to be a
good reader will also work for becoming a good writer. In fact, the better a reader
you become, the better a writer you will be, and conversely, the better a writer you
become, the better a reader you will be because you will start to understand more
completely the nature of text structure and writing conventions in your foreign
language.

Listening

Like reading, listening is a receptive, though not a passive, skill. In
the case of listening, we have little control over what comes our way in terms of
auditory input. Moreover, more often than not, in real life, we have little control
over the speed at which we receive the input or the number of repetitions, if any,
we get. At home, though, we often have the option of replaying an audiotape,
film, DVD, or interactive computer lesson. In this way, it is possible to gain a
modicum of control over the input, at least temporarily.

There are a number of strategies that you can use to build listening skills.
More of these will be discussed in future chapters, when you can put them
into the context of what kind of learner you are. In general, though, listening
skills are acquired by putting yourself in positions where you can hear real language in progress. For planning purposes, you might consider how that can best
occur:

- by making the most of study abroad; or
- by looking for listening opportunities at home.

Listening abroad

If you have the opportunity for study abroad, especially once you have acquired a basic set of language skills, take it and make the most of it. Go out – anywhere (and do anything). Go to movies and the theater. Go to parties. Eavesdrop on fellow bus riders and make small talk with shopkeepers. Take a long walk with a new friend. Interview a range of people on topics that interest you. Watch television. Listen to the radio – and to music.

Listening at home

Whether or not you go on study abroad, then consider where you might have the chance to hear authentic language use around you. Perhaps you can develop friendships in the local émigré community. Look for local theaters that show films from countries where the language you are studying is spoken. There is usually some way, given a little thought, that access to authentic speech can be acquired. You can also listen to radio via the Internet. Voice of America and BBS are also available on the Internet in dozens of languages. Some universities have access to SCOLA broadcasts; these are regularly televised shows of a variety of genres from around the world. Sometimes university departments have weekly roundtables where the foreign language is used. From time to time, some foreign-language departments bring in guest lecturers who make presentations in the foreign language.

Speaking

Speaking is another productive skill; as in writing, we *encode* language, though more rapidly. We have few opportunities to slow down or repeat without sounding uncertain or foreign. In encoding messages into words, sentences, and texts, we have to use sufficiently clear phonetic forms that interlocutors understand us.

As with other skills, the enabling knowledge that supports good speaking includes building a good lexical reserve (i.e. a large vocabulary) and using proper grammatical forms regularly enough so that mistakes and errors do not interfere with communication. At higher levels, of course, you will need to exercise great precision in your choice of words and sophistication in your choice of structures, and cultural knowledge will become even more important.

Specific strategies for developing speaking skills will be discussed in subsequent chapters. Listed below are a few that you might think about right now:

* Speak a lot
* Read voraciously
* Work on accent reduction

Speak by speaking

Much of learning to speak involves habit formation. Habits are formed by doing the same thing over and over. In this case, talking about the same or similar topics over and over, and using some of the same terms and structures, can do much to build smooth and easy speaking skills – at least, on those topics. Similarly, using new structures and terminology over and over in a range of different contexts will also build fluent speech.

Read voraciously

One might be tempted (as we were, above) to say that one learns to speak by speaking, as we have said about other skills, and that would be true in general. However, research studies are beginning to show something else that is quite interesting. Many good speakers did not acquire their speaking skills by a lot of speaking practice; rather, they acquired them by doing a lot of reading (Badawi, 2002; Leaver, 2003a), then using what they had read in speaking.

Accent reduction

Listening to someone with a heavy accent talk can be very tiring. You have probably felt some discomfort in speaking to non-native speakers of English whose accent is so strong that you have to work very hard to understand them. This can be so tiring that after a while you just give up. The same is true in reverse. If your accent is strong, people will get tired of listening to you, and if they speak English themselves, they may switch to English, depriving you of speaking practice in your language. Develop a more native-like accent. It may take a lot of time in a language lab, working with a native speaker, and comparing your taped speech to that of a native speaker, among a host of other strategies. The time, however, will be very well invested.

In working on accent reduction, our suggestion is to start with trying to produce intonation that is close to native-speaker patterns. Often, books and tapes are available to teach *intonational contours* (patterns of intonation within a specific language – usually there are several patterns, depending on whether you are asking a question, making a statement, expressing anger or surprise, etc.; see chapter 6 for a discussion of intonation). We recommend starting with intonation because incorrect intonation has a greater impact on both understanding and perception of a speaker as a foreigner than do incorrect sounds here and there.

Once you have mastered intonation – through listening to tapes and comparing your own intonation to that of native speakers or perhaps through work on into-nation in your classroom – start to work on the sounds. Find out exactly where to place your tongue and how to move your lips for each sound. Many of these positions will feel very strange to you. That is because your muscles are not used to moving in this way. Therefore, once you know exactly how to make the sound (and a native speaker confirms that it sounds close to the native-speaker version), you will need to practice making it over and over until your muscles do it for you

---

CASE STUDY

Problem

Sam is experiencing difficulty understanding his teacher in class. The teacher uses only Farsi, and Sam just cannot understand what it is she says to him. It is even worse when she speaks directly to him or asks him what sounds like a question. It is so embarrassing when he cannot respond adequately! What can he do?

Possible solutions

There are a number of things that Sam can do to help him survive a teacher who uses immersion techniques in the classroom.

(1) He needs to build his listening skills in general. (The pronunciation section in chapter 6 may provide some hints.) He needs to listen to many spoken authentic texts outside the classroom – films, tapes, lectures by and talks with native speakers, etc. Simply listening may not be enough, however, and it might help him to have the scripts to the texts so that he can start associating words with how they sound. One strategy that has helped a number of students has been to have the teacher record texts that will be discussed in class later; that way students can listen to them ahead of time and be prepared to discuss them. This latter approach is an example of *advance organization* – something that is very helpful to nearly any student.

(2) Sam needs to develop some good listening strategies. It is easy to get lost in a stream of sound. Sam will survive better if he lets the words that he does not know simply slide past his ears. If he listens for words he does know and uses them to piece together the meaning of what the teacher is talking about, he should be able to figure out the general thrust of what is being said.

(3) Sam can prepare in advance for class. If he knows, for example, that educational systems will be an upcoming topic, he can become acquainted with much of the vocabulary and grammar in advance through reading ahead in the textbook or finding authentic written materials on the topic.

(4) Some students have found that if they work on improving their pronunciation, their listening skills improve correspondingly.

Figure 1.2

automatically. Pay special attention to sounds that do not exist in your language (such as the flap sound that sounds like a little of both /l/ and /r/ in Japanese or the *yerih* sound in Russian), as well as those sounds which are similar to your language but made in a different way (such as long vowels in Czech and long consonants in Arabic). The latter will be the most difficult for you because your brain and mouth are used to processing and interpreting the same sounds differently. (Chapter 6 contains a more in-depth explanation of phonemes, phonetic and phonemic difference, and other language features that influence accent.)

Finally, if your university offers a course in phonetics, take it! It may be one of the best courses, long term, that you will ever take. These courses often focus on where and why accents occur – the differences between how your language and the foreign language makes and interprets sounds and intonational patterns.

Differences between child and adult foreign-language learning

If you started studying a foreign language when you were small or in the lower grades at school, you have probably noticed that studying it then was different from studying it now. Why is that, and does everyone experience the same reaction? How is studying a foreign language as an adult different from learning or studying it as a child?

A number of years ago, language teachers and researchers believed in a critical period for language learning (Scovel, 1988). That period was said to end with brain lateralization (early theorists posited age five as the time of lateralization; the theory was later amended to suggest that this occurs during the teenage years). Brain lateralization refers to the brain's finalizing the location of the functions that will be accomplished in either the right or left hemisphere – or cross-laterally. Before lateralization, functions can be picked up by the other hemisphere, e.g. speech, which is generally a left-hemisphere function, can be taken over by the right hemisphere when the left is damaged in a young child. After lateralization, this cannot happen. Lateralization is also considered to be responsible for the finalization of the range of sounds that a person can hear or learn and an explanation for why children generally acquire foreign languages without an accent and most adults have a moderate to severe accent when they speak.

Children have also been said to have a *Language Acquisition Device* (*LAD*), or "black box," in their heads (Chomsky, 1998). This LAD is envisioned as an unseen, uncharted part(s) of the brain (or perhaps just a manner of synaptic functioning) that allows children to acquire the structure and words of a language without conscious effort. After childhood, the LAD seems to cease functioning, although the authors have heard of some instances of adults reporting LAD-type activity and at least one of us has experienced it personally as an older adult. The fact is that in childhood language acquisition, whether a native language or a foreign language, is closely associated with a developing mind (Golinkoff and Hirsh-Pasek, 2000), whereas adult acquisition of language is associated with a developed mind.

Contrary to these earlier suggestions, the role of age in language acquisition is a very disputed aspect of language learning theory. Some adults have been able to do everything a child does – pronounce words with a native accent, learn language in context, and the like (Birdsong, 1999; Leaver, 2003a). Moreover, a cognitive advantage has been found for adults – knowing one language and its lexico-grammatical system can sometimes create impediments through its influence on a learner's expectations of how another language will work, but a good grasp of the systems behind one's native language can also provide the learner with basic linguistic categories that are useful in learning a second language. Often, too, the learning is faster because of this cognitive advantage (Schleppegrell, 1987). The discussions below explore the relative advantages of child and adult language learning.

Pronunciation

Researchers have found (and nearly every language learner has noticed) that children learn to pronounce words better in a foreign language than adults. Most adults who learn a foreign language have accents; in some cases, the accent can be quite strong and noticeable. Children, on the other hand, pick up the sounds pretty much as the native speaker makes them, seemingly without much effort.

Adults, however, can improve their pronunciation. It just does not generally happen easily or quickly. Typically, it takes much time working in language laboratories, with tapes, and with native speakers. There are adults with very good language skills – you may be able to think of some famous ones – whose speech clearly gives them away as foreign because they have never mastered the sounds of the language or its intonational patterns. There are other adults who have been able to master the sounds well enough to pass as native speakers, perhaps not all the time and in all circumstances, but frequently often enough to allow them to do the kinds of things that language learners with strong accents cannot do. Perhaps you can think of some adult learners who have largely eliminated their accents.

Now, think about those adults you know with strong accents. Is it sometimes difficult to understand them? Do you sometimes feel uncomfortable with them? Do they seem really foreign to you, i.e. not someone you would choose to pal around with because they are *so* different from you? Do you sometimes have to put out more effort than you are willing to in order to get their point? For all these reasons and more, it is important for you to try your best to develop good pronunciation – and the sooner the better. Cole (2004) suggests that good pronunciation from the beginning speeds up language acquisition and that poor pronunciation not only slows down the acquisition by limiting the amount of time native speakers are willing to talk with someone whom they have difficulty understanding but also becomes fossilized, making the work of acquiring a good accent later much more difficult.

Sounds

For producing more native-sounding language, adult learners have two chores: to learn to *hear* sound differences that do not occur in their own language and to *make* sounds that do not occur in their own language. Additionally, knowing the conventions of standard and dialectal forms can help the foreign-language student develop consistency in speaking that does not mark him or her as a foreigner. Some institutions offer accent reduction courses; these can often help. Where these are not available, noticing, training the ear to hear, and practice will go a long way.

Words

In developing better pronunciation, there are many things to consider. Learning to make new sounds is only the beginning. There are also word boundaries. In some languages, e.g. in French, words are elided (or run together) in specific ways. In some languages, e.g. in English, parts of words are not pronounced by native speakers, talking informally. If you are learning a language or a dialect of a language that uses a lot of elision, you may have to spend a good deal of time with authentic texts (those writings, broadcasts, or speech events prepared by native speakers for native speakers) before you can understand elided language, even though you can readily understand language that is well enunciated. Children in the process of language acquisition often can hear and process elisions quite readily; adults may find that they need to work at this harder and spend time in deliberately studying and practicing this particular aspect of language. (See chapter 8 for more information about this.)

Intonation

Native-like intonation is another area that is often difficult for adult learners to acquire and that seems to come readily to a child. Typically, the intonational patterns that are present in one's own language strongly influence one's intonation in a foreign language, including, sometimes, even at pretty advanced levels of foreign-language proficiency. Often, the babbling of babies sounds like real language, mainly because intonation is one of the earliest features of language that is picked up by babies. Tempo, pitch, and inflection are all part of intonation; chapter 8 will explain these features to you in more detail.

Vocabulary

As has been mentioned in the discussion of acquiring language skills (reading, writing, listening, and speaking), vocabulary learning is one of the sets of enabling knowledge and a critical aspect of developing the ability to use your foreign language in useful ways. One can never know too much vocabulary. One should also know how words are formed in a foreign language, what international words (e.g. *radio*, *television*, *computer*), if any, are available to make the vocabulary acquisition task easier, and where semantic differences in words occur. Chapter 6 will guide you through the specifics of vocabulary acquisition.

Grammar and syntax

Knowledge of target-language grammar, sometimes called structure (or forms), and syntax (word order) is an equally important aspect of second-language acquisition. Words alone are not enough to communicate. The words must come, in most languages, in a certain order and take a certain shape, or they will not be understood and your message will not be conveyed. For example, if someone said to you, "the book sees I," you would not understand what the speaker meant unless you knew the context. If the speaker used correct word order (syntax) in English – "I sees the book," you would understand much better, but you might think he or she meant, "I seize the book" because "sees" is not the correct form (grammar) to use with the word "I." Similarly, unless you understand the grammar and syntax of a foreign language you will miss the message (and, with more sophisticated levels of grammar and syntax, the nuances, which can sometimes be very important, too). This is a part of language that the LAD, discussed above, supposedly helps children to acquire with relatively small amounts of conscious effort. You will very likely find that as an adult you will need to spend much conscious effort to learn the grammar and syntax for your foreign language, beginning with the same activities we recommended for acquiring good pronunciation – noticing and practice. Chapter 6 will explain aspects of grammar and syntax to you in a more comprehensive format to spend time noticing (or to look for).

Literacy

Some studies indicate that adults are better at developing literacy than children (Atwell and Leaver, 2002). What do we mean by literacy? We mean the ability to communicate in the language in ways that are considered educated. In a foreign language, we often refer to a literate person in a foreign language as communicatively competent.

Although adults develop literacy as well as children, if not better and more quickly, they do learn somewhat differently from children (Schleppegrell, 1987). In developing literacy, adults have some very important advantages over children. First, they are already literate in one language – their native language; this allows them to transfer some skills into the second language. For example, it is not necessary to learn how to read again, that is, to learn that letters form words, words sentences, and sentences thoughts. Similarly, adults already have cognitive processing skills – they know how to think analytically and critically, and they have background knowledge they can apply to reading and writing tasks.

Planning language study

Planning is perhaps one of the most important things you can do if you want to make the most of your language learning opportunities in or outside of a classroom. Knowing how you learn (see chapters 3 and 4), how you feel about various situations and kinds of interactions (see chapter 4), and how you work with others (see chapter 5) is very important. This volume will help you understand all of these things, and that understanding will and should influence your planning.

CASE STUDY

Problem

John Smythe started studying French relatively late – when he was fifteen years old. He has found it difficult since then to develop a good French accent. Some of his friends, who started studying at a younger age, have accents that are much better than his, and this makes him embarrassed to speak French with them. By comparison, his German accent is quite good, but he started studying German when he was quite young, and besides, German is the native language of his mother. John knows that his French may never "sound" as good as his German, but he would like to reach the level of his friends' French accent.

Possible solutions

It is possible for John to improve his accent, even though he is now an adult. Some of the actions he might take include:

(1) spending time in a language laboratory, completing exercises on phonetics and intonation that both "sharpen" his ear and "limber" his tongue;

(2) asking a native speaker of French to give him feedback and suggestions;

(3) taking accent reduction courses in France;

(4) making recordings of his voice that he can compare with those of native speakers (and re-do many times, trying to come as close as possible to the native speakers' sounds);

(5) using a spectrograph (a special machine that records the frequency of sounds and produces a spectrogram – chart of the sounds) to compare the sounds he makes to those that a native speaker makes;

(6) reading about tongue and lip movement in a text developed for second-language learners of French and monitoring his own physical formation of sounds.

Figure 1.3

What should you plan? Everything you can! You can plan what you want to get from the course and how you will do that. You can plan how you will study and interact in the classroom. You can plan how you will study at home. You can plan how to find native speakers to talk with who are not teachers. The better you plan, keeping in mind your own learning needs, personality, and goals, the more likely you are to be a good learner, to succeed in your course, and to meet your goals.

Planning language study for a course

When you decide to take a language course, you are usually motivated to do so by one or more reasons. Those reasons should have objectives attached to them. Just what do you want to get out of the time that you spend in language study? What would you like to be able to do with your second language at the end of the course? The better you can define your goal, the more likely it is that you will reach it.

In defining your goal, you might try using the same kinds of behavioral objectives that teachers use in lesson planning. This means that you should identify:

- the outcome that you want,
- the condition under which you want to be able to accomplish the outcome, and
- the criterion or standard by which you will judge your success.

For example, in an intermediate course, as one goal (of several), you might say that you would like to be able to read contemporary short stories in the foreign language (outcome), given texts whose authors use a straightforward narrative style that is not entirely dissimilar from everyday speech (condition), and without having to resort to a dictionary (criterion/standard). With this amount of specificity in stating your goal, you will not need a teacher, native speaker, or test to tell you how well you are progressing; you will be able to measure your progress yourself, using the outcomes, conditions, and standard you have set for yourself.

Once you have defined your objective, you can decide how you will approach the course. Certainly, the teacher's objectives and syllabus will influence much of what you do. Still, you can also do what you yourself want, if you keep your ultimate objective(s) in mind.

Planning language study for the classroom

If you leave all the language study planning to your teacher, you may achieve what the teacher has set out for you to achieve, but you may not achieve all that you would like to achieve for yourself. Further, you will have given control of your learning over to someone else. The deepest and most effective learning, though, comes from controlling for yourself as many aspects of the learning process as you can.

How can you control your learning process in the classroom? Here are a couple of suggestions:

- organize yourself before class, and
- pay attention in class.

Advance organization

Plan before class to improve your performance in class, as well as to increase the amount of "intake" you ultimately get from the teacher's "input." You will probably choose techniques, called "learning strategies," based on your preferences for how to learn, i.e. learning styles. (Styles and strategies are addressed in chapter 3.)

Advance organization (Ausubel, 1960), which is a learning strategy in itself, is more than just planning ahead and knowing what strategies you will need to use for any given class hour. It also involves looking ahead at the topics you will be studying and finding out what you can about them *before* you go into the classroom.

Attention in class

Pay attention to what is going on in your class in order to be more aware of the process in the classroom. That will help you make more informed choices in and out of class. What is the teacher doing now? Why? What are the students expected to do now? Why? What do you think will happen next?

You should also notice the language concepts that are being presented. Not all will be presented overtly. Some will be present in texts that you read or listen to; make sure you understand the key elements of the text and not just have a fuzzy understanding of overall meaning before you move on to other texts. That does *not* mean that you have to understand every single word, and trying to do so would be inefficient, if not ineffective. It *does* mean that you should understand how your teacher or classmates arrived at the general meaning of the text.

While in the classroom, the most successful students use a number of *metacognitive* strategies. The term *metacognitive* is simply a way of saying that one deliberately pays attention to his or her thinking processes. What are you doing now? Is it effective? What else might you be doing that might be even more effective? Planning itself is a metacognitive strategy; so are evaluating your ways of studying and assessing how effective they are. (You will read more about metacognition in chapter 2.)

Planning language study outside the classroom

Equally important is what you do outside the classroom. For the most efficient use of time outside the classroom, planning is required. Some of the things that you can and should plan include answers to questions that you have probably heard many times before in many different venues: what, when, where, how, and how much. Here are some such questions that you might consider answering:

- *What* do you want to learn?
- *How much* do you want to learn?
- *Where* do you want to learn?
- *When* do you want to study?
- *How* do you want to learn?
- *How much* can you take in at once? (The lower your proficiency, the faster you will experience *language fatigue*, or lack of ability, attention, and strength in continuing to speak and listen to the language.)

Your answers to the above questions and others like them can help you do effective language-learning planning. You will have a chance to try this out in the practice exercises at the end of this chapter.

CASE STUDY

Problem

Susan is studying Afrikaans. She is currently at an intermediate level of proficiency and wants to get to an advanced level as soon as possible. She is quite flexible as to where she studies, and if necessary, she can study foreign language full time. The problem is: she does not know how she should go about getting to the next higher level of proficiency. What should she plan as her next step?

Best possible solution

Given Susan's personal flexibility and her desire to reach a higher level as fast as possible, along with the fact that she is currently at a level on which study abroad experiences can have a strong influence, Susan's best plan will be to take a semester abroad (or a year, if she can manage it).

Figure 1.4

Duration of language study

Sometimes students want to know for how long they should study a foreign language. Much depends on what level of proficiency they want to reach and how quickly they learn. Much depends, too, on whether or not they will have access to the foreign country and/or native speakers; both kinds of access usually increase the level and the rate of learning, reducing the overall amount of time needed for study.

The US government has gathered statistics over the past thirty or more years, and it now has a good idea of how much time (and aptitude) it takes to learn how to "speak like a diplomat" (or soldier). The chart below provides information on how long it takes a typical US government employee to reach the Superior level in a program with five or six teacher contact hours daily and a class size of 1–6 (US Department of State) or the Advanced Level with six teacher contact hours daily and a class size of ten (Department of Defense) – class size has been shown to have a direct and proportional influence on the level of proficiency that can be reached in a specified period of time. The term *Superior* refers to the American Council on Teaching Foreign Languages (ACTFL) proficiency level scale (available on the Internet at www.actfl.org). This level has other names, depending on which scale is being used. The Federal Interagency Language Roundtable (FILR) scale (also available on the Internet at www.govtilr.org) calls this Level 3/Professional Level Proficiency, and the Council of Europe (see www.alte.org) calls this Level 4/Competent User. The differing lengths of time are not reflective of the inherent "difficulty" of any particular language, but of the "language distance" from English. In other words, in Arabic, there are many more new things to learn for a native English speaker than there are in French, and, therefore, it will take

Table 1.1

category	sample languages	length of study (goal)
I	Afrikaans, Basque, Danish, Dutch, French, Haitian-Creole, Icelandic, Italian, Norwegian, Portuguese, Spanish, Swedish	6 months / 720 hours (FSI) 6 months / 720 hours (DLI)
II	German, Indonesian, Malay, Romanian, Urdu, Swahili	6 months / 720 hours (FSI) 8 months / 960 hours (DLI)
III	Albanian, Armenian, Belarusian, Bengali, Bulgarian, Burmese, Cambodian, Croatian, Czech, Dari, Finnish, Georgian, Greek, Hebrew, Hindi, Hungarian, Lao, Latvian, Lithuanian, Macedonian, Pashto, Persian, Polish, Russian, Serbian, Slovak, Somali, Tagalog, Turkish, Ukrainian, Vietnamese	1 year / 1320 hours (FSI) 1 year / 1440 hours (DLI)
IV	Arabic (all dialects), Chinese (all dialects), Japanese, Korean	2 years / 2640 hours (FSI) 18 months / 2160 hours (DLI)

longer for most English speakers to acquire Arabic than to acquire French. The chart reflects the relative language distance and, therefore, length of time required to acquire the language to a useful level for most of the major languages (USMC, 1998; USAF, n.d.). (We would note that the categories reflect the Department of Defense organization; the Foreign Service Institute uses a three-category system, in which Category I and Category II above are collapsed into Category I.)

Planning for lifelong language learning

If your only goal in taking your current foreign-language course is to complete a requirement, then this section is not for you. If you just want to do a few courses to get a "feel" for the sounds and a sense of the culture of a language of your ancestors (but not one spoken in your home today), then again this section is not for you. This section is for those language students who have already made the decision that language must be a part of their personal or professional lives (perhaps for career reasons).

Having made such a decision (or determination), it is important to understand that language learning is not a one-course activity. Nor is it a short-term activity. If you want to become truly proficient in a foreign language, you will need to invest many years and much effort in the endeavor. This time will be spent in many venues: the classroom is only a start. Interactions with native speakers in many environments and for many purposes will be necessary to achieve higher levels of proficiency and inescapable for those who plan to use high-proficiency language in their careers. Independent learning will also be critical. In other words, planning for lifelong learning is like making a strategic plan for the language portion of your life. While many people do not bother to do this, among language learners who reached near-native levels of foreign-language proficiency, a significant percentage did, if not formally, then informally (Leaver, 2003a, 2003b).

The first stage of the typical student's language learning endeavors usually, but not always, takes place in the classroom. Classroom learning can come at nearly any age, but there is some advantage, particularly for the development of good pronunciation, in starting at a younger age (as you will recall from the chapter 1 discussion of age differences in language learning). Besides, the younger one starts, the more years one has for learning!

Courses and class work are not only helpful for language learning; they are usually essential, even at very high levels of foreign language proficiency (Leaver and Atwell, 2002). However, a collection of courses is less helpful, in general, than a fully thought-out and cohesive program that includes multiple activities, like those listed in the next section.

How do I organize lifelong language learning?

For many, the most important tool to use in lifelong language learning is an Individualized Study Plan (ISP). ISPs can take many forms. They can be in a date book, as a checklist, or in some form of diary that you keep. Whatever works for you is an adequate format for the plan.

Your ISP should reflect your objectives, learning experiences, desires, style of learning, and financial/time possibilities (Leaver, 2003b). While essential for advanced students who wish to exceed some of the possibilities of language study in a classroom, they can be equally important for serious language students from the very beginning of language study.

ISPs should also be cohesive. That means that everything in them should reflect another step toward your ultimate goal. There should also be a mechanism (or maybe more than one) for assessing your progress on a periodic basis; otherwise, the plan will be much less effective. ISPs take into account some or all of the following:

- Courses
- Study, work, and travel abroad
- Independent study
- Reading
- Use of the Internet
- Work with a native speaker
- Friendships with speakers of the language
- Writing to pen-pals (and/or friends and relatives)
- Practica and internships

- Watching television
- Listening to the radio and tapes
- Becoming acquainted with arts and art forms
- Foreign assignments
- Periodical assessment of progress

Making the most of the classroom

No two students get the same results from the classroom. Some students learn far more in a semester or year or two than other students. Some reasons for this may include motivation (see chapter 3 for a discussion of motivation), aptitude (aptitude will be discussed later in this chapter), and knowledge of how language works in general (an overview is presented in part II). Another reason can be learning styles and how they interact with teachers' and classmates' learning styles, and with the learning strategies selected for use. Most important, some students simply plan better how to use their classroom time experience and choose their courses more selectively.

While you may not be able to change your aptitude, you can certainly change your attitude. This means not assuming that you can't learn just because learning is hard for you (see the discussion on self-efficacy in chapter 4). A "can-do" attitude can go a long way toward overcoming aptitude handicaps. Furthermore, aptitude isn't a monolithic barrier. There are various components to learning aptitude; some people may have better memories, for example, whereas others may be better mimics. So it's possible that you can compensate for your weak areas through your stronger ones.

Course selection, where an institution allows it, can be more important than many students realize. For example, if you want to learn a language to use in an overseas job, you probably shouldn't take a large number of literature courses because the language of focus in such courses is not as useful for daily work as more business – and daily life – oriented language would be. When making course selections, think ahead to what knowledge and skills you need to develop in order to reach your ultimate goals.

Making the most of study, work, and travel abroad

Simply being abroad is rarely enough to improve language in and of itself. *What* you do when you are abroad is very important. Whether you will study, work, or travel abroad, it is important to engage in that all-important planning (thinking about what you will do to learn and how you will do it). It is also vital that you put *effort* into your language learning. Just being there and letting it wash over you simply doesn't work for most people. Tips on how to make the most of your out-of-classroom learning are found throughout this book. For starters, however, you will need to seek out learning opportunities while abroad. In addition to the experiences which can be handled by formulaic language, such as buying food, mailing letters, and the like, find some friends with whom you can discuss a wide range of ideas. Do things together with these friends and leave time for sharing opinions and thoughts. Students who have actively sought out opportunities while abroad to learn their language and who have spent more time with friends have been shown to have experienced greater gain in their language proficiency (Brecht, Davidson, and Ginsburg, 1993).

Making the most of independent study

Independent study can, and probably will, occur at a number of different times during your language-learning career. It is a key to getting the most out of your homework when you are taking a class; it is equally essential if you are truly on your own without access to a teacher, or at least to a trained, experienced teacher. In either case, the kinds of things that you do independently can do much to improve your language learning. For example, reading as much authentic literature as possible (including not just newspaper articles, but the classical literature of the culture you are studying) builds reading stamina, a deeper lexical and grammatical base, and greater cultural understanding and knowledge. Extensive reading has been shown to be the single best thing that one can do to improve one's reading skills (Krashen, 1993) and general foreign-language proficiency (Badawi, 2002).

What kinds of things should you read? That depends on your proficiency level and your personal interests. Generally, find things that you think you'd enjoy reading and take every opportunity to dip into them. In general, you might start with the same kinds of things that you read in your own language – if there are parallel materials in the foreign language. Carry these materials around so you can read on the bus or if you are stuck on an elevator.

At the earliest stages of your learning, you may not be able to get much meaning from a passage or a text; in that case, see how many words you recognize (such as words borrowed from English or languages you already know) and how many you can guess. Later on, you are likely to know most of the words in a given passage; in that case, try to figure out what the unknown items are before you look (a few of) them up. Rarely should you look up every word. At the higher proficiency levels, it will be more important for you to develop precise understanding; at lower levels of proficiency, a general overall understanding is sufficient. Once you have more than a few words at your command, you will be able to get this general understanding from the passage itself. Until then, select passages on topics that you know something about. That will make it far easier to guess from context; you will know what the likely possibilities are, and you will know what is absolutely not possible.

Making the most of Internet programs

The Internet has given quite a boost to language-learning activities in a number of ways. It offers access to up-to-date texts in a wide variety of languages. Most countries have sites in the language of the country, and so do many enterprises and groups within them. If you have a hobby, you may be able to find a target language site about the hobby. The Internet is also a very convenient way to develop friendships and find "pen-pals" who will exchange email or even chat with you in real time. You can also often find on-line dictionaries and many other resources (just type the name of your language and the words "online dictionary" into Google, Yahoo, or other search engine). If you are studying a language that uses a foreign alphabet, you may even be able to sign up for a free email account on a site that is located in a country where your foreign language is spoken, making it easier to write to someone in the foreign script. (This can be a problem with some American Internet service providers.) For example, for the ability to use the Cyrillic alphabet, www.mail.ru is a very good source. We cannot, of course, provide a complete list of sites for all languages with a foreign alphabet. However, your teacher or some of your teacher's colleagues are likely to know about sites, so if this is something that interests you, ask your teacher about it. You can also check on www.mindsolutionsinternational.com (click on the foreign language page).

Making the most of native speakers

Native speakers may know very little about language teaching, but they can serve as models of various kinds of language use and can provide practice to language learners. Some of them will be able to answer your language questions directly; in other cases, you may have to try things out and see how they react.

Some university programs use native speakers who are also students (and generally without teaching experience) to teach languages that would otherwise have too low an enrollment to be offered; the Critical Languages Program (CLP) in the United States is an example. This program came into being in the late 1960s; it is less widespread today than in the past but can still be found at such leading universities as the University of Pennsylvania and the University of Connecticut. Originally, the CLP used foreign graduate students and others to help independent and self-motivated students to develop foreign-language skills; today's CLP formats are more varied. Most recently years, university, government, and private school programs have begun to use local immigrants to supplement their classroom activities either by inviting these people to class from time to time to interact with students or pairing students up with them for the completion of out-of-class tasks. In all these cases, motivated students can take advantage of this kind of access to native speakers to improve their own language tremendously.

Additionally, some very successful language learners who have not been able to travel abroad for various reasons have sought out local immigrants on their own for practice and language improvement. You can often find immigrants who might be willing to help out in various aspects of language-learning endeavors.

We would add a word of advice here. Learn all you can about how interpersonal interactions take place in your culture before proceeding in developing friendships. In some cultures, effusive, warm, and touching behaviors are expected; in others, they create estrangement at worst and misunderstanding at best. Knowing and following the rules of interpersonal behavior in the culture you are studying will make friendships develop that much more rapidly. In this way, your native speaker(s) can become your friend(s), which will provide you with very important insights into the culture you are understanding beyond those you can learn in a book.

Developing foreign friendships

As mentioned in the section above on study abroad, foreign friendships can be a very powerful tool for building language proficiency. Developing foreign friendships is not easy, but it is possible. Perhaps the most traditional way is through finding a foreign pen-pal, a person to whom you write on a regular basis. Pen-pals can be located through a number of sources. The Internet is a very good resource for developing foreign friendships. It provides resources for chat, email, and instant messaging with friends and e-pals. Some URLs you might want to check out for pen-pals are the following:

Youth Venture: worldcomputerexchange.org/schools/international_pen_pal_program.htm

People to People International: www.ptpi.org/programs/student_program.jsp

We would add a few words of caution, however, when using the Internet for this purpose. Keep in mind that there is much scamming that takes place over the Internet. Even if everything seems above board, it is always unwise to give out personal or financial information to anyone over the Internet.

You might also experiment with "tandem learning." This is an attempt by two native speakers of different languages to teach each other their L1 via email. You can find out more about it here: www.shef.ac.uk/mltc/tandem/.

If you are studying a heritage language (a language originally spoken in your family), friends and relatives who live in a foreign country can be a very good source of information about the culture and an excellent resource for practice in using the foreign language. They are even better than pen-pals because they may know a lot about you and your family and may know what will be interesting and useful for you.

The same words of caution apply to pen-friends and Internet pals as to making friends among native speakers. Learn and follow the rules of culturally appropriate behavior, and you will be much more successful in your efforts at making friends, as well as at language learning.

Making the most of practica and internships

Like study abroad, a good practicum or internship in a foreign country can be extremely valuable. The difference between a practicum and an internship is that with a practicum you will probably be guided by a teacher in your home country, as well as overseen by a teacher in the foreign country who is connected with your home university, and you will have specific requirements to meet as a result of carrying out the practicum. The course of your study is, in part, controlled by these teachers.

Internships, on the other hand, are often simply arranged by the home institution or study abroad program through standing agreements with various foreign businesses or agencies. Typically, what you gain from an internship depends very much on you. The better your language skills on entering an internship, the more likely the organization is to give you a solid learning opportunity where you can use and continue to improve your language.

If you have a specific reason for taking a practicum or internship, explore all aspects in advance. For example, find out whether you have access to the level of society, the amount of interaction with native speakers, and the kinds of language use that you want and need. Ask questions – lots of them – before making the final decision. Sometimes you can get an internship or practicum changed onsite, if you find out that it is not what you expected. However, this is not always the case, so it is better to resolve all issues in advance.

Making the most of television, radio, and tapes

For listening comprehension, many resources are available nowadays. Satellite television from a wide range of countries is available in many large cities; these broadcasts can include a wide variety of genres – news broadcasts, movies, game shows, talk shows. You do not have to be in the country of broadcast; many are available in your home country, either through satellite broadcasting or in the form of videotape or digital media. Enclaves of speakers of the language you are studying are likely to have shops where such media are available on sale or for rental.

Radio and television and other forms of media will also introduce you to the popular culture (what is often called "pop culture") of a nation. Pop culture sheds light on mindsets and gives us common topics of conversation. Much "pop culture" derives from the US and western European media; it may be of interest and use to you to observe how it has been assimilated into the host culture. Pop culture includes the movie *du jour*, the latest "in" expressions and clothing styles, and the like. Depending on your age and the kind of people you want to interact with, you may want differing levels of acquaintance with the popular culture of your target language.

Becoming acquainted with arts and art forms

Low culture refers to the everyday ways of behaving that make one set of people different from another, such as shopping, riding on local means of transportation, and eating out. You will quickly become familiar with artifacts of low culture through study abroad, friendships with émigrés, and other actions that are listed here as part of a good ISP.

On the other hand, high culture – the music, arts, dance, philosophy, religion, and literature of a nation – is different from everyday culture, and not every member of a society is thoroughly familiar with high culture. Nonetheless, high culture is a good entry into understanding the mindset of people who speak your foreign language. High culture reflects everyday life, as well as the values and thinking of native speakers of the language, in its art forms. Likewise, everyday life incorporates citations from literature and references to various forms of art into its aphorisms and ways of expressing ideas.

Making the most of foreign work assignments

Foreign work assignments, if you are lucky enough to get them, can be a huge boon to your language-learning efforts and lead to a great deal of success. Some possibilities include work as a diplomat, diplomatic attaché, foreign business offices, the Peace Corps (for United States residents), non-government organizations, or as a teacher of English abroad.

Unfortunately, many language learners who have had the opportunity to work abroad have not made the most of that opportunity and have actually ended up losing foreign-language proficiency even during the time that they were living among native speakers (Goodison, 1987). This happens when language learners associate with people from their own country and do not force themselves to participate in the larger, local community. It takes a deliberate effort to become a part of the foreign community, but your language skills will improve immeasurably if you do.

Periodic assessment of progress

No ISP can be fully effective unless you periodically stop and measure where you are. In measuring your progress, there are a number of ways to assess your current language skills. These are discussed below.

After you have assessed your progress, you may find that you have a different set of learning needs. At that point, you will need to re-evaluate your ISP itself to make sure it reflects these needs. Keeping your plan current is a good bet for reaching your goals.

How do I assess my progress?

There are several ways to assess your progress. Some are formal, and some are informal. Once you have decided on one or more measures for assessing your progress, you should probably stay with them throughout your language-learning study in order to be able to compare your ability before and after any point. (Instruments can measure somewhat differing things and define levels in slightly different ways, so a consistent standard is a good idea.)

Each time you assess your progress, you will need to make a determination of whether or not you are on target for your objective. If you are moving too quickly to assimilate what you need or too slowly to meet your goals in a reasonable time, you may want to adjust your plan to optimize your learning experiences, based on evidence of your strengths and weaknesses to date. That means that assessing your progress also means assessing your own language strengths and weaknesses.

CASE STUDY

Problem
Mary is in the process of developing a lifelong learning plan for herself and is lost in the details. She just does not know where to start. What can she do?

A possible solution
Before Mary can make a plan of this scope, she needs to know where she stands right now – what skills does she have and which ones does she still need to develop? She can find out this information by checking can-do statements online. She could also ask a teacher to provide an assessment, or she could take a formal test. (She also needs to know how she personally goes about learning – something that will be discussed later in this volume.)

Figure 1.5

Formal measures

There are a number of tests that are available for measuring progress. Not all will be available to you. It all depends on what your personal circumstances are and where you are studying or working.

Formal proficiency tests can test either some form of global, that is, overall, proficiency (through representative activities) or specific proficiency (through performance requirements). Examples of formal proficiency tests are those given by the Federal Interagency Language Roundtable (available to anyone working for the US government) and the American Council on Teaching Foreign Languages (ACTFL). The ACTFL test is considerably less comprehensive than the government test, but it is available to students enrolled in foreign-language programs at US universities, as well as through Language Testing International (www.languagetesting.com). Other kinds of proficiency-oriented foreign-language tests in the United States are available through the Center for Applied Linguistics in Washington, DC (www.cal.org). In Europe, the Association of Language Testers Europe (ALTE) has established its own set of testing rubrics for use with foreign-language learners.

Informal measures

There are also a number of ways in which you can get an informal assessment of your language skills. One way is to ask a teacher or other knowledgeable person to give you feedback. A second way is to take note of your successes (and failures) in actual language use or to keep a diary of your progress. A third way is to compare your skills against an established scale. You can use the ACTFL scale for this (www.actfl.org), the Federal Interagency Language Roundtable (FILR) scale (www.govtilr.org), or the Council of Europe/Association of Language Testers Europe scale (www.alte.org) to see how you measure up.

purpose(s) of language study:

    ultimate objective:

    coursework (and approximate dates) planned:

    out-of-class activities planned (and approximate dates):

    activities abroad (planned, with approximate dates)

    mechanisms for measuring progress (with approximate dates)

Figure 1.6

Checklists are a very helpful way to assess your progress. For example, using the FILR proficiency scale, the Defense Language Institute has developed a series of "can do" statements. By answering questions about what you can do (and, of course, cannot do), you can get an idea of your proficiency level. These can-do assessments exist at a number of sites. Examples of can-do statements can be found at the LangNet site (www.langnet.org) and at the ALTE site (www.alte.org), among other places.

Practice what you have learned!

1.   How many purposes of language study can you think of? Use the list in this book as a starting point. Interview some friends who are studying foreign languages other than the one you are studying and find out their reasons for studying a foreign language and for choosing the particular language(s) that they are studying. Compare your responses with those obtained by your classmates.

2.   Let's do some work on planning your language study. To begin, answer the following questions:

    a. Why do you want to study a foreign language? Of the reasons given in this chapter, which ones match your reasons? Do you have a different one? Write it down.

    b. What is your ultimate objective? Based on that, make a list of the kinds of courses and activities that you will need to take/do.

    c. When and how will you assess your progress?

    Now, fill in the chart shown in figure 1.6. You may want to type the chart into your computer, so that you can keep a record of it via a tracking program or change it at will or upon need. This document can be amended in any way – and the categories used are not sacrosanct. You can include your own categories, as well as the ones on the form or instead of the ones on the form. If you decide to change the categories, explain why.

3.   Try a very sketchy and informal self-assessment. If you already know something of the language you are interested in, assess where you are now, looking at:

- *Vocabulary*. What content domains (e.g. geography, history, political science, everyday life, etc.) can you express yourself in? What other content domains would you like to be able to talk about?
- *Structure*. Which constructions can you handle easily? Which give you trouble? Which have you decided you aren't ready to work on yet?
- *Discourse*. Can you speak in connected sentences? Can you tell a story or make an explanation?
- *Pronunciation*. How much trouble will most non-teacher native speakers have with understanding your pronunciation? (You may have some experience in talking to native speakers and know the answer to this question; if not, you might want to ask your teacher or a native speaker you know.)

4.   Analyze your local newspaper. How many genres (e.g. letters to the editor, sports items, news items, advice columns, etc.) can you find? How is the text organized? If you were to write a letter to the editor or a news report, how would each of these need to be structured? Where do the main points come? Where are the supporting details given? Now, with your teacher's help, do the same with a newspaper in your foreign language. How many differences can you find between your local newspaper and the foreign one?

Review

In this chapter, you considered a number of questions. The answers to these questions can be summarized as follows:

The purpose of language study
(1) Obtaining a job or performing a job better
(2) Gaining access to foreign bodies of knowledge
(3) Traveling abroad
(4) Studying abroad
(5) Working abroad
(6) School requirements
(7) General edification and interest in linguistics
(8) Understanding your heritage
(9) Parental influence
(10) Understanding people in your neighborhood
(11) Maintaining knowledge

The nature of language study
(1) Developing skill in listening, reading, writing, and speaking
(2) Acquiring enabling knowledge of grammar, vocabulary, pronunciation, and culture

The differences between child and adult language learning
The differences between how children and adults acquire languages are, as a minimum, the following:
(1) Children have a better "ear" and can spend more time on task.
(2) Adults already know one language and learn more efficiently.
So, the situation is not one-sided, at all. Adults do have some advantages of their own.

Planning language study
Planning language study includes developing:
(1) goals and objectives for studying;
(2) plans for the classroom; and
(3) plans for outside the classroom

Duration of language study
Based on government studies (see the chart in this chapter), we can say the following:
(1) In general, Romance languages are more quickly learned by adult native speakers of English than are Slavic languages or Arabic.
(2) In general, Germanic languages take somewhat more time than do Romance languages for adult speakers of English to learn.
(3) In general, Slavic languages take twice as long to learn to the same level of proficiency for native adult speakers of English as do Romance languages.
(4) In general, Arabic and Altaic languages take four times as long to learn to the same level of proficiency for native adult speakers of English as do Romance languages.

If you want to learn more about the topics in this chapter, consult the following sources: AATSEEL Publications Committee (2001); Champine (1999); Council on International Educational Exchange (1994–1995); Frantz (1996); Gliozzo and Bishop, eds. (1994); Krannich and Krannich (1994); Leaver (2003b); Leaver and Champine (1999); Modern Language Association (n.d.); Shryock (n.d.).

2 Understanding the role of cognition in the learning process

Preview

This chapter introduces you to the science of learning – in this case, as applied to learning foreign languages. While we do not yet know everything about how the brain processes foreign language and builds proficiency, much is known and much more is being discovered every day. Topics that this chapter will address include:

- **Cognition**. Cognitive processes will differ, depending on whether this is your first, second, or third language. In any case, you will fare better in your language-learning activities if you understand such concepts as coding and encoding and the difference between knowledge and proficiency.
- **Memory**. Memory has a number of components. These include sentient memory (or awareness), short-term memory, long-term memory, and working (or activated) memory. Activated memory is important for recognition, recall, and reconstruction of others' expressions and construction of our own (new) expressions. Good memory depends on memory strategies and body chemistry; both of these can be improved by learners.
- **Aptitude**. Aptitude refers to the ability to learn a foreign language, much of which may be innate or at least developed over a long time. Some students just seem to learn languages more easily than other students. There are a number of components of aptitude, and even students with low aptitude can learn a foreign language by being aware of their strengths and knowing how to compensate for their weaknesses.
- **Metacognition**. Metacognition is that which is "above" cognition. In other words, it is "thinking about thinking." Being aware of one's own progress, actions, and thinking processes can do much to improve language-learning success.

Cognition

Cognition, simply put, means thinking. There are many processes involved in thinking, and all of them are considered part of cognition. Some examples are noticing, paying attention, making guesses and hypotheses, monitoring what you say, interpreting what you read or hear, and so on.

Cognitive processes will differ, depending on whether this is your first, second, or third language. In any case, you will fare better in your language-learning activities if you understand the concepts behind the learning of foreign languages.

Aspects of cognition: second language vs. third language

There are some advantages that accrue in learning a third (or fourth or fifth) language over learning a second language. Students who are aware of what these advantages are can exploit them wisely.

A third language may be related to a language you have already studied (either your native language or your second language). If so, you have quite a head start, especially if you do not overgeneralize. For example, the L3 grammar may be very close to what you already know in L1 or L2 grammar. In this case, your greatest challenge will be not to make the assumption that *all* the grammar is the same and to keep your eyes open for subtle, as well as gross, differences in the linguistic systems of L1, L2, and L3 (or L4 and/or L5). Let's consider a concrete situation:

> In Spanish and Portuguese, tenses are generally the same, yet some of the difficult moments for students of English who are studying both languages, such as the choice between two different verbs expressing to be, *ser* and *estar*, are intensified in that Spanish and Portuguese sometimes use these verbs in the same way and at other times where Spanish requires *estar*, Portuguese requires *ser*. The tendency of the learner who has learned Spanish as a second language and is learning Portuguese as a third language is to overgeneralize the Spanish rules to Portuguese – and in this way to make some kinds of mistakes that learners of Portuguese as a second language might not. Similarly, students of Portuguese can make the same erroneous overgeneralization when learning Spanish.

Another advantage in studying a third language that is related to a language you already know is that some of the vocabulary will look and sound similar, creating a sense of instant familiarity. However, you may tend to overgeneralize and use words from the second language in the third language, marking your speech as anglicized (if English is the source of influence), gallicized (if French is the source of influence), and so on. To avoid this, look for generalities you can make about the differences; these generalities will allow you to acquire a large reserve of vocabulary very rapidly. Again, let's take a concrete example:

> Many French words ending in -*tion* are the same as the English words, except for pronunciation. (This is a result of historical influences of French on English, dating from 1066 and the days of William the Conqueror.) Similarly, you might notice that these words are often the same in Spanish, but that they end in -*ción*. However, not all English words that end in -*tion* end in -*tion* in French or -*ción* in Spanish.

Table 2.1

Language family	Languages
Afroasiatic	Amharic, Arabic, Berber, Egyptian, Hausa, Hebrew
Altaic	Altay, Azeri, Bashkir, Chuvash, Japanese, Kazakh, Korean, Kumyk, Kyrgyz, Manchu-Tungus, Mongolian, Tatar, Turkish, Turkmen, Uyghur, Uzbek, Yakut
Austroasiatic	Khmer, Vietnamese
Caucasian	Chechen, Georgian
Dravidian	Tamil
Indo-European	Afrikaans, Albanian, Armenian, Bosnian, Bulgarian, Catalan, Croatian, Czech, Danish, Dutch, English, Flemish, French, German, Greek, Icelandic, Italian, Lithuanian, Norwegian, Polish, Portuguese, Romanian, Russian, Serbian, Slovak, Slovenian, Spanish, Swedish, Yiddish
Indo-Iranian	Baluchi, Bengali, Dari, Farsi (Persian), Hindi, Hindustani, Kurdish, Ossetic, Marathi, Panjabi, Pashto, Urdu
Malayo-Polynesian	Hawaiian (Polynesian), Indonesian, Malay, Maori
Niger-Congo	Dinka, Fulfulde, Ganda, Gikuyu, Shona, Swahili, Twi, Yoruba, Xhosa/Zulu
Sino-Tibetan	Amdo, Burmese, Chinese, Horpa, Pao, Pumi, Sajalong, Tibetan
Tai/Daic	Lao, Nung, Tho, Kam-Sui, Shan, Thai (Siamese), Yuan
Uralic	Erdzya, Estonian, Finnish, Hungarian, Ingrian, Karelian, Khanty, Kola, Komi, Lapp (Saami), Livonian, Mansi, Mari, Moksha, Mordvin, Skolt, Udmurt, Veps, Votic

You will encounter more items in common, including basic roots, if you study a language in the same language family. Thus, if you study Russian and already know English, both of which are Indo-European languages although not closely related, you may not immediately recognize similar words, but you can use the roots of words to your advantage (roots are often similar throughout the language family, even though the words themselves have developed differently in each of the languages). Thus, knowing that _video_ in English has to do with seeing something will help you understand the word _videt'_ (to see) in Russian. Similarly, the English word _visual_ shares a root with the Russian word _vizhu_ (I see). Table 2.1 identifies some basic language families and their members (it is not meant to be inclusive – there are over 100 language families with, in some cases, many members – but to show you some of the relationships that you might encounter in your language study). Within individual language families, there are branches, for example, the Romance branch (Latin, French, Italian, Portuguese, Romanian, Spanish, etc.); within the branches, the languages are even more alike and, in some cases, mutually intelligible.

Even if your third (or fourth or fifth) language has little in common with any other languages you have ever studied, you still have a head start because you already have developed a set of strategies to use in language learning. For example,

- You know how to figure out the meaning of new words based on the context in which you see them.
- You know how to figure out grammar rules by seeing specific forms in several contexts.
- You know how to ignore what you don't know yet and use what you do know in order to decipher meaning.
- You know the kinds of actions you need to take in order to remember vocabulary and grammar rules.
- You know what to do in order to communicate with a native speaker – both when you know all the expressions you need and when you do not.

This is just a little of what you already know if you have studied a language before. If you think about it, you have quite a full toolbox of implements for use in learning yet another language – and the more languages you study, the bigger that toolbox of strategies becomes. (See chapter 3 for more information about learning strategies.)

Aspects of cognition: knowledge, accuracy, and fluency

There is a considerable difference between knowledge and speaking accurately and fluently. For example, you may well know a lot of grammar rules and words. This information is considered knowledge. It is in the background of your ability to communicate, but it rarely results directly in communication.

The amount of information you have does not determine your level of fluency, or even accuracy, in a foreign language. In other words, it is not what you know that counts in foreign-language proficiency, it is what you do with it. There are people with very limited knowledge of a language who are able to negotiate all kinds of things in the language with native speakers. Other people know a lot about the language, but fail miserably if asked to accomplish something that requires real communication, such as negotiating a contract, because they have almost no fluency. You probably have met both kinds of people – those who know a lot and can accomplish little and those who know little but can accomplish a lot.

For proficient speech, knowledge is just a stepping stone to being able to use the language – and some learners actually develop the knowledge from the experience of using the language and not vice versa. What is specifically needed for proficient speech (and understanding) is a combination of accuracy (saying things correctly and understanding them the way speakers or writers meant them) and fluency (speaking with a normal tempo).

CASE STUDY

Problem

Jacqueline has studied Japanese for a number of years. Now, she is studying Korean, and she gets confused a lot. When the words and grammar are similar, but not exactly the same, she forgets which is which, and Japanese begins to encroach upon her use of Korean. As a result, Jacqueline has decided to try to forget her Japanese while learning Korean, as she is afraid that it will interfere.

Possible solutions

The real problem is that Jacqueline is using her knowledge of Japanese in a negative way, not a positive way. Instead of trying to learn Korean as an independent language and, thereby, starting from scratch – which allows Japanese to seep into the learning process in distractive ways, Jacqueline should consider her knowledge of Japanese to be an asset and begin to look for ways in which it can help her with Korean. She can control the negative influence and bolster the positive influence of Japanese by doing the following:

(1) Change the way she looks at Japanese from being a nuisance and source of confusion to being an advantage;

(2) Find the patterns of similarity between Japanese and Korean words and grammar that she already knows, then try applying those to new Korean communications to see if those patterns can be generalized;

(3) Analyze the situations where she has overgeneralized – determine whether there are commonalities among them that she can avoid in the future; and

(4) Accept the fact that occasionally she will overgeneralize, applying patterns from Japanese to Korean not only in cases where the two languages match but also in cases where they do not match – that this is not a fatal mistake (and often may not even interfere with being understood).

Figure 2.1

Aspects of cognition: memory

Researchers and cognitive psychologists have developed a number of classifications of memory that can be helpful to the foreign-language learner. Further, as time goes on and more research is accomplished, we gain better insights into how memory works, what role chemicals play, and what happens to information once it enters memory.

Psychologists look at memory in several ways – and at the possible taxonomies of memory types. Some of these taxonomies are discussed below.

Episodic, procedural, and semantic memory

One way of looking at memory is based on what kinds of information the memory works with. In this taxonomy, there are

- episodic memory (remembering events, such as what happened at a party you attended two weeks ago);
- procedural memory (developing habitual processes, such as driving a car or riding a bike); and
- semantic memory (remembering content information or linguistic elements and their meanings).

All three kinds of memory play a role in language learning, with semantic memory usually considered the most important, because it is in fact memory for language. However, you need episodic memory to store learning events and procedural memory to make what you learn automatic (a key to fluency). Remembering grammar rules and developing a knowledge base about your language will require semantic memory. All of these kinds of memory work together to make you a good language learner.

Attention and awareness

Attention and awareness are often referred to as sentient memory. This is the very first step in the process of storing information in memory and making it available for later use (Cowan, 1997). For example, if we do not notice something – such as the color of the sky as we walk to class – there is no way that we are going to be able to tell someone later about it (i.e. to recall it from memory) because it never entered our cognitive system to be stored (D. Broadbent, 1982; D. E. Broadbent, 1952, 1958). (We will see in chapter 3 that there are some learning styles that take advantage of an ability to absorb some such information without conscious knowledge of doing so, but usually there needs to be at least awareness that the phenomenon to be picked up exists and is of some importance.)

Beyond simply noticing (paying attention), we normally have to understand something we hear or read in a foreign language in order to remember it later (i.e. we must be aware of what it means). Yes, we can sometimes repeat strings of words we do not understand in choral drills, and we can sometimes remember, even for years, a word that we did not understand (and years later some situational context finally makes the meaning clear). We can, in fact, remember many things without understanding meaning: intonation, sounds, rhythm, sometimes entire songs. These are, however, isolated moments and no more than the tip of the iceberg in language acquisition. Generally, if we do not understand something in another language, we are not able to remember, let alone reproduce, it later. Since there is no understanding, there are very limited ways to store the information, which generally needs to be linked with other knowledge and schemata (systems of knowledge) that already exist in our heads (Piaget, 1967; Piaget and Inhelder, 1973).

How sentient memory works and whether it is a prelude to short-term memory store or whether there are two parallel initial entry ports into long-term memory – sentient memory for information that can appeal to the senses and short-term memory for the abstractions, both of which are also referred to as transient memory

(Cowan, 1997) – are areas that neuroscientists do not yet agree on. What kind of rehearsal is needed, how much, and its effectiveness are also hotly debated by psychologists working in the area of memory today. What seems to be clear is that sensory memory is very short – from a few milliseconds up to twenty seconds and cues directed toward information perceived via the senses can create recall of the larger picture, whether perceived visually (Turvey, 1973) or in an auditory manner (Massaro, 1972).

So, what does this mean for you, the foreign-language learner? Until we learn more, it would appear beneficial to do all of the following:

- pay careful attention to the environment in which you learn language elements;
- pay attention to as many aspects as possible of the language you hear and see;
- try to use as many senses as possible in learning a new language; and
- attempt some sort of rehearsal.

The latter, rehearsal, is something you do all the time. For example, you may "rehearse," by repeating a telephone number aloud or silently a few times in order to fix it in your head. The same tricks that work to store general information in your brain (i.e. to move it into long-term memory store, which can last from minutes to months) can work when learning a second language.

Short-term, long-term, permanent, and working memory

Short-term, long-term, and permanent memory are what psychologists call *memory store*. They are less a "place" than an "action." Usually, cognitive processing that involves these three kinds of memory is considered to begin with sentient memory, as described above.

Once information is in some form of transient memory, it is either lost forever or transferred to long-term memory through a two-step process (from sentient to short-term to long-term) or a one-step process (from sentient or short-term to long-term), depending on the view of memory processing. Losing information will be discussed a little later in this chapter. The important things for you, as a language learner, to know are that:

- some information/language can and should be lost (otherwise you will be overwhelmed with too much information that you cannot sort through), and
- paying selective attention to the things you want to be able to recall will do much to make sure these items reach your long-term memory.

Then, for memory to "work," these memory stores must be activated. That activation is accomplished via working, or activated, memory. Let's look at each of these in a little more detail.

Short-term memory

Short-term memory is a holding tank of up to twenty seconds, in which information is rehearsed long enough to be sent off to long-term memory. An example would be holding a phone number in your head long enough to dial it – after which it is forgotten. Another example is listening to a teacher give a brief explanation of an odd word. Once the teacher moves on to something else, the information about the word will be forgotten unless it is moved to long-term or permanent memory.

Moving information from short-term to long-term
(or permanent) memory

Moving information into a longer-lasting memory store can take place in several ways. Sometimes an association with other information in long-term or permanent memory will be made, and this "binding" of new information with old information can become a short-cut to permanent memory for the new information (Terrell, 1986). Here is an example:

> One of the authors wondered for many years what a *tygach* was in Russian. The translation always was "prime mover," but she did not know what a prime mover was in English. So, while she was able to translate these words back and forth between the languages, she had no idea what she was saying – until one day at an airport, she saw one of the little machines, a prime mover, pushing the plane away from the gate. That was an "Ah-hah!" that she will always remember and be able to retrieve from memory easily because the experience connected brand-new information (a visual rendition of a prime mover) with the verbal information already in permanent memory.

One of the reasons that cognates (words that are similar in two languages) are helpful in learning a new language is that they connect short-term memory to permanent memory in one fell swoop: if I am an English speaker, for example, it will be easier for me to remember the word for information, *información*, in Spanish than it will be for me to remember the word for city, *ciudad*. The first is almost the same as the word I already know, and if I read it, it will be even easier than if I hear it because I may not yet be familiar with the differing sounds of the phonemes (see chapter 6 for a definition, if you do not know what a phoneme is) and the differing patterns of stress between the two languages. Similarly, learners can help create a shortcut to permanent memory by associating sounds of new words with sounds that already have meaning for them, even if the grammar is not equivalent. Thus, in Arabic, someone named John could introduce himself, saying *Ismee John*, or *My name is John*. Trying to remember *ismee* (name) will be much easier if John associates it with similar sounds in English: *(it) is me*. There is no end to the ways in which such associations can be made in order to improve memorization.

Long-term memory

Typically, long-term memory lasts up to three years. An example of long-term memory is the information you learn for a test and forget the next day or the next semester. Long-term memory generally holds information that you need right now and for the next little bit, but unless there is further use and repetition (i.e. further need for use), this information will not stay with you for a lifetime. Information can be lost from long-term memory through trace decay (one loses the thread of the information), stroke, and other things that interfere with retention. (We will discuss some of these kinds of interference later in this chapter.)

What this means for you as a language learner is that you need to use what you have learned and you need to have many opportunities for reading the same kinds of things, hearing them, speaking them, and writing them over a long period of time. You have probably heard some of these sayings:

> Use it or lose it.   (American proverb)
> Povtorenie – mat' ucheniya (repetition is the mother of learning).
> (Russian proverb)

You can create non-boring opportunities for repetition and prevent language loss through initiating conversations on similar topics with a range of conversationalists. You can also find some topics of interest to you and read as much as you can on those topics, then write a letter to someone about what you have been reading or write a report on it for your class. Consciously making an effort to return to topics you have not concentrated on in a while will help you keep the vocabulary and grammar associated with them fresh in your long-term memory; at some point, they will become part of your permanent memory store.

Permanent memory

Permanent memory lasts, theoretically, forever, though it may become latent, requiring refreshing and activation when needed. (This is often the case for knowledge you have not used for quite a while but which never really goes away.) What remains and what disappears may be very situational and very much dependent upon individuals. The more information that gets into permanent memory, however, the easier it will be to recall the information you need – even after a hiatus in using it. Research, for example, as well as much personal experience of teachers who work with students who have high levels of foreign-language proficiency, indicates that students who surpass professional levels of proficiency and approach near-native levels can bring back their skills very, very quickly, even if they seem nearly tongue-tied during the first hour or two that they try to talk or write (Leaver, 2003a). (Receptive skills – reading and listening – seem more accessible than do the productive skills, and that makes some sense. If you have not ridden a bike for some time, when you first ride again, you may need to reorient yourself to bike riding; at the same time, receptively you know what it is all about before climbing back on the bike.)

We talked about how association of new information with permanently stored information can move the new information into permanent memory faster. The reverse is also true. New information is more accessible and short-term memory tasks more readily accomplished if some of the "new" elements are similar to or the same as elements in permanent store (McCauley, Kellas, Dugas, and DeVillis, 1976). What this means is something that is probably good commonsense: if you read or hear a passage in which you already have acquired 80 per cent or more of the words, it will be easier to learn the other 20 per cent than if everything in the passage is new. This is another reason to do extensive reading and listening on a limited range of topics. The more you read within one topical domain, the more likely it becomes that each new reading will contain relatively fewer new words or grammar points.

Activated (working) memory

Activated memory is sometimes called *working memory*. Activated memory is the activity of pulling together information from short-term, long-term, and permanent memory store for the purpose of processing information. Processing activities generally consist of one or more of the following:

- recognition
- recall
- reconstruction or
- construction of information.

In order to recognize words, grammar, or ideas, we need to have related information about them stored in memory already. Activated memory pulls up this information so that we can use it in a variety of ways, such as using context to guess the meaning of a new word or using background knowledge about a topic to figure out the gist (general meaning) of a text.

Activated memory pulls together the pieces of information that we need at the time. It is pretty rare that we recall information as a whole. This is because information is not generally stored some place as a whole. Rather, specific characteristics are "peeled off" and linked to similar kinds of information. Thus, information about the color of an object would be more likely to be linked with information about color about other objects. Size information would more likely be bound to other size information. Or, at least, so contend contemporary psychologists (Reiser, 1991). Even in sentient memory, for immediate recall, categorization seems to be significant (Greene, 1986; Greene and Samuel, 1986; Morton, Crowder, and Prussin, 1971). What this means for you as a language learner is that it will often help you to group lexical items for learning by different characteristics. Multiple groupings will provide multiple associations to help them stay in long-term memory. Also, thinking about related things can sometimes stimulate recall. For example, if you are trying to remember the word *ball*, you might group it with other words for toys, with words that start with the letter *b*, with words that rhyme (*fall, hall, mall*, etc.), or, even better, all of these.

In processing language, we do something beyond simple reconstruction. We make up new sentences and even occasionally new words. That would be considered construction, or generation. How does this happen? We recombine stored information in new ways.

Aspects of cognition: forgetting

Understanding why we forget is every bit as important as understanding why we remember. Both help us become better learners. In fact, forgetting is, surprisingly, essential to good learning. This is because if you forget something you have learned, you can relearn it in a somewhat new context, and it will be combined with traces of the previous learning. Forgetting is also necessary when you are overwhelmed with new material to learn. It's like a storm drain: it prevents flooding.

There are a number of things that can go wrong in the storage, recall and reconstruction process. When they go wrong, we simply do not have access to the information, whether we know it or not (the "it is right on the tip of my tongue" phenomenon) or knew it and lost it. Some of the things that can go wrong are retrieval errors, lost data, and overwritten information. Each is described below, and the reference list at the end of this chapter provides additional reading for those interested in more detail.

Retrieval errors

Retrieval errors occur when you know something but just cannot seem to remember it. You have probably experienced retrieval errors before – not just in foreign-language classes but in other subject areas, too. The answer may be on the tip of your tongue, but you just cannot get it to come out right. This is pretty normal, and while it is frustrating, there is little that you can do about it (at least until psychologists do some more research in this area and come up with some aids), so you might as well shrug it off and find an alternative way to say what it is you had in mind. Since the expressions *are* in your memory somewhere, if you do not obsess about what happened, you will most likely be able to recall the "forgotten" item the next time you need it. If you just cannot let go of the fact that you do *know* the word or information you are after, sometimes association will help: where did you hear the information, what else is related to that information, what even might sound like the information? All the ways in which you use association to store information in long-term or permanent memory can work in reverse to help you recall it. If you are in the middle of a conversation, however, you will need to decide whether it is worth the time and trouble to do that right now or whether a circumlocution or paraphrase would work best to keep the conversation flowing. If you know the information, it will come to you later – isn't that always the way? – and you can reinforce it for the next time by using it in a number of new situations so that there are even more associations that you can make when you next need it.

Lost data

Sometimes information really is lost. This may be because it never made it into permanent memory in the first place. Perhaps it did not stay long enough in short-term memory and the "trace" of the information decayed to the point that it became unrecoverable. Perhaps it did make it to long-term memory, but was not used enough and had no associations to place it into permanent memory. In any event, lost data must be relearned; it will not show up again in the future on its own. In some cases, part of the information may be remembered. Then the relearning is much faster than the original learning. You will lose data from your language banks from time to time; that is to be expected. Just take this situation in stride and relearn the information. Even the best language learners experience this situation from time to time.

If you do not study or use your foreign language for a long period of time, whole chunks of data may seem to be lost. In some cases, they are lost, and they must be relearned, but relearning rarely takes more than a fraction of the time of the original learning. In other cases, the information is not lost at all, but the pathways for retrieving via activated memory may be hard to find because they have not been used recently. Once found, however, more and more intersecting paths will become accessible very quickly. Most language learners who had good proficiency in a language that they have not spoken for a number of years can reclaim that language in pretty short order.

One of the authors of this book had this experience. Having achieved native-like proficiency in French, she did not speak, hear, write, or read a word of French for twenty years. Suddenly, she needed good French proficiency almost immediately. It took only fourteen hours of intensive study with a native speaker to open up almost all the closed pathways – at least, enough of them for her to be able to use French at a professional level. Another had a similar experience: decades after learning French and Spanish in secondary school, she was called on to travel (on separate occasions) to France and Spain. In both cases, she was amazed at how much returned when she spent fewer than ten hours in conversation with a native speaker. She was able to function comfortably in both countries and continue learning.

Overwritten information

Memory researchers have found that human memory has a number of characteristics in common with computers. One characteristic in particular is unfortunate: new information can overwrite (i.e. eliminate) old information. Some well-known studies have been made of people who witnessed accidents or historical events but later changed their testimony without even realizing it. What caused this was the introduction of distorting information, for example, a question such as: what did you see next to the white house? (Only there was no white house.) Later, people remembered a white house that never was there. Human memory is now considered so unreliable and so prone to being overwritten

memory processes

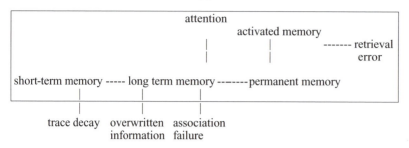

Figure 2.2

that many states will not allow the testimony of eyewitnesses alone to serve as evidence in court cases (Luus and Wells, 1991).

If some of the information you learn in language class is overwritten by new information (e.g. after you learn the past tense, you find that you have forgotten present-tense forms), there is nothing to be done except to relearn the old information – without blaming yourself for having a bad memory. The memory itself is not at fault here; it is normal for related information to overwrite information that already exists. One way to prevent this from happening to you in language classes is to repeat old information (e.g. continue to use the present tense on a regular basis) while learning new, related information. That way, your brain should perceive both elements as distinct pieces of information and not overwrite one with the other.

We would be remiss not to point out a positive aspect of overwriting information. It is fortunate that this phenomenon happens, especially in language learning, because we can continually overwrite previously learned inaccurate or inadequate language on our way to being more precise.

Aspects of cognition: memory strategies

There are a number of strategies that can help the brain function more efficiently. These include directed attention, repetition, association, clustering, key words, and mnemonic devices, to list just a few. All of these have been discussed above, but we will look at them in greater detail here.

Directed attention

Directed attention, sometimes called selective attention, lets you focus only on the information that you need. This is a blessing because if you are reading an article or watching a film in your foreign language, especially when proficiency is not very advanced, there are probably many words and expressions that are simply meaningless to you. Getting "stuck" on each new word is not an efficient use of your time. Nor is using the dictionary to look up everything you do not understand or know. Using the strategy of directed attention requires that you decide ahead of time what you want to learn from what you are hearing or reading and to look for that information specifically. It also lets you pass by whatever you do not understand and focus on what you do understand. Piecing together the elements that you do understand can often help you get the gist of an entire passage.

Practice and rehearsal

Sometimes you just cannot get past the fact that memory needs rehearsal and practice. Before you go to meet a foreign conversation partner for coffee, think about the things you might talk about – and practice them in advance. You may end up with somewhat different topics, but some things will be similar or even the same, and the conversation will be much easier for you. You will also be improving your memory for these expressions.

There are times, too, when you just cannot seem to remember a particular word, no matter how you try. You see it in a passage. You recognize it as something you should know, but you cannot recall its meaning. In fact, you cannot even divine its meaning! Or, you hear it in a television show, and even the context does not help. In fact, you may need that word, in particular, in order to make everything else make sense. Or, someone asks you a question in which that word is the most important element, and you just simply cannot respond. Here is where repetition, repetition, repetition may help out. Repeat the expression at every opportunity. Make a game of walking to a rhythm and repeating the word or expression – especially if movement helps you learn (see chapter 3 for more information on kinesthetic learning). Come up with a rhyme for it that you then repeat *ad nauseam*. There is a funny poem about just this approach. A little girl had studied her "tables o'er and o'er and forward and backward, too," but she "couldn't remember six times nine and didn't know what to do." Her mother tells her to call Mary Ann, her favorite doll, "Fifty-Four" for a while. She does it and learns the answer to 6 × 9 with no trouble – except that when the teacher asks her the answer to six times nine, she unthinkingly responds, "Mary Ann" – obviously, by association. (See Fig. 2.3.)

Association

We have talked much about association earlier. This may be the strongest strategy you have for getting information into memory. It works faster and lasts longer than other strategies. Moreover, other strategies, such as clustering, key words, and mnemonics, have aspects of association. So, whenever you want to remember something new, find as many associations for it as you can. Listed below are a few kinds of associations that you might make. You can probably think of dozens more.

- Does it look (spelling) like anything you already know?
- Can you put a picture with it in order to remember meaning?
- Does it sound like anything you already know?

Fifty-Four

I studied my tables o'er and o'er and forward and backward, too,
But I couldn't remember six times nine and didn't know what to do
Till mother said to play with my doll and not to bother my head.
"If you call her Fifty-Four for a while, you'll learn it by heart," she said.
So I took my favorite Mary Ann though I thought it a terrible shame
To give such a perfectly lovely doll such a perfectly horrid name.
But I called her my dear little Fifty-Four a hundred times till I knew
The answer to six times nine as well as the answer to two times two.
Next day Elizabeth Wigglesworth who always acts so proud
Said six times nine was fifty-two, and I nearly laughed out loud.
But I wish I hadn't when teacher said, "Now, Dorothy, tell me if you can."
And I thought of my doll, and, sake's alive, I answered, "Mary Ann!"

Author unknown

Figure 2.3

- Do you already know any parts of the word or expression?
- Can you make up a rhyme or ditty that would go with it and use part of that ditty for recall?
- Are there any connections with other languages you know, including your native language?
- Can you associate it with a person, place, or thing that might assist recall?

Clustering

Clustering lets you remember whole groups of information by treating the group as one piece of information. For example, the numbers 18396745062 would probably be pretty hard to remember. There are ten separate numbers in a specific order. Research shows us that to remember this number, then, is beyond the capability of the average person, in that most of us have memories that can handle seven digits, plus or minus two (Miller, 1956). However, if you were to organize these numbers into the structure of a telephone number, it would be much easier to remember the full string: 1-839-674-5062. Now, there are only four pieces of information to remember, and within any group there is never more than a string of four numbers to remember. This makes the task possible. What makes the task even easier is knowing the "script" or format. All long-distance numbers in the United States start with 1, so that number makes sense and is already part of every American's permanent memory. Recall is immediate and effortless. Of the remaining three groups, 839 is an area code. It is pretty likely that the person memorizing this number is either familiar with this area code or lives in it. Again, this represents fairly effortless recall from permanent memory. The remaining seven numbers are a little harder, but often the first three of them are similar for an entire city, and if the person memorizing that number lives in that city, this is once again an effortless retrieval from permanent memory. So, the real task boils down to remembering four numbers, and in this case, even that is easy. One really only has to remember 51 and the fact that the last two numbers are plus one: 6 (5+1) 2 (1+1). So, of ten numbers, the real memory task is two numbers and a formula! Piece of cake! Not all numbers will be this easy, and not all information will be this easy to cluster, but much will be.

Let's now take a verbal example, for which there are many approaches. To remember the word *ball*, you might cluster it together with words that sound alike: *call, fall, mall*. You might even make up a ditty that is somewhat mnemonic in nature (see Mnemonic Devices below): "I will call the mall in the fall about a ball." Similarly, let's say you want to remember the following ten words: *antidote, antecedent, antipathy, anteroom, antenatal, deformation, demobilization, deflection,* and *antiphon*. You could cluster these into three groups: *ante-*, *anti-*, and *de-*. You could even reinforce the meanings of these words, by seeing which ones can use synonymous suffixes, as in *antenatal* and *prenatal*, *antecedent* and *precedent*. You could also remove the prefixes, in your attempts at manipulation and clustering, to see which words exist without their prefix and which do not. Which ones can use the opposite prefix to change meaning? An example would be *postnatal*. Which ones take other prefixes that cause their specific meaning to change, while the basic meaning stays the same? Examples would be *immobilization*, *inflection*, and the like. You could go on and on with these kinds of clusters; as you play with the words, you will learn not only these words but also something about how your foreign language constructs words, along with many new related words.

Key words

Key words is a popular device for remembering long speeches (Lorayne and Lucas, 1996). These are words or short phrases that are used to remind the speaker of whole passages of text. The same kinds of things can be used to memorize speeches in a foreign language. Let us say, for example, that you need to talk about your biography frequently. You can memorize the phrases, sentences, and even full paragraphs of information, then recall how to string them together through the use of guiding key words, like "born," "school," "work," "travel."

Mnemonic devices

We have seen some forms of mnemonic devices already. These are the use of rhyming words or alliterative words (those that start with the same letter) to remember things. If, for example, you want to remember to buy five things at the store: cookies, ham, ice, potatoes, and sugar, you could select the word chips. Each letter in chips stands for one of the items that needs to be purchased.

You can use a similar strategy in learning words. Let us say that you need to remember the words *knockout, boxing, score, out*. Using the first letters of each of these words, you could use the nonsense word *boks* to remember these four words. Some learners find mnemonics complicated to use. If that is you, use other strategies (described here and elsewhere in this book) to help you remember what you need to remember. Many people, however, find mnemonics fun and useful. Try using mnemonics for a while. You may find yourself in the group that really likes using this strategy.

Aspects of cognition: state-dependent learning

The research that has been accomplished on state-dependent learning can be very important information for language learners. What state-dependent learning theory (and research) tells us is that the context in which we learn new information can be important in helping us remember it (or preventing us from remembering it). For example, some students have problems taking tests if they are moved to a new seat. Part of the "state" in which they had learned the tested information was associated with the desk at which they were sitting when they were learning it. Similarly, those who have spent much time in-country will often claim that they speak better language in-country. They may well be right in that perception: part of the state in which they learned a rich and complex set of vocabulary was the in-country environment and the everyday realia. If you understand state-dependent learning, you can use it to advantage by recreating, as much as possible, the state under which you learned the new information originally.

Aspects of cognition: taking advantage of the chemistry of memory

Chemistry really does play an important role in the efficient functioning of activated memory. Putting the situation in simple terms, memory is moved about the brain thanks to glucose. The production and use of glucose (blood sugar) is facilitated by the chemical epinephrine, which is released by potassium, among other things. What does this mean in concrete, useful terms? If you eat a banana, your now-potassium-rich memory might improve. Any food that is rich in potassium (for example, potatoes) is a better choice for breakfast before a test than those foods that give you a quick energy boost (often, the energy disappears before the test is over). If the food you eat is high in sugar, it will temporarily increase your glucose level in an intensive way, insulin will be released to deal with it, and then the blood sugar level will drop – leaving you in a "crash," just when you need to be at your most alert. It is much better to eat foods that contain the chemicals that facilitate the efficient *use* of blood sugar, rather than to raise the blood sugar level itself, especially on a roller-coaster basis. In the same way, it is better to eat a complex carbohydrate, such as a bagel, than something that will release sugar immediately into the blood stream, such as chocolate. Also eating excessive amounts of glucose-rich foods in the morning is not an efficient way to handle your memory-related glucose needs; the best way is to eat moderate amounts throughout the day.

CASE STUDY

Problem

Sally always does poorly on tests. Although she really has studied in each case and really does know the new vocabulary and new grammar rules quite well, when she gets into the test room, she forgets it. When she walks out the door, however, she can usually remember what she should have answered on the test. How can Sally help herself do better on tests?

Possible solutions

There could be more than one reason for Sally's predicament. Sally might be experiencing test anxiety; she also might have an inefficient memory. In either case, there are steps that Sally can take.

(1) There are a number of ways that Sally can overcome test anxiety; one of these is knowing that she has done all she can to make her memory efficient; another is to learn all she can about the format of the test and practice that format ahead of time; yet another is not to cram for the test the night before but rather to study a little bit every night so that she develops good control over the materials well in advance of the test and can get a good night's sleep right before the test, allowing her body and memory to function at peak levels.

(2) Sally can assist her memory by eating a banana or potatoes before her test, nibbling on a bagel during the test, and avoiding foods, such as chocolate, that raise her blood sugar rapidly and then send it crashing, and coffee that provides temporary stimulation that wears off rapidly.

(3) Sally can use mnemonic devices for helping recall specific information.

Figure 2.4

One thing that many learners forget is that chemicals – and one's body – react to the internal environment. Processes slow down when tired. Cramming for an exam might make you feel that you are gaining important last-minute information but all too often that information will not be accessible to you on the day of the test because you are too tired for your brain to process the information efficiently. It is much better to get some good sleep the night before a test, even if you do not feel ready for the test, so that your brain can make efficient use of what you do know. Of course, it goes without saying, that the best way to prepare for a test is to start on the first day of class and learn a little every day! Then, right before the exam, all you have to do is to review.

Aptitude

How many people have you heard say, "I have no aptitude for foreign-language learning"? Maybe you are even one of them. Before you can evaluate the truth of such statements, it is important to know more about aptitude.

Defining language aptitude

Language-learning aptitude is often thought of as what is assessed by language aptitude tests (more about these below). For the most part, these tests address such cognitive abilities as making correspondences between sound and symbol, auditory discrimination (between sounds), native-language vocabulary, memorization, and linguistic analysis, especially inferring grammatical patterns from information provided on the test. There is increasing understanding, however, that current forms of tested language aptitude are only part of the picture when predicting learning success in foreign-language learning.

However, there appears to be more to effective language learning than the factors that are tested by aptitude instruments. Some of these non-tested factors are related to personality, learning style, and emotional factors, which are treated in subsequent chapters in this volume. These are not traditionally considered aptitude factors at all, yet they have much to do with language-learning success. Among these, tolerance of ambiguity (especially comforting in situations where you cannot understand everything) is a major element in language learning both inside and outside the classroom. For example, in a situation that demands rapid comprehension and response, even a learner who does very well on an aptitude test might freeze or panic at the first new words, missing everything that is said thereafter. With a greater tolerance of ambiguity, that learner would be more likely to keep listening until more information comes in and permits a good guess at the likely meaning. Similarly, a learner who tolerates ambiguity would be more likely to try out a response even knowing that it might not be exact.

There is consensus among some experts (Ehrman, 1998, Sternberg, 2003, Robinson, 2002) that more investigation is needed of variables representing a broader definition of language aptitude. In addition to tolerance of ambiguity, they could include such factors as previous learning history, motivation, and learning style. They recommend that these be investigated to supplement traditional tests and especially for use in counseling and advising students on how to make the most of their strengths and work around their less strong points as learners.

For the purposes of this book, the most general definition, which takes into account all the current and potential uses of language-learning aptitude, is that *it consists of relatively stable factors within an individual that promote successful language learning.*

Language aptitude testing

The best-known test for language aptitude is the Modern Language Aptitude Test (MLAT, Carroll and Sapon, 1959); it is used in universities and in the government for a variety of purposes, including selection for classes. Other aptitude tests that you might encounter include the Defense Language Aptitude Battery (Peterson and Al-Haik, 1976), the VORD (Parry and Child, 1989), the Pimsleur Language Aptitude Battery (Pimsleur, 1966), a language aptitude test

prepared some years ago by the Modern Language Association, five language aptitude tests produced by the collaboration of the University of Wales at Swansea
and Leonardo da Vinci Programme of the European Commission in Brussels
(Meara, Milton, and Lorenzo-Dus, 2000), and the Oxford Language Test, which
was prepared by the colleges of Oxford University and is available online at
www.sun.rhbnc.ac.uk/Classics/ cUCD/test.html. You should be able to find information about these tests online and/or in your university library.

Aptitude tests provide valuable information about learner ability to cope with
language learning, especially in classrooms. Aptitude tests can provide considerable data about an individual's learning skills and learning styles. The MLAT, for
example, evaluates skills and abilities related to auditory memory, making inferences, focusing on what is most important, cognitive restructuring of information,
sensitivity to grammatical structure, and effective rote learning. This information
has proved very useful in helping learners (Ehrman, 2000).

Language aptitude and you

In looking at your language-learning ability, think about *all* of your
assets, not just the ones that show up on aptitude and classroom tests. Do you
think fast on your feet? Are you good at making others understand what you
want to say, even if it is not completely grammatically accurate? Do you listen
well? Are you confident in your ability to solve problems, practical as well as
academic?

If you have a low tested aptitude and no previous language-learning experience
to indicate that the test score is not indicative of your ability, you may need to
work closely with your teacher or other guide. Together, you can put your learning
into a format that takes advantage of your strengths and compensates for your
weaknesses (or builds the lacking skills) – what these are, in particular, will depend
on your learning style and your study skills in general. Your teacher should be able
to analyze your answers on whatever aptitude test you have taken and determine
the areas in which you will need help. Language learning is not an arcane science,
but it does take thinking, work, and planning.

The important thing to remember is that a language aptitude score is not an
infallible diagnosis of whether or not you can or should learn a foreign language.
Look at the skills required to do well on an aptitude test: holding sounds in
short-term memory, comparing sounds and letters, understanding how grammar
works, understanding how words are formed, and the like. All these things can
be learned. Almost invariably, someone who has studied four to five languages
does well on aptitude tests. Why? Because they have acquired these skills while
learning the various languages. Not having these skills can hold you back, so
finding out which of the skills you lack and developing that skill will go a long
way not just to increasing your aptitude score but also and more important to
improving your classroom and out-of-class performance. Many of the topics in
this book are aimed at helping you do just this.

CASE STUDY

Problem

Robin is struggling with the first semester of Swedish. On the advice of the teacher, Robin has taken the Modern Language Aptitude Test, to see what the problem might be. It turns out that Robin's strengths are in auditory comprehension, word learning, and matching sounds to symbols. On the other hand two parts – (1) word recognition and assignment of a synonym and (2) grammatical sensitivity – were very low. What can Robin do about it?

Possible solutions

(1) Robin should examine the strengths the MLAT has revealed and work with the teacher to see how she can take advantage of these.

(2) Knowing that she has a weakness in spotting and mentally reorganizing what is important, Robin should work with the teacher to practice doing this with easy things at first (such as differences in word suffixes and prefixes), building up to more difficult ones (spellings that are in free variation, reading between the lines, even finding the topic sentence in a text – it is not always at the beginning in some languages, as it is in English).

(3) When she feels overwhelmed, Robin should find things about the language and its study that maintain her motivation, perhaps keeping a diary that elicits positive self-talk and records her successes.

Figure 2.5

Metacognition

Metacognition, as mentioned in chapter 1, is "thinking about thinking." It refers to being aware of your language-learning behaviors and progress, self-monitoring, and planning. Metacognition plays a very important role in language learning. Not only is it important for the long-term planning of learning activities, perhaps even throughout your career and/or life, but it is also important for ensuring the most successful use of your time during courses of study.

When we discussed planning in chapter 1, we were describing one of the most important metacognitive activities. Planning, or forethought, is just the first metacognitive step. In addition to planning, you will need to monitor and set priorities, two more important metacognitive strategies.

Monitoring

Monitoring refers to paying attention to what you are doing while you are learning. Tracking what you are doing permits you to remember it when it comes time to evaluate it. (The tracking doesn't need to be intensive, but you have to pay enough attention to be able to recall something of what you did later.)

For example, when you are sitting in the classroom, are you paying attention to what the teacher is saying? What do you think the teacher will do next? How are you doing? Are you keeping up? Are you having problems? If you are having problems, what are you having problems with? If you can identify your problems, you can *plan* to work on them as part of your homework or you can ask the teacher for some additional help.

Monitoring your progress can provide tremendous insights into what you can and should do to improve your own success in language acquisition. Done well, it usually provides wonderful insights that you can use in any planning that you undertake. What should you monitor? Everything, including, but not limited to, the following:

- Your overall progress
- Your specific successes (and any lack of success)
- Your learning-strategy use
- Your materials
- Your use of time
- Your feelings

Progress

As mentioned in chapter 1, there are expected rates of progress in acquisition for individual languages. How does your progress stack up? If you do not know, arrange to take a proficiency test. Slower than the average? See if you can find out why. What aspects of language learning are troublesome for you? Talk to your teacher. Determine whether your progress really is slow or not when you compare it to that of your classmates. It could be that the class is moving more slowly as a whole. On the other hand, if you are moving faster than others in your class and/or than the average expected, do not just pat yourself on the back. Find out what has helped you be successful and become even more successful.

Specific successes

Besides overall progress, it is important to know in what aspects of language learning you are succeeding well and where you are not succeeding as well. Evaluate the success of the language items you are working on. If you are focusing for now on the past tense, evaluate in general terms how fluently and how accurately you are using it. At a higher level, you might assess how well you are using the right register (social style level) for the people you are talking to. An advanced language user should not be using a register implying familiarity with high-status strangers, for instance.

Learning-strategy use

Every so often, you should evaluate the learning strategies you are using. Some of them may be no longer useful because you have learned new ones or because you have reached a level of proficiency where they no longer help and you need to develop new ones. For example, at lower levels, you may need to look up some words in a dictionary or guess their meaning from context. At higher levels, however, you might be able to figure out their meaning based on the meaning of their roots, your knowledge of word formation, and/or comparison with vocabulary that you already know.

Materials

Evaluate the materials you are using. Can you find better ones? Are you playing it too safe and using things that are too easy for you? Or are they too hard, so that you use too much energy for figuring things out or looking information up in the dictionary when, with different materials, you would need less time for these activities and could spend more time on the information itself, remembering the vocabulary, and exploring the grammar through application of what you already know?

Use of time

Take a look at how much time you are spending on your language-learning activities. In fact, you might want to keep a diary for a week in order to track your time use better. Total time is important, of course. If you are spending four hours in order to learn ten words, you may need a different learning strategy. Specific use of time is important, too. Where does the greatest amount of time get spent? On vocabulary? On grammar? On application? If you are spending more time on knowledge (grammar and vocabulary learning) than on use (application), you might want to reassess and see if you can find more opportunities for application. If all your time is spent on knowledge activities not by choice but by necessity, then your overall progress in learning the language may be affected, and you should examine what is holding you back. Take a look at the four skills, too. Do you spend more time speaking, reading, writing, or listening? Is the relative balance one that works for you? Would a different mix work better for you? Sometimes it is not *how much* time you spend studying that matters but rather *how* you spend time studying.

Feelings

Assess your feelings. Are you feeling discouraged? If so, take a look at why and think about how you can get yourself out of the doldrums. Are you feeling pleased and successful? If so, find ways to give yourself more of the same. Rewarding yourself for your successes – even when the successes are small – can be highly motivational.

CASE STUDY

Problem

Alex has been struggling with homework. The teacher is very helpful in class, guiding him and his classmates through the material presented, but he assumes that the students will know how to study the text and what has been done at home on their own. The teacher seldom gives explicit assignments, and Alex is sure he isn't using his time well. He feels he is drowning in new things to learn.

Possible solutions

(1) Alex needs to develop some metacognitive skills. He needs to work on planning (suggestions listed above will help him a lot).

(2) An especially important metacognitive activity is examining the whole field of what he has to do every day and selecting only the most important things. He should select the three most important things, and then the next three. When he finishes the first set, he can then move on to the next set.

(3) Even if he is a learner who likes to organize things for himself and feels restricted when forced to learn things in a step-by-step manner, he may benefit from taking a relatively sequential approach here because he needs to limit what he attends to and stick to one thing at a time.

(4) While he is developing these skills, he should consult with his teacher to confirm his priorities.

Figure 2.6

Setting priorities

Setting priorities is just as important in language learning as it is in many other aspects of your life. Setting priorities will be far more effective if you base your priorities on the results of monitoring and evaluating. If you find, for example, that you are weak in speaking and yet you spend less time on speaking than on the other three skills, you might want to make opportunities to speak a higher priority in your learning plan.

Setting priorities may also lead to redoing your learning plan. This is not bad; this is good. Learning plans should be redrawn periodically. In fact, if you apply the metacognitive strategies described here, you will find that metacognition is the key to independent learning. It is the essence of what is called "self-regulation" in chapter 9. A self-regulating learner plans, monitors, evaluates, and replans (setting priorities, in that process). There is a list of specific self-regulating strategies you can use in the section on self-regulation in chapter 9.

Review

In this chapter, you considered a number of themes. The content of these themes can be summarized as follows:

- **Cognition**: the process of thought
- **Memory**: the storage of information
- **Language aptitude**: the ability to learn a foreign language
- **Metacognition**: thinking about thinking

Cognition

(1) Second language learning can differ from third language learning in that the more languages you study, the more schemata you have to assist your language-learning efforts.
(2) Knowledge is not necessarily fluency; one has to do with how much you know and the other with how quickly you can recall it.

Memory

(1) There are several kinds of memory and ways of classifying memory:
  - Episodic, procedural, and semantic memory
  - Attention/awareness
  - Short-term, long-term, permanent, and working memory

(2) *Forgetting*
  - Forgetting contributes to learning in the long run
  - Memory can be overwritten.
  - When memory of previously known information fails, it can be because long-term memory has been overwritten or because activated memory momentarily cannot retrieve the information.

(3) Memory can be assisted in several ways:
  - Proper nutrition
  - Proper rest
  - Repetition
  - Association

Aptitude

(1) Aptitude is not a single, monolithic construct.
(2) Some aptitude-related skills can be learned.
(3) It is possible to compensate for weak areas.

Metacognition

(1) Planning
(2) Setting Priorities
(3) Monitoring
(4) Evaluating

Practice what you have learned!

1. You have a foreign-language test tomorrow, and unfortunately you have not kept up with your assignments. Which of the following steps might you take to improve your chances of a passing grade on the test? Exactly how will you do it? Explain why you decided to take a specific approach or not to take it. (Think about your own personal strengths and weaknesses, as you answer and explain where they matter and where they do not.)

    a. It's never too late – stay up late, cramming.
    b. Review what you do know and make sure that is solidly under your control.
    c. Learn as much of the new material as possible in time to get a good night's sleep.
    d. Get up early to study and review.
    e. Drink a strong cup of coffee before heading off to the exam.
    f. Eat a balanced breakfast, to include bagel and banana, before heading off to the exam.
    g. Assess whether you will be reviewing oral or written materials, so that you can play to your own strengths.

2. Do you consider your language learning aptitude good, bad, or middling?

    a. On what grounds? (Experience? Comparison with others? etc.)
    b. Aptitude is a complex thing. Consider what you do well in language learning and what isn't so easy with you. List these in two columns.
    c. What do you do to cope with the items in the weaknesses column? What can you do that you are not doing now?

3. Quickly assess your tolerance of ambiguity.

    a. What do you do when you hear or read a word you do not understand?
    b. How do you react when you come across a word that looks like one you already know but means something either a little or a lot different?
    c. What is your response to grammar that is completely different from what you are used to, such as number classifiers or politeness levels in Asian languages, or different kinds of passive voice in Indonesian or Philippine languages? (You might need to take a trip to the library and find a grammar book on a very different language to be able to answer this question; you might do this in combination with task 4 below.)

4. Take a look at the language family chart in chapter 1. First, find a language related to the one you are studying and find out four or five things it has in common with your language. Then, select a language from another family and find out at least three ways in which it differs from your language.

If you want to learn more about the topics in this chapter, you might consult the following sources: Carroll and Sapon (1959); Ehrman (1998a); Golinkoff and Hirsh-Pasek, eds. (2000); Goodison (1987); Leaver (1999a); Leaver (1999b); Restak (2002); Restak (2003); Robinson, ed. (2002); Robinson (2002); Schachter (2002); Skehan (1998); Skehan (2002); Sternberg (2002); Sternberg (2003); Stevick (1996).

3 Learning styles and learning strategies

Preview

This chapter introduces you to the concepts of learning styles and learning strategies. These are important concepts that we will refer to throughout this book and have, in fact, made allusion to in chapters 1 and 2. Learning styles and learning strategies affect the nature and quality of learning, whether or not the learner knows anything about these concepts or not. Therefore, it is better to have an understanding of them, so that you can consciously use this information to good advantage. Topics in this chapter include:

Definitions of learning styles and learning strategies.

- **Learning styles**. Learning styles are habitual patterns of perceiving, processing, or reacting to information.
- **Learning strategies**. Learning strategies are the specific actions one takes and/or techniques one uses in order to learn.

Kinds of learning styles. This chapter divides learning styles into the following categories:

- **Sensory preferences**. Sensory preferences refer to the channels through which we perceive information which consist of visual, auditory, and motor modalities, as a minimum.
- **Cognitive styles**. Cognitive styles refer to individualized ways of processing of information. Many models of cognitive styles have been proposed. This chapter presents the E&L Construct in detail; this particular model organizes most of the work on cognitive styles into one system of cognitive profiles.
- **Personality types**. These are another kind of learning style. Since they involve affective (emotional) factors, they are discussed in chapter 4, along with other affective variables.

Learning strategies. In addition to memory strategies, which were discussed in chapter 2, and communication strategies, which will be discussed in chapter 10, there are comprehension strategies and production strategies. This part of the chapter is divided into the following subtopics:

- **Deep and surface strategies**. This dichotomy includes strategies that require maximum thinking (i.e. much cognitive activity and attention); these are called deep strategies. There are also other strategies that require minimal thought; these are called surface strategies.
- **Taxonomies of learning strategies**. A number of authors have attempted to organize the myriad of possible learning strategies into systems, or taxonomies. Several of these are overviewed here; for the learner who wants more information about learning styles, any one of these taxonomies is worth exploring on one's own.

- **Comprehension strategies**. Specific strategies are useful for achieving success in listening and reading activities in the classroom and in real life. Some of those are presented in this chapter.

- **Production strategies**. Specific strategies are useful for achieving success in speaking and writing activities in the classroom and in real life. Some of those are presented in this chapter.

- **The relationship between styles and strategies**. There is a close relationship between styles and strategies. Individuals with one set of styles, for example, probably use very different strategies from those with another set of styles.

Use of learning resources. This section explains how to make good use of the aids that you have at your disposal. These include dictionaries, flashcards, and more.

Learning styles and strategies: a definition

When you run into trouble in completing an assignment or in making progress in general in gaining proficiency in your foreign language, it is often useful to look at what you are doing when you learn. The activities and techniques you use to learn are called *learning strategies*. These strategies tend to fall into various groups, which are considered to represent a more abstract set of tendencies that we call *learning styles*. Learning styles are convenient shortcuts for talking about patterns of what an individual is likely to *prefer* as a learner. For example, some people like to follow a syllabus or textbook chapter by chapter when they learn. This approach is referred to as *sequential* style because people with this style like to follow a sequence of predictable or predetermined steps to get where they are going. The contrasting style is called *random*; people with a random learning style tend to prefer to follow whatever thread of learning seems relevant or interesting at the time. Their sequence is not predictable, often not even to them. So random and sequential are *styles*, or habitual, general approaches for which the observable behaviors are certain specific learning *strategies*, such as looking for patterns within a mass of information (random), remembering events by putting them into chronological order (sequential), or any of the memory or other strategies that were presented in chapters 1 and 2.

Keep in mind that no one can actually *see* a learning style. Instead, we see behaviors that seem to have something in common and we *infer* a style. The same behaviors can be interpreted in various ways, as we will see later in this chapter. For example, a preference for reading over talking can indicate a visual style (rather than auditory), a preference for introversion (versus extraversion), and so on.

Learning styles

Learning styles come in several flavors or, using a different metaphor, we might say that there are a number of ways to slice the learning-style pie.

Leaver (1998) suggests that we slice it in at least four ways: sensory preferences, cognitive styles, personality types (see chapter 4), and environmental needs. For some people, one of these categories may be more important than others. For other people, the categories have more or less equal valence.

Sensory preferences

Sensory preferences are sometimes called kinds of memory (as in "visual memory"), KAV (referring to the types of sensory preferences: kinesthetic, auditory, or visual), and perceptual styles. They are the physical channels through which students take in and perceive new information: ears, eyes, and touch, and directly relate to the perceiving (or attentional) aspects of cognition. The typical categories used by specialists in learner differences are visual, auditory, and motor – these are described below. Sometimes, though, you might also hear the word *haptic*. Haptic learners use their hands and their sense of touch to learn through how things feel to them. Examples include working on a foreign alphabet by tracing sandpaper letters, using block letters to spell out words, and forming letters with clay. There are also categories for sense of smell and taste, but these are minor styles. We describe the most common ones here.

Visual learning

Visual learners acquire new vocabulary primarily through sight; they understand grammar better when they can read about it in a book. Leaver (1998) defines two kinds of visual learners: imagists and verbalists.

When imagists hear or read something in a foreign language (or in their native language, for that matter), they see a picture of what they have heard or read. In other words, they make an image of it. They understand through that image, and they typically store the information in their memory as an image. The image, then, is more likely to help them recall the words or grammar than is a verbal prompt.

Verbalists, on the other hand, see words. If they hear the French word, *soleil*, for example, they will not necessarily see a picture of the sun; that is what the imagists would do. Rather, the verbalists will see the letters s-o-l-e-i-l in their heads. Verbalists store the letters, and when they have difficulty remembering a word, they can usually remember the initial letter or some of the letters in it. They do not associate the word with an image but with the letters that compose it. For verbalists, reading is a key to remembering – much more so than with imagists. Verbalists, not surprisingly, are much better at correct spelling (and very likely the winners of most spelling bees are verbalists or people who have learned the kinds of memory strategies that come naturally to verbalists).

Visual learners can cope with and even take advantage of non-visual activities that come up in the classroom by applying strategies that are used by auditory and motor learners or by turning an auditory activity into a visual one. An example of the former is using rhythm or ditties (as mentioned in chapter 2) to remember new vocabulary words. An example of the latter is remembering phrases for a role play by imagining that you can see these phrases on the ceiling, then reading them aloud.

Auditory learning

Auditory learners acquire new information through sound; they hear grammatical endings, and they associate new words with sounds they already know. Even pitch, tempo, and intonation provide them with clues to the meaning of what they are hearing, and they are very quick to learn to make these differences when they are speaking the foreign language. Leaver (1998) divides auditory learners into two groups: aural learners and oral learners.

Aural learners learn by listening to others. They tend not to take notes in class because they usually remember what they hear. They are usually pretty good at listening comprehension tasks; can figure out either the essence of broadcasts and films or the details contained in them – or both, depending on their learning style; and have generally pretty good accents.

Oral learners learn by listening to themselves. Oral learners, then, like to talk. Talking and hearing themselves talk is often essential to their ability to comprehend information and store it in memory. Whereas aural learners need auditory *input*, oral learners need auditory *output*, which becomes their input. Simply put, they get to learn by hearing when they hear themselves speak. As classmates, they can be perceived to be interruptive because they talk "all the time." However, if they were to stop talking, the quantity and quality of their learning would diminish.

If you are an auditory learner, you may become confused or impatient if you are asked to learn through written materials. Most auditory learners have varying tolerances for visual input. Since much of language learning is visual, with a good half of the activities that students are asked to accomplish being reading and writing, chances are that you will have to learn to cope with non-auditory requirements. You can do this by using some of the same strategies that visual learners use or by turning a visual requirement into an auditory one. An example of the former would be to learn how to encode sounds into letters and words. One way to facilitate this is to ask your teacher or a native speaker to record some of your reading texts for you – then read them as you listen. To turn visual activities into auditory ones, try reading aloud or subvocalizing (saying the words to yourself under your breath); you can use this latter strategy not only when you are reading but also when other students are answering in class.

Motor learning

Motor learning is sometimes called kinesthetic learning. While the terms are sometimes used interchangeably, doing so does not represent an accurate description of learning style information. Kinesthetic preferences are only one kind of motor learning. Quite obviously, given the terminology, motor learners acquire new information through movement. The differences among motor learners, according to Leaver (1998), are based on the kinds of muscles being used: gross motor muscles (arms, legs, or whole body) or fine motor muscles (fingers or hands).

CASE STUDY

Problem

Marilyn is usually alert and interested, but sometimes she finds herself drifting off in class. She is vaguely aware of the need to do more than read and speak, but it wasn't until she heard about learning styles that she started to suspect that she is a motor learner. Now that she may have discovered at least one possible cause for her lapses of attention, what can she do about it?

Possible solutions

(1) Marilyn can volunteer for movement tasks, from the mundane job of passing out papers to going to the library to research a disputed word.

(2) She can work on flash cards, making her own cards rather than buying them ready-made.

(3) Marilyn might take the initiative in proposing and organizing excursions or role plays.

(4) She would do well to enlist her teacher's support for the occasional change in routine to enhance the learning environment for her.

Figure 3.1

Kinesthetic learners are in perpetual motion. They use their entire body for learning. In language classes, role plays and total physical response activities (those that require some kind of physical response, such as carrying out commands) help them learn and remember new vocabulary and grammar.

Mechanical learners like to write. They also like to draw and doodle. In class, their fingers are rarely idle. They learn by taking notes, writing compositions, and even copying.

Unfortunately, most classrooms are not well set up for the motor learner. Much work is done in the same seat with only occasional breaks. If you are a motor learner, you may need to find ways to move while seated. One way you can do this is by using your hands. Some kinesthetic learners, while preferring to use their arms and legs, find that taking copious notes can provide enough activity to keep them from fidgeting. (By the way, doodling really is okay as an assist to learning for mechanical and kinesthetic learners – but keep in mind that some teachers do consider it rude.) Let your teacher know that you like field trips and role plays. When studying on your own, find ways to move with the rhythm of the language, even to the point of dancing a little to sentences.

Cognitive styles

The terms *learning style* and *cognitive style* are found throughout the literature on learning. They are often used interchangeably, though some researchers make a distinction between them. In this book, we treat learning style as a more general term. Cognitive styles, then, are specifically preferred forms of activity associated with information acquisition and processing.

As with other kinds of learning styles, cognitive styles are habitual patterns of processing information. In this case, we are talking about thought processes (as opposed to perceptual ones, as with the sensory preferences, or to emotional ones, as in the case of personality types).

Interest in cognitive styles is not new. Dating from the days of Hippocrates and his protégé, Galen (Itsines, 1996), the differences in individual approaches to learning have fascinated researchers. In the twentieth century, many new concepts were introduced to the field of cognitive styles research, and a number of kinds of pies (learning styles constructs) have been suggested. Some of your teachers may have introduced you to brain dominance (Torrance, 1980), Learning Styles Inventory (LSI) and being a master student (Ellis, 2002; Kolb, 1985), 4-MAT (McCarthy, 1980), Gregorc's Information Acquisition Inventory (Gregorc, 1982), Sternberg's mental government model (Sternberg, 1994). and the E&L Construct (described below). The latter incorporates many of the elements of the previous style models and is the one that is used throughout this book.

The E&L construct

The E&L model originated from dissatisfaction with existing approaches to cognitive styles, which were leading to misdiagnoses and confusion about the meanings of terms. Ehrman and Leaver (1997, 2003) selected a variety of cognitive style scales, most of them from the research and models mentioned in the above section, that were informative to them in their work with students. Looking for a way to organize the many concepts that had been floating about over the past twenty years, they sought – and found – overarching categories that could organize the various proposed cognitive styles into a streamlined model. They called these overarching categories *synopsis* (adjective – *synoptic*) and *ectasis* (adjective – *ectenic*), using the Greek words for a process that is holistic (*synopsis*) and extended and atomistic (*ectasis*). In foreign-language learning, synoptic learning is reliant on intuition and subconscious control whereas ectenic learning generally occurs under the conscious control of the learner. Each of these "poles" is composed of ten cognitive scales that are subscales in the E&L Construct. Thus, the E&L Construct can be graphically portrayed as shown in table 3.1.

As seen in the diagram, the umbrella scale is synoptic and ectenic learning. This scale is composed of subscales that reflect various aspects of synopsis and ectasis. Each subscale contributes different and important information to a learner's profile.

Descriptions of the ten subscales follow; they are listed in alphabetic order, with the synoptic pole named first. Consider yourself and what you are most comfortable with as you read the descriptions.

Table 3.1

synoptic learning	(definitions)	ectenic learning	(definitions)	category source
digital	*literal and factual learning*	**analogue**	*learning through metaphor*	*Ehrman and Leaver*
abstract	*learning through ideas and books*	**concrete**	*hands-on learning*	*Gregorc*
field independent	*decontextualized learning*	**field dependent**	*contextualized learning*	*Witkin and Goodenough*
field insensitive	*lack of osmosis in learning*	**field sensitive**	*learning through osmosis*	*Ehrman; Ramírez and Castañeda*
global	*oriented toward the big picture*	**particular**	*oriented toward details*	*Ehrman and Leaver*
impulsive	*simultaneous thought and reaction*	**reflective**	*reaction following thought*	*Messick*
inductive	*understanding rules from examining examples*	**deductive**	*learning rules, then understanding examples*	*Pierce*
leveling	*noticing similarities*	**sharpening**	*noticing differences*	*Holzman and Gardner, Messick*
random	*preferring to self-organize materials*	**sequential**	*preferring materials to be pre-organized*	*Gregorc*
synthetic	*assembling pieces into wholes*	**analytic**	*disassembling wholes into pieces*	*Kant*

(1) Analogue–digital scale. Ehrman and Leaver (1997, 2003) also introduced this scale. It addresses the degree to which a learner tends to seek connections of meaning among words, structures, or other units or, on the other hand, the degree to which a learner prefers to work at a more surface level.

- *Analogue* learners gravitate to the use of metaphors, analogies, and conceptual links among units and their meanings. These learners tend to have a clear preference for learning material in meaningful context.
- *Digital* learners take a more surface approach, dealing with what they can see or hear directly. Their understanding is generally literal and under the kind of conscious control typical of ectenic learners.

Sometimes, it is important to use metaphoric approaches; this can be especially important when learning in country where synoptic/analogue learners may have a distinct advantage. There are also times when it is appropriate to use literal approaches, e.g. rote memory strategies.

(2) Concrete–abstract scale. This scale was introduced by Gregorc (1982). He suggested an interrelationship between the concrete–abstract scale and the random–sequential scale (see below). The E&L Construct, however, treats these two scales as separate and subordinate to the greater, overarching categories of synoptic and ectenic learning. The concrete–abstract scale, in general, considers the amount of hands-on experience that an individual learner prefers.

- Concrete learners use real materials and examples for learning. They are hands-on, experiential learners. The learning (input, materials, procedures, etc.) are generally consciously controlled either by the learner or, more frequently, by the teacher.
- Abstract learners, on the other hand, prefer pictures and explanations. They learn through lecture and concept. They accept theory well. They are, in essence, "book learners." Some are able to apply the book learning to real life easily; others have more difficulty doing so.

The venue of where you are learning a foreign language will determine whether concrete or abstract learning preferences will be advantageous or disadvantageous. In study abroad situations, as well as for field trips, synoptic/concrete learning can be a considerable advantage. On the other hand, when working nearly exclusively with a textbook, an ectenic/abstract style can have a distinct advantage.

(3) Field independent–field dependent scale. The concept of field independence has been around for a long time (Witkin and Goodenough, 1981). The usual instrument used to assess field independence is a test that looks at how rapidly a person can find a simple geometric field within a more complex diagram (i.e. can find a particular object within a larger object, known as "the field"). The more rapidly you can distinguish the object you are seeking from the field around it, the more field independent you are. You may have taken such a "hidden figures" test in your elementary school days. If you did not, you may have had a chance to self-check your preference for these styles by doing any number of puzzles that asked you to find hidden objects or animals in a picture. Figure 3.2 is an example of a hidden figure. Look at the shape on the left and find it in the shape on the right.

The concepts introduced by Witkin and Goodenough were more related to mathematics than to foreign language. More recently, some researchers have looked at the relationship between the Witkin–Goodenough concepts and success in foreign-language learning (Stansfield, 1989).

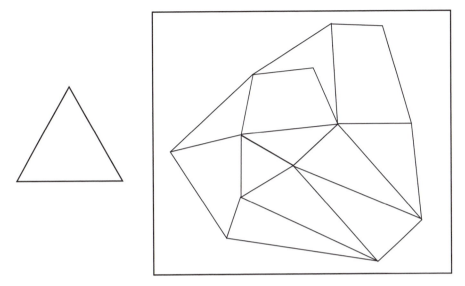

Figure 3.2 Sample Embedded Figure Test Item: Find the simple shape on the left in the complex figure on the right.

- Field independence, in foreign-language learning, means being able to select something of importance or interest for focus. The process is automatic.
- Field dependence, following Ehrman (1996, 1997), is construed as the absence of field independence.

Let us take some examples to see how field independence and field dependence influence language learning. Perhaps the study of plurals is on the docket in your class syllabus. If you are a synoptic/field independent learner, you will probably instinctively notice plural forms wherever you encounter them, without consciously searching for them. You may also find yourself unconsciously selecting plural forms that are new to you from among all those that you encounter and then organizing the different forms so that they are easier to deal with. If you are field dependent, then you may rely on your textbook, teacher, or syllabus to organize these forms prior to your setting about learning them. One of the most important functions of syllabi and instructional guidance is to point out the things that matter; if you are an ectenic/field dependent learner, you can use these items to good avail.

More than the other dimensions, field independence is often considered to be an ability and is tested as one through hidden figure instruments. For purposes of the Ehrman and Leaver model, however, we are treating it as a processing preference. (To be sure, preferences often lead to abilities through frequent practice.)

(4) Field sensitive–field insensitive scale. In an effort to avoid the apparent pejorative implications of the term *field dependence*, Ramírez and Castañeda (1974)

coined the term *field sensitivity*. Ehrman (1996, 1997) built on preceding work on the field independence-dependence construct to unpack field dependence into two scales instead of one. These scales are (1) field independence vs. the absence of field independence (called *field dependence* in her system, presented above) and (2) a separate approach, for which she adopted the term *field sensitivity*, with the resultant scale being field sensitivity vs. field insensitivity. The difference between the two scales can be summarized in this way: whereas a field independent learner focuses on a part of the whole, a field sensitive learner stays aware of the whole learning environment, including social relationships and background phenomena, and absorbs a great deal from what is around and in language, i.e. from what is heard or read.

- Field sensitive learners use the full language environment for comprehension and learning.
- Field insensitive learners do not focus on the language environment but rather pay attention to a particular language element being studied.

Classrooms tend to be information-poor environments. This can be a problem for field-sensitive learners. If you are a field-sensitive learner, you can take advantage of your learning preference by finding opportunities to overhear the teacher talk to others, listening to native speakers talking on tapes or videos, reading, noticing posters, overhearing the questions and conversations of other students, and the like. All of these opportunities will provide you with the rich source of information, replete with all kinds of additional details and content, i.e. a "field" of information, that you may need for understanding new words and grammatical usages that you have not seen before.

Field-insensitive learners will probably fare better in classrooms that treat language as isolated grammar rules and vocabulary items for rote memorization than they will in classrooms where the teacher uses a communicative approach. If you are a field-insensitive learner in a communicative classroom, you might ask your teacher or peers to help you develop the kinds of strategies that you will need to take advantage of the wealth of additional information that accompanies the authentic texts and tasks that are typically used in communicative classrooms. For example, you might try to become adept at the strategies of applying background information, hypothesis formation and confirmation (for confirmation, you may need to look at the bigger picture), and finding supporting details for your hypotheses (looking for these will also help you start to use surrounding information on a regular basis).

(5) Global–particular scale. The global–particular dimension was first suggested by Ehrman and Leaver (1997). It refers to the learner's breadth of focus.

- Learners who prefer global processing attend to an image as a whole (as opposed to its parts). For them, the most important thing is seeing and understanding the "big picture." Informally, we often distinguish between people who "see the forest" and those who "see the trees."

Global learners are the ones who see the forest and may miss the trees. They process information in a "top down" manner, focusing on overall meaning first and details later – if at all. If they miss enough details, the meaning that they "invent" can stray quite far from reality.

- Students who display particular processing are attentive to discrete items and details. They are aware of the various kinds of "trees," rather than the forest *per se*. Their processing of information is "bottom up," seeing the form first and the general meaning second. Sometimes the details become important to them independently of any relationship to larger concepts, creating a different kind of difficulty for them.

If you are a global learner, you are likely to want to start with an overview of the material, and, if very extreme in preference for global processing, feel that the job is done when the main ideas are understood. First, you should always ask for the overview since it will help you understand better. Second, having received the overview, spend some time thinking about the details and how they work together to build the big picture. For example, in writing you may want to re-read your work more than once because global learners often look at their own mistakes and see as they should have been written, not as they have been written. Sometimes, it is even better to do your writing at night and check it over in the morning when it is no longer fresh in your mind.

In contrast, if you are a particular learner, you will probably plunge into the specifics of the material at hand, focusing on the words, sounds, or grammatical components. If extreme, you may not take the details to a more abstract level where they are instances of generalities (e.g. you may try to learn the conjugation of each new verb you encounter when you could learn just 2–3 different patterns that would account for nearly all the regularly conjugated verbs) or relate them to a larger context (e.g. treating the sentences in a passage as isolated examples without understanding what they contribute to the meaning of the whole text). One thing you might like to do is prepare an outline of the content of any passage you are reading; that will force you to put the details into a larger format so that you will begin to see the big picture.

(6) Impulsive–reflective scale. Impulsive–reflective differences are yet another learning-style domain important to the classroom. This concept relates to the speed and manner of processing a response to a cognitive stimulus (Messick, 1984).

- Impulsive learners think and respond nearly simultaneously. They tend to complete their work more quickly but often with less accuracy than reflective learners. They often give facile answers.
- Reflective learners think, then respond. They tend to show more involved and deeper levels of thinking. Reflective learners more often than not work accurately, but their slowness sometimes means that work is incomplete.

In language classrooms, reflective learners experience the same kinds of problems that they experience in other subject-matter courses. Although many of them are highly accurate, they are handicapped on speeded tests that do not allow them to turn material over in their minds. In classroom exchanges, they may lose out to more assertive and impulsive classmates. If you are a reflective learner, you may want to look through your lessons in advance, predict some of the questions that will come up, and prepare your answers in advance so that at least some of the time you can compete with your impulsive peers. You may also need to learn to accept the fact that making errors in class in a foreign language is okay – there is really no way a foreign-language learner can avoid making mistakes at times. (In fact, if you think about it, many native speakers make small mistakes in their language performance at times.)

In language classrooms, impulsive learners generally do well. In language learning, however, impulsivity can lead to a lack of monitoring (paying attention to what you are saying). As a result, if you are an impulsive learner, you may develop ingrained habits of speaking with mistakes that you ignore, and this can lead to your being "stuck" at lower levels of proficiency. We call this phenomenon "fossilization." If you find accuracy to be a problem for you, you might deliberately work on building a monitor by recording your own talk, then listening to it, correcting it, and saying it again correctly.

(7) Inductive–deductive scale. Induction–deduction differences were first used in the field of logic (Peirce, 1878), to indicate going from examples to hypothesis (induction) vs. going from hypothesis to examples (deduction). In foreign-language learning, induction generally means using examples to figure out rules and deduction as using rules to identify and understand examples.

- Inductive learners form hypotheses, then test them. They may only rarely seek teacher support. They enjoy seeing a multitude of examples and intuiting what the rule should be and sometimes cannot get enough examples during class.
- Deductive learners study the rules, then practice applying them to examples. They prefer to get these rules either from the teacher or from references. Like sequential processing, deductive processing can save some cognitive load (the amount of material the brain is expected to process simultaneously) because the learner does not need to work out the rules.

Whether inductive learning or deductive learning will be advantageous in a particular language program depends very much on the teaching method of the course. If you find yourself as an inductive learner in a deductive classroom, perhaps the most typical mismatch, there are some things you can do that will allow you to learn through your preferred style. For example, if the teacher's explanations fill the quiet time you need for processing in your head and figuring things out for yourself, do your induction in advance at home. Look through the next day's materials and learn whatever you can and want from them. That way, you will often have better control of your classroom output the following day.

If you are a deductive learner, you may experience difficulty sometimes in working with authentic materials, especially where you do not know all the words and have to "guess" some of them from context. One military officer we know who was in a foreign-language program insisted that he "did not become a captain by guessing." This is probably true, but some guesswork will be essential in foreign-language classrooms. You can use what you already know to guess better. If you are reading a text and do not know a key word, think about the subject matter and what you have read so far in the text. Based on that, what do you think the word might mean? If this does not help, think about word composition; can you guess now? If you are still lost as to meaning, let the word go. Read ahead in the text; it might become clear then. If you have access to a dictionary, you will probably find yourself wanting to look it up. That is okay. Other times, in real life, you may not have a dictionary, so try, first, to figure it out without a dictionary if you can.

(8) Leveling–sharpening scale. Leveling and sharpening represent an important difference in cognitive processing that has a substantial effect on how learners handle fine distinctions and how they remember information (Holzman and Gardner, 1959; Messick, 1984).

- When learning new information, levelers meld together information that may be distinctly different and come from a number of sources. Therefore, when it comes time to retrieve specifics, the details of the pieces that formed the melded concept are no longer available to the learner (Lowery, 1982). Levelers remove distinctions instinctively; frequently they see only similarities.
- Sharpeners look for distinctions among items. Everything that we said about levelers can be reversed for sharpeners. They readily retrieve details because they store them in different "compartments." They do notice differences, and they write well when the assignment allows them to use their tendency to notice and describe differences.

The leveling–sharpening distinction can be important for learning foreign language to very high levels of proficiency. Both preferences include approaches that are useful for language learning. Sharpeners often naturally notice and remember the subtle distinctions of form and meaning that characterize native-like language, especially if they have high language aptitude or previous language-learning experience. Levelers tend to notice the patterns in the language and, thereby, "see" the underlying linguistic system. Both approaches are useful for language learning, and sharpeners can teach levelers some of their strategies and vice versa to good avail.

Let us take a typical language-learning situation. You are assigned the task to write an essay about the differences between your country's political system and that of another country. As a leveler, you may find it difficult to write the essay not because you are a poor writer (perhaps you are a very good writer) but because you cannot find the differences. Similarly, if you are a sharpener and asked to write an essay about the commonalities between the two systems, you may experience difficulty with the nature of the task. Both levelers and sharpeners can build facility in accomplishing tasks requiring the opposite learning styles by using Venn diagrams before writing. Make a list of all the traits you can think about the two governments. If you find traits in common, write them in the section where the left-hand and right-hand circles of the Venn diagram overlap. Write the other traits into the left-hand circle if they pertain only to your government and in the right-hand circle if they pertain only to the foreign government. Using this technique prior to starting a writing assignment can help you develop style flexibility in the leveling–sharpening domain.

(9) Random–sequential scale. Random–sequential learning differences is the second scale that Gregorc (1982; see above) used in his four-dimensional model of learning styles (see the suggested reading list at the end of this chapter for bibliographic information on this model). In the E&L construct, the random-sequential scale is treated as a separate, independent subscale. This subscale refers to the amount of external organization that a learner wants or does not want.

- Random learners generally prefer to develop their own approach to language learning and organize assignments in their own way, often completing them in no apparent (to the outsider) order. (Likewise, in reading a novel, many random learners report reading the ending first or skipping out in the book. Extreme random learners have sometimes reported even reading the ending of a mystery before reading the story itself.)

- Sequential learners generally prefer to receive materials that have been organized in some fashion: a syllabus, lesson plan, or programmed tutorial. While they may adjust the organization to fit their own needs, these learners tend to feel uncomfortable when handed a collection of authentic materials with no guidance on what to do or how to use them. (In reading a novel, most sequential learners report that they prefer to start on the first page and read the subsequent pages in order; they generally do not understand why anyone would want to read the end of a mystery before reading the story itself.)

Both random and sequential learning have advantages in foreign-language study, and much will depend on the teaching method and textbooks as to whether one or another type of learner will be comfortable in the classroom. The World Wide Web is a random learner's paradise. If you are a random learner, you have an advantage in your greater tolerance for surprises and the unexpected. Assignments of much authentic material (passages from magazines and newspapers, for example) will allow you, as a random learner, to use your learning preference. On the other hand, textbooks in which everything is presented as a series of steps can be boring and even confusing for you if you are a random learner. You might use some of your free time to read books that let you handle the same language features in a more random manner; e.g. if you are studying the past tense, you might read a historical novel or an essay about some aspect of history.

If you are a sequential learner, you may be daunted by the mass of input from the World Wide Web; in this case, you might ask the teacher to give you some questions to think about in advance before you go online, so that you can use your sequential style to advantage. On the other hand, unlike random learners, you may be very happy to have a textbook in your hands, especially one that explains everything in a step-by-step manner.

(10) Synthetic–analytic scale. The synthetic–analytic difference is another important domain. This difference refers to the directionality of processing: putting together or taking apart, and was first introduced into the field of philosophy (Kant, 1781/1998). The overall difference lies in whether you prefer to assemble old information to make something new or to take apart new information in order to understand it better.

- *Synthesizers* assemble something new (knowledge, models, stories, ideas, etc.) from known information. They do this by using the given pieces to build new wholes, e.g. making up new words, using typical roots and prefixes or rewriting a paragraph from a different point of view, using the sentences already there as models. Synthesizers typically put together disparate ideas easily and not only make sense out of them but also develop new models with them. Synthesis as a learning style has several characteristics: (1) hypothesis formation is experienced or intuited; (2) processing is unconscious; (3) process and product are simultaneous; and (4) the synthesizing learner goes from insight to construct.
- *Analyzers* disassemble known information into its component parts and are usually aware that the "big picture" is composed of small pieces. They like rules because they can break them down into component parts and use them to explain phenomena. They like word study because they can break the words into etymological pieces: roots, stems, affixes. Analysis as a learning style has several characteristics: (1) hypothesis formation is built up consciously; (2) processing involves discrete steps (setting up the hypothesis, looking at components, and organizing them); (3) process and product are experienced as consecutive; and (4) the analytic learner goes from construct to insight.

In language classes, if you are a synthesizer, you may well want to use or even play with new words or features of the language as wholes, rather than take them apart. So, faced with a list of new words, make up sentences or stories that go with these words to help remember them. You might also like to make up new endings for stories that you read or rewrite a story from another point of view, using some things you know and other things that you learn new from a text in the foreign language.

If you are an analyzer, on the other hand, you will probably want to zero in on what needs to be figured out, so that you can understand it and feel confident that it is "yours" before you try to use it. Some things you can try doing in order to use new words is to apply contrastive analysis (how these words look and act differently from words in English) and word attack (how you can break these words down into meaningful parts).

Learner profiles

So far, we have treated the E&L subscales as if they were even– or choices and the overarching categories of synopsis and ectasis as if every related subscale would be represented in a learner of one or the other style. In reality, the situation is much more complex. Each of the scales is a continuum; you would then be more or less synthetic or analytic, for example, not entirely synthetic or entirely analytic. If you think of the continuum as a line extending from the synoptic attribute (any of the ten subscales) to the ectenic attribute, you might find yourself anywhere along that line. For example, you might be in the middle when it comes to synthesis and analysis, which would mean that you probably are very situational in your preference – where synthesis is needed, you are more synthetic and where analysis is needed, you are more analytic. This kind of situational application is generally what is meant when someone refers to learning-style flexibility. On the other hand, you might find yourself at the extreme synoptic pole on the random–sequential line, which means that you are almost always random, even in cases where it might be more advantageous to be (or act) sequential.

When you find your scores for each of the subscales on the E&L construct, you will find that you have a unique collection of ten different styles. We call this collection your learning profile. Nearly everyone in your class will have a very different or slightly different learning profile from you.

You may notice some things that seem rather odd at first. For example, perhaps you are synoptic, but you are a sharpener, not a leveler. Since sharpening belongs to the ectenic pole, it does not seem to "fit" your profile well. Such profiles, however, are pretty typical. Most people are not purely synoptic or purely ectenic. Where the "impurity" exists is in one or more style preferences that fall into the opposite domain. Being able to see how many preferences "cross over" to the opposite learning style will tell you much about yourself as a learner, where your

---

CASE STUDY

Problem

Andrew has been a very successful student in almost all his classes. He is quick to zero in on what the teacher wants and find it, process it in his head, and produce it in exams. This makes for a high level of achievement in subject classes, but it is proving not to be enough in his language class. His program includes a great deal of authentic language through reading, listening and field trips where the language is spoken. He has a lot of trouble making fully effective use of the out-of-classroom portions because it all goes by too fast for him to use his normal pinpoint focus techniques. Andrew is aware that he will need to make the most of the language environment when he leaves the classroom and goes out to study and work overseas. How can he start preparing for this now?

Possible solutions

Andrew is probably field independent but field insensitive. He is good at pinpointing but doesn't do much in the way of naturalistic learning (i.e. learning from the environment). Listed below are some things that he can do now to prepare for situations that require field sensitivity.

(1) Andrew and his teacher can do some advance preparation for field trips and immersions. They can imagine the situations Andrew will be in and think of things that he should prime himself to pick up one way or the other. Later, he can do this for himself.

(2) Some form of relaxation may help Andrew feel less in need of getting everything. He is more likely to pick up material if he isn't trying too hard.

(3) A listening or reading focus may be of help; if he is listening for descriptive adjectives, for example, his self-judging part may be distracted, permitting him to use more naturalistic learning.

(4) Speaking with someone about the nature of language learning and the limitations of focusing on knowledge alone might help him see the importance of developing some new strategies that can be useful with authentic materials.

Figure 3.3

flexibilities are, and where you may experience some rigidity in your approaches to learning.

Your learning-style profile tells you even more. It shows you specifics about your approach to language learning and indicates in advance where you may have a mismatch with your textbook, your teacher, or the teaching method in your foreign-language program. Knowing where these mismatches occur means that you can develop strategies for the opposite, needed style, a topic that we will be addressing in the next section of this chapter.

Learning strategies

Learning strategies is the term applied to the various behaviors or tech-niques we use to learn. Some are consciously employed, and others are automatic. As mentioned above, most learning styles are expressed by observable learning strategy behaviors. In a nutshell, learning strategies are:

*   things we do;
*   relatively easy to change;
*   different, depending on our learning styles;
*   effective or not effective for specific situations; and
*   frequently under some level of conscious control.

Some learning strategies will be specific to each of the four skills. The receptive skills of reading and listening can share certain strategies, as can the productive skills of speaking and writing. Let's look at some concrete examples of learning styles in each of these areas:

*   Comprehension/receptive strategies can include such things as using background knowledge, analyzing word parts, using context, asking for help, using a dictionary, and the like.
*   Production strategies can include such things as adhering to the known, paraphrasing, using an authentic text as a guide, asking for help, using a dictionary, rehearsal, and the like.

Strategic thinking can make an enormous difference to learning success, espe-cially outside the classroom, where there is much less direction. The key to strategic thinking is metacognition (cognition is thinking, and metacognition is thinking about thinking). Metacognition for strategy use includes such things as monitoring, evaluating, and refining your use of strategies and deliberately selecting appropriate strategies for specific tasks. Other metacognitive strate-gies include planning and rewarding oneself for specific kinds of progress. These latter strategies are perhaps the most significant way to achieve suc-cess in autonomous (independent) learning because it is up to the learner to decide what to learn, when to learn it and how (O'Malley and Chamot, 1990). While strategic thinking may appear to be a conscious approach and/or atti-tude toward learning, for some learners metacognitive processes can be quite intuitive.

You will find specific learning strategies in several of the following chapters. Take note of those that seem like they will suit you or be useful to you and try them out. Keep them in mind for when you find you need some new strategies later on, too.

Strategic competence

Strategic competence is the ability to select the appropriate learning strategies for the learning or communicative situation in which you find yourself. There are two ways of looking at strategic competence. One is from the point of view of learning; the other is from the point of view of communication. From the point of view of learning, we talk about *learning* strategies – those actions that help you to learn more effectively (see, e.g., Chamot and O'Malley, 1994; Chavarriaga-Doak, 1999; Messick, 1984; Oxford, 1990; Schmeck, 1988). From the point of view of communication, we talk about *communication* strategies – those actions that help you manage when you do not understand something or do not know how to express something, i.e. to cope with new and unfamiliar linguistic situations (Canale and Swain, 1980; chapter 10, this volume). In the case of both learning strategies and communication strategies, strategic competence refers to (1) being able to deal with situations where you are in over your head, and/or (2) taking control of your learning and linguistic behavior. The first kind of strategic competence is very important at lower levels of proficiency; the second kind is more important at higher levels of foreign-language proficiency.

Taxonomies

There are countless learning strategies, so many people find that it is helpful to group them when thinking about them or learning to use them. Over time, a number of different taxonomies (groupings) of learning and communication strategies have been suggested; some samples are given in Appendix B, along with information about tests to determine learning/communication strategy use. We suggest that you use one of these tests to see what learning strategies you are now using. Test results will tell you whether you have a wide set or a limited set of strategies; if the latter, you might want to think about trying out new strategies. Whether or not your strategy use is appropriate for your learning tasks will be determined through one of two means: (1) your success (or lack of it) in completing the task and (2) your teacher's observation of your strategy use.

Some taxonomies contain purely learning strategies; others combine learning and communication strategies. Taxonomies *per se* are of most interest to theorists and researchers. For you, the most important things are knowing about the strategies that are listed in each of them, using a variety of strategies in your language-learning endeavors, and selecting the one(s) that is/are most appropriate for any given learning task. The research on the "good language learner" (Naiman,

Fröhlich, et al., 1978; Rubin and Thompson, 1994; Stern, 1975) indicates that the number of overall strategies used in learning a new language is less important than that the proper strategies be chosen for each task.

Deep strategies and surface strategies

If you study the taxonomies in Appendix B, you will notice that many learning strategies are in the service of getting material into memory. Research (Schmeck, 1988) has shown that the most effective such strategies are what are called *deep strategies*. The opposite of deep strategies is *surface strategies*.

- Deep strategies make connections among things: unknown to known, among unknowns, new connections among knowns. These activities normally involve investment of personal energy and attention and thus impose something of an additional cognitive load. Examples of deep strategies include making associations among concepts, elaboration (making more of something than what you initially received, such as turning a sentence like *The house is on the corner* into *The white house with green blinds is on the corner of Main and Prospect*), and reconceptualizing into hierarchies or diagrams.

- Surface strategies do not make much of an investment in the material being learned. They are of a "just get it done" nature. Although they tend to be less useful for bringing material into long-term memory, they can be very helpful when there is something that needs to be dealt with in the short term. Rote memory is often a surface approach, because it may not make use of connections to other things. Reading through word lists without much thinking about the contents can also be a surface approach.

Use of deep strategies means more time spent on study while the associations and elaborations are made, but it is an investment with long-term payoff.

Let's look at what happens now in a classroom setting. The teacher assigns a reading; it has twenty-five new words, and there is a word list that follows that translates each word into English. As you read the article, you look back at the word list. That is a surface strategy. Later, you learn that your teacher might give you a quiz, and you are worried about knowing these twenty-five words, so you spend a half-hour memorizing the word list by first covering up the English and telling yourself the meaning of the word and then covering up the foreign word and, using the English as a prompt, writing it down. These are also surface strategies.

What, however, would happen if you were to take a different approach, one using deep strategies? In this case, when you encounter an unknown word, you do not look at the word list right away. You try to figure out the meaning on your own. If it is near the beginning of the article and you are not sure yet what the article is all about, you could skim the article for that information (that is something that you might instinctively do if you are a synoptic learner; skimming is a strategy typically used by students with a global learning style preference); if you are an ectenic learner, you might put aside global meaning for a moment and look at the structure of the word. In doing so, you may notice that it has two parts – one part is an ending, which you recognize as typical for past tense and another part (the stem) looks like another word you know. Putting this information together, you can figure out the meaning on your own. If you are strongly ectenic, you will probably want to confirm your hypothesis by checking with the word list (reflective strategy). That is okay. You have used a deep strategy to get the meaning, and that meaning will probably stay with you much longer than through simple memorization. You may even find that it does not take you any time at all to prepare for that quiz because you have already learned the words in the process of figuring them out on your own.

Comprehension strategies

Comprehension strategies are used when you need to understand something that has been said or written. Perhaps there are new expressions in a text. You can use a number of strategies to understand them. You can guess their meaning from context; this is more instinctive for inductive learners. You can break the words apart and see if you can analyze their meaning; this is more natural for ectenic learners. You can apply background knowledge of the topic to determine what the limits on the range of possible definitions of these words would be; this is a naturally synoptic strategy. You could also look up the word in the dictionary – something that an ectenic learner is more likely to do than a synoptic one. These are all cognitive strategies.

You could use social strategies, too. Appealing for assistance from a teacher or a peer is just such a social strategy.

The taxonomies in Appendix B contain a number of comprehension strategies. So do chapter 10 and other chapters of this volume.

Production strategies

Strategies for production are used when you need to say or write something. There are a number of other kinds of strategies that can be used as well. Of those, at lower levels of proficiency, the ones that are most useful will very likely be the compensation strategies – how to communicate when you do not have the words to express what you need to be able to say.

One compensation strategy is to substitute similar words that you do know for words that you do not know. A friend of ours lived for a while in Spain with his wife who spoke only a little Spanish. He tells the story of her needing to buy a chicken at the market one day. She wanted the head and feet to be cut off, but she did not know the right words, so she asked the seller to please remove the chicken's hat and shoes. He understood – and told this funny story to his friends. This was a compensation strategy.

In the case of analytic strategies, one might use description in lieu of a specific, unknown word. For example, if someone wants to buy a nail file, he or she might ask for the long, sharp thing for nails. One of the authors did just that in a foreign country recently – and learned the word for nail file in the process.

Many more learning strategies can be found throughout this book. In addition, Appendix B contains a list of taxonomies with sample strategies.

Using learning strategies effectively

How can you use learning strategies effectively? Let's take some examples. If you are an ectenic learner and you need to express something for which you do not have the words, then an analytic compensation strategy may be perfect for you. As in the case with the nail file, describe any aspect of what it is you want to say, and you will probably be understood. Then take note of the "correct" word for next time. If you are a synoptic learner, you could do the same thing, but probably a holistic compensation strategy would work better for you. Try using similar ideas and analogies, as in the case of the chicken and its shoes and hat. You, too, should take note of what the word is when you get it, but make sure you have it right. Often, synoptic learners come close but are not precise when they learn new things in real-life contexts. Ask again, if you need to. If you are not an auditory learner (regardless of your other learning styles) and you get this information in an auditory fashion, take the first opportunity you have to write it down (and, if necessary, to look it up in a dictionary). You will need to figure out for yourself which strategies are the most effective for you. You will get feedback on your strategy use by monitoring your success in specific tasks.

The influence of learning style on learning strategies

We have mentioned above that learning styles are expressed by learning strategies; they are what you can see and hear. Another way to look at it is that learning styles – habitual patterns of preference – influence choices of learning strategies. So, for example, the synoptic learner will prefer to get the gist of a listening or reading passage first, whereas an ectenic learner may want control of the specifics before seeing how they relate to the whole picture. Thus, the global (synoptic) learner will gravitate to top-down (big picture to details), and the particular (ectenic) learner will want to go from bottom up (details then whole). Of course both will need eventually to use the opposite strategies. If the ectenic learner never sees the whole picture, he or she will have a hard time navigating the language. If the synoptic never gets the details, she or he may flounder about in vagueness.

CASE STUDY

Problem

When he was asked to complete a survey about which learning strategies he uses in studying Urdu, Eric selected nearly all of the activities on the survey. He was puzzled by the fact that he was having trouble learning when he does so many different things to learn.

Possible solutions

Eric needs to understand that it is not the number of strategies he uses that makes a difference, but rather whether they are appropriate to the circumstances and done in a deliberate way. He can work on making this change in his approach by:

(1) Working with a teacher or other helper to outline the different kinds of learning situation he encounters and then decide on the one or two most appropriate strategies for those situations to focus on until they become automatic;

(2) spending more time developing his metacognitive skills of planning, monitoring, and evaluating, in order to pick the right cognitive strategies at the right time; and;

(3) testing himself periodically to determine where and when he is having problems and determining what strategies will be helpful for those particular situations.

Figure 3.4

An important point to be derived from this example is that everyone needs some flexibility in the strategies used. (The term used for switching styles as needed is *style flexing*.) If you stick only to strategies that are consistent with your learning style, you are likely to find your learning quite limited. A good example is the sequential learner who never adopts random strategies. You can doubtless imagine the trouble such a learner may have in a situation where there is little English spoken and no teacher or syllabus. On the contrary, a random learner who never uses sequential strategies may waste a great deal of time with a new topic or skill that could be saved by following a tutorial or lesson series.

A note on using language resources

Probably the best-known resource is the dictionary. Dictionaries can be either monolingual or bilingual. Monolingual dictionaries are those that native speakers use. In English, these would be reference aids like the *American College Dictionary* or *Webster's Dictionary*. Bilingual dictionaries are made for language learners and for translators (although professional translators generally prefer specialty dictionaries, monolingual dictionaries, technical glossaries, and authentic texts on the topic in the foreign language). Bilingual dictionaries usually have two sections: English–Foreign Language and Foreign Language–English, although some (the better ones) come in two volumes. Dictionaries and glossaries can be wonderful helps, or they can be the source of difficulties. It is all in how you use them.

General caveats in using a dictionary

For the most part, unless you are doing close translation work with specialized vocabulary, it is usually wise to use dictionaries sparingly. There are three reasons for this:

- inaccuracy in dictionary use
- inequivalence in languages
- inefficient use of time

Inaccuracy in dictionary use

Dictionaries, especially bilingual ones, can be very misleading. Words, in any language, have more than one meaning, and simply picking a word from a list may lead to the choice of the wrong word. This is less of a problem in looking up something you are reading or something you have heard. You can usually figure out which is the correct translation from the context. In speaking and writing, however, you can create texts that no one can understand or that are hysterically funny in the misuse of words. At the very least, if you select one word of several in a list in an English–Foreign Language dictionary. One can easily think of all kinds of words in English that can be mistranslated into another language. Think of something like "that's a tall tale," meaning it stretches the imagination and does not conform to reality. The word you are likely to find in any foreign-language dictionary is one about size – and in another language, which does not use "tall" to mean "far-fetched," you will both confuse and amuse your reader or listener. In a case like this, you will need to look something up by meaning, not but expression, i.e. look up the word *far-fetched*, not the word, *tall*.

Inequivalence in languages

Sometimes reference aids simply will not work because a concept in one language does not exist in another language. Privacy, for example, is very important to people who live in the United States. Even our children ask for their privacy at times. In Russia, however, people would not understand what this is. There is no such thing as privacy, and no desire for it. It is an alien concept. Translating it is nearly impossible unless you know both cultures very well and *explain* it, rather than translating it. Similarly, there will be concepts in your target culture that do not exist in your native language, and until you get to know the target culture very well, you may not understand these concepts. In such cases, reference aids are not very helpful.

Inefficient use of time

If you have to look up every word you do not know, you are probably working with material that is too difficult. That is, its difficulty level is requiring you to spend more time in preparing to learn by finding meanings than in actually learning. This is an inefficient use of your time.

Ideally, you will be working with texts (written and oral) in which you know enough that you can guess at the meanings of the new items. It is best to try to guess at the meaning of the paragraph or passage, then of the sentences before looking up much of anything. We call this a "top down" approach, as opposed to a "bottom up" approach in which the reader uses the meaning of words to put together an understanding of the whole text. A top-down approach is essentially synoptic, but it is an approach that all learners will probably need when you are using language in real life, not in class or for homework. After you have taken whatever guesses you can, then select one or two words that, if you knew what they meant, might clarify large chunks of the passage. Look those up. Then try again to see if you can figure out what the passage and its components mean, and look up the next set of key items. Repeat a time or two. If you are doing "intensive" reading or listening, in which you need to understand a text thoroughly, you will go through this process more times than if you are seeking an "extensive" (broad understanding of a long text or texts).

Using the dictionary by learning style

Your learning style will have a direct influence on you prefer to use a dictionary. It will also probably determine how well you make use of the dictionary and when and how you use it.

Ectenic dictionary users

If you are an ectenic learner, you may feel a "tug" to use the dictionary for every unknown word. This is a natural feeling but not a helpful one. If you are very uncomfortable with the top-down approach (reading whole texts, getting the gist, and determining meaning of words from the gist), you can attack the task by noting all the new words and making some decisions about the ones that you want to look at first. It's still best to do this with the context in mind, because even if you prefer bottom-up processing, you will still need to reach and deal with the text as a whole and with words you do not know and how they fit into the larger context.

Synoptic dictionary users

If you are a synoptic learner, you may find that you refer to the dictionary far too infrequently and trust your hypotheses far too often. Especially at lower levels of foreign-language proficiency, you may need a "reality" check of some sort from time to time; this could be the dictionary, your teacher, or other resource (bilingual books are great reality checks for synoptic learners – they handle the language of the text better than dictionaries and let you swim on your own as much as you want).

Other resources

Other resources include grammar books, books and lists of verb conjugations, pre-made flash cards, and word lists, as well as the electronic resources available on the Internet. You will probably like some of these better than others; your learning style will probably play a role in these preferences. Like reading a text, you can use these resources in surface or deep ways. Surface strategies would include such things as glancing at the reference and learning by rote. Deep strategies would more likely involve the making of associations between the items or between them and what you already know.

Practice what you have learned!

1.   Try this experiment. Write your name with your right hand, then write it with your left hand. Were you equally comfortable both times? Probably not. This is what it feels like to work in accordance with your preferred learning styles and to work in your non-preferred styles. Of course, you could learn to write with the opposite hand, and you can learn to work with non-preferred styles, but that will take time, practice, and the development of new muscles (strategies).

2.   Using the E&L or any other learning styles scale, determine your own set of learning styles (learning profile). What does this profile tell you about how you might best go about learning a foreign language?

3.   Pick one area in which you have experienced learning difficulty. Analyze your difficulties from the point of view of your learning profile. If you find there is a conflict between your learning styles and the learning styles required by the task, select 2–3 strategies from styles that are required for the task that you do not now use and find some opportunities to use them.

4.   Using Appendix B to identify possible strategies, make a three-column list. In column 1, write those strategies that you use regularly, in column 2 those you use occasionally, and in column 3 those you never use. Over the next 2–3 months, try to move a couple of strategies from column 3 to column 2 and a couple from column 2 to column 1. Be sure to include the use of reference aids in these lists if you do use them.

5.   Make a list of expressions such as "tall tale" that could cause problems with a word-for-word translation. Then, figure out how you could possibly look up ways to translate these. Check out your translation with your teacher or a native speaker.

Review

In this chapter, you considered a number of themes. The content of these themes can be summarized as follows:

Definitions of learning styles and learning strategies.

- **Learning styles**: habitual patterns of perceiving, processing, or reacting to information.

- **Learning strategies**: specific actions and/or techniques taken to learn.

Kinds of learning styles: sensory preferences, cognitive styles, and personality types (the latter, personality types, will be covered in chapter 4).

Sensory preferences: visual, auditory, and motor modes of perception

Cognitive styles: synoptic vs. ectenic traits

- **Synopsis**: concreteness, induction, field independence, field sensitivity, leveling, globality, randomness, synthesis, analogue, impulsiveness

- **Ectasis**: abstraction, deduction, field dependence, field insensitivity, sharpening, particularity, sequentiality, analysis, digitality, reflectivity

Learning strategies: memory strategies (chapter 2), communication strategies (chapter 10), deep and surface strategies, comprehension strategies, production strategies

Taxonomies of learning strategies: ways of organizing and grouping strategies (see Appendix B for specific strategies)

The relationship between styles and strategies: Each style category is accompanied by a range of strategies particular to that category.

Use of learning resources. This section explains how to make good use of the aids that you have at your disposal. These include dictionaries, flashcards, and more.

If you want to learn more about the topics in this chapter, you might consult the following sources: Chamot and O'Malley (1994); Claxton and Murrell (1987); Dunn and Dunn (1978); Ehrman (1996); Ellis (2002); Keefe (1982); Kolb (1985); Leaver (1998); McCarthy (1980); McCarthy (1996); Oxford (1989); Oxford (1990); Ramírez and Castañeda (1974); Rubin and Thompson (1994); Sternberg (1994); Torrance, Reynolds, Riegal, and Ball (1977).

4 Understanding feelings and personality in language learning

---

Preview

This chapter introduces you to the affective variables in learning – your feelings, personality preferences, and relationships with others involved in your learning process such as teachers and other students. Topics that this chapter addresses include:

Foreign language anxiety is the fears and uncertainties that arise when you think about studying a foreign language, There are useful coping strategies for it.

Performance anxiety is closely related to foreign language anxiety and refers to completing acts in the foreign language, such as using it in front of others in class or in the society. This chapter suggests some coping strategies.

Test anxiety is the nervousness that accompanies test preparation and test taking. This chapter will help you understand the source of this nervousness and will provide you some guidance in dealing with it.

Motivation is reflected in the reasons you study a foreign language and the reasons you do (or do not) work hard in class. There are a number of kinds of motivation, several of which are discussed in this chapter.

Self-efficacy is your feeling of competence, that you can do something. This chapter will help you understand the sources of these feelings.

Personality can have a strong effect on how you approach language-learning situations, in-class work, peer interactions, and interaction with the culture. In this chapter, you will be helped to understand not only your personality traits but also those of your classmates.

Ego boundaries refers to receptivity to external input. You will learn about thin and thick boundaries and their significance for language learning.

Defense mechanisms are the things we do to protect our self-esteem. Sometimes, these things get in the way of learning. This chapter will help you recognize the defense mechanisms that you use.

Many learners are intuitively aware of the cognitive factors described in the preceding chapter: after all, if you are having trouble remembering how to put together a sentence in the language you are learning, you are likely to know it.

If you are among those having difficulty, you may want to try out some of the suggestions made in the previous chapter. At the same time, however, you are also likely to have some feelings about your difficulties.

The truth is that the line between the cognitive and the affective (feelings) factors in language study situations is not as firm as our splitting them into two chapters suggests. There is considerable overlap. For example, if you are usually optimistic, your thinking, as well as your feelings, will tend toward the positive, and this will have an influence on the efficiency and success of your cognitive processes. If you think you can learn a language, then, usually, you more likely to be able to. So, what your feelings are and how you deal with them will make a great deal of difference to your learning success. Here we talk about anxiety (related to fear), motivation (desire to do something), and self-efficacy (the feeling that you can do something).

Your feelings and your cognition are frequently influenced by your personality, which filters how you interpret experience and act on your interpretations. If you tend to have a strong need for orderliness in your life, for instance, you may find the open-endedness of language learning "messy," and this may cause you irritation, as well as make it more difficult for you to deal with the new material. It is important, then, to understand these preferences, mental filters, and habits, which are discussed in detail below.

Foreign language anxiety

Specific sources of foreign-language anxiety

Everyone feels anxious some of the time. Most of us feel some anxiety before going to the dentist or during a job interview, for instance. Anxiety is a kind of nervous-system arousal that is very functional when there is danger, but it can get in the way when we have a task to do, like learning a language. The key is that *anxiety uses up cognitive and emotional resources that then are not available for learning.* A small amount of anxiety can be helpful when we need to get going on a project, but when there is too much, it gets in the way. Many learners feel a special kind of anxiety when they are learning a foreign language. There are several reasons for this, each of which is described below:

* the amount to learn;
* the difficulty in communicating at lower levels;
* self-consciousness about mistakes; and
* the foreignness of foreign language.

Amount to learn

There is a vast body of information to learn. A language takes years to master to near-native ability. There will always be something you do not know.

Thinking about this, especially if you want everything immediately, can create immense amounts of anxiety. However, if you make a long-term learning plan and start to see how your daily steps add up to larger and larger gains in foreign language proficiency, you will probably reduce that anxiety to a great extent.

Sometimes you may find yourself approaching burnout (inability to work or focus). Under these circumstances, the best thing you can do for yourself is often to give yourself a break from study and any further input. Do something completely different for a while. If you forget a little bit, do not worry, you will have many chances to relearn it even more solidly afterward.

Difficulty in communicating

For adults in particular, the early and intermediate learning stages can be very frustrating because they want to express adult concepts but do not yet have the necessary foreign expressions. This lack of language results in a feeling of being tongue-tied and can, of course, create anxiety, as well as frustration, especially if you are in an immersion program.

Some people can accept this situation as a natural step in the language-learning process. For others, however, just accepting the fact that beginning language learners can appear tongue-tied does not help. In this case, there are ways to handle your awareness of your communication gaps.

Simplification. One way is to learn strategies for simplification. Instead of trying to say, "The obfuscation in the writer's text organization confuses me," or, in a different register, which you may also not yet possess, "This author's writing is so messed up that it is impossible to understand it," you could use a couple of short phrases to make yourself fully understand and get your message fully across: "The author writes poorly, and I cannot understand the text."

Islands. Another way to handle this situation/reality is to work out and learn some more advanced ways of speaking about several of the topics that you know you will be speaking about frequently. These are sometimes called "islands" (see chapter 10), and they can give you moments of fluency at a level higher than your typical proficiency. (Your teacher or any native speaker can help you work these out, but you will have to practice them so that they will be under your full control and available to you when you need them.) Knowing how to simplify and having a set of islands at your beck and call can do much to allay anxiety.

Focus on the known. Perhaps the most powerful tool at your disposal is to focus on what you *can* do. For example, you might give yourself a good pat on the back for finding roundabout ways to get your meaning across when you do not have the right words for getting yourself to a popular landmark from a hotel or getting a shopkeeper to sell you what you need. You may have had to work hard and have been less than precise, but you used the language and made it work for you.

Self-consciousness about mistakes

In most language classrooms, you are expected to try to speak the language. As a learner, you make mistakes, and then you are likely to feel self-conscious about them.

It is not only common to all learners to make mistakes, it is also necessary, or you are probably playing it too safe. Nevertheless, many of us come to learning experiences expecting perfect performance. When we can't achieve 100 per cent, we can get anxious, yet it is rarely possible to achieve 100 per cent accuracy when speaking a foreign language. (Full accuracy does not occur in our native language, either; we just do not notice mistakes there in the same way that we do with foreign languages.)

If you can adopt the motto of the concrete-random learner (remember the styles we discussed in chapter 3), who learns through trial and error – a mistake is just the next step in learning, and the more mistakes the more opportunity for learning – you will be further ahead than you will if you cower in fear of the inevitable mistake. Mistakes can be your friend. This changed attitude will not only help reduce your anxiety, it will encourage you to speak and write more so that, in the long run, you actually will make fewer mistakes, thanks to all the practice.

Inside the classroom, mistakes can be more threatening to your sense of self-esteem than outside of it. You may feel judged by your teacher and classmates for your performance, and of course in some ways everything is a test, not only formally named tests. A good way to deal with the inevitable anxiety of feeling judged is to focus on *your* performance, not that of others. Put effort into observing your own progress and patterns of errors, and relate them to your learning plans. For example, after you notice that you are getting the pronouns for superiors and inferiors in Asian languages wrong regularly, put some special activities for practicing them into your study plans for the week. Your learning style will help you with starting points for these activities: for instance, an analytic learner might want to build a table of the pronouns and the situations where they should be used. On the other hand, a synthetic learner might well decide to write some dialogue among characters of different social status.

Outside the classroom, remember that the native speakers with whom you speak are not interested in judging your performance. They are interested in communicating with you. If it is not too much work for them to understand you and make themselves understood, your mistakes will not matter much and are in fact expected in a non-native speaker. Of course, if they have enough motivation to talk with you (to sell you something, to help you learn, or because they like you), they will work with you even if it does require effort on their part.

Foreignness

Foreign languages reflect foreign ways of thinking. Learning to think in different ways can upset comfortable patterns. Then we may become anxious because things are not as predictable as they used to be.

Foreign customs offer opportunities for fascinating exploration, but they also can be fraught with pitfalls that might cause you to give offense without intending to. As a decent, sensitive human being, you may feel anxious about doing the "wrong thing."

There are ways of managing this, too. Learn as much as you can about these foreign cultures and foreign customs. The more you know, the less likely you are to make a *faux pas* – and the less anxious you are likely to feel about doing so. Also, try to think about the unfamiliar customs as adventures, not as threats, and native speakers and teachers as wanting to help you rather than criticize you. Even if you make mistakes in etiquette, most people will know you are foreign, and they will make allowances. They want to have a good relationship with you, just as you do with them.

Some learners also report not liking the language they are studying. It might be the combination of sounds that does not sound pleasant to their ear, or perhaps the manner of expressing ideas seems inaccessible or just plain weird. In some cases, learners like the language but not the culture. In both these cases – not liking the language and not liking the culture – you can experience mixed emotions (and mixed motivation) toward your learning tasks, your classmates, your teacher, and native speakers. Being aware of the source of your aversion or irritation can help, as can being clear on why you are taking the language. If your reason is not related to the language *per se*, such as wanting to spend time with a friend who is in the class, you might consider whether or not being in this particular language course is a good use of your time and whether you could perhaps accomplish your goals in some other way with fewer negative emotions.

Managing generalized feelings of anxiety

What if your anxiety is more generalized than these specific situations? What if you are almost always feeling a sense of dread and nervousness when you think about your foreign-language class or about using foreign language in a community? First, remember that anxiety is not always bad. If it is in small amounts to get you moving, or if you really are in a dangerous situation, then it's appropriate. It is only when anxiety gets in your way that you should be concerned. There are several ways in which anxiety can be managed before it becomes debilitating: through acceptance, reframing, goal-setting, and game playing.

Acceptance

Franklin Roosevelt said "We have nothing to fear but fear itself." Similarly, if you get anxious about being anxious, you may end up multiplying the negative effects of your anxiety. Accept that you are anxious, analyze the source, and if it is one of the sources identified in the previous sections of this chapter, follow some of the suggestions there. If it is more generalized, accept that you are anxious and take one or more of the following steps.

Reframing

One of the most powerful strategies you can use is called *reframing*. What this means is that you try to see something threatening as something helpful. The comment above about the importance of making mistakes is a good example. You can look at mistakes as failures, but this will damage your learning efforts. You would do much better to think of mistakes as a natural part of the learning process and realize that if you do not make mistakes, you are not learning as much as you could. The same is true for the example given about being overwhelmed by the amount to be learned. Reframing the whole into smaller pieces can take away the sense of failure and replace it with a sense of success. Reframing is a cognitive strategy in service to an affective purpose: it has to do with changing how you think about something and, as a result, how you feel about something.

Goal-setting

Perfection of language control is not necessary. *You do not have to speak like a native* to do the things you want to do in the language. So another strategy you can use is setting goals, by deciding what you want to do with the language. That will indicate how close to native-like language you need to aim for, and it can be another way to forgive yourself for making mistakes. You can evaluate your progress and performance in terms of your goal, not some kind of abstract perfection. For example, if you are learning the language in order to make foreign friends, you would aim at being able to express yourself well enough to say what you want and be understood without a lot of work on the part of the person you are talking with.

In setting goals, make them realistic. If you are a beginner and are trying to read something written for native speakers, be glad when you can figure out what the passage is about in general or even if you can understand 5–10 per cent of it.

Game playing

Make a game of trying to say as much as you can with what you know. One of the authors will try to say something with a native speaker knowing that it is probably wrong and then feel pleased when she is corrected, especially when she is working with someone who might not explain it to her if she asked directly. (This would probably be because the native speaker considered the concept too difficult for the learner's level of foreign-language proficiency.) In this case, making a mistake is strategic.

CASE STUDY

Problem

Alex has come to the university from a small town high school, where he graduated first in his class. He was used to "acing" tests and was disappointed when he got less than 100 per cent. However, his high school had no foreign language courses. Now he has to meet a foreign language requirement. Feeling that he was a strong learner who wanted to try something different, he signed up for Swahili. Now, Alex is feeling overwhelmed by the amount he is having to learn in his Swahili class, and furthermore, the system of infixes and use of aspect doesn't make sense to him, so that he often makes mistakes in class. He has become so anxious that he doesn't want to study French at night, and he is in danger of poor performance in class and in the exam.

Possible solutions

(1) Within the larger framework of course goals, Alex needs to think about his personal goals in learning Swahili. If he had none in reality (other than wanting to take on a challenge), perhaps now is the time to set some, such as wanting to get an "A" in the course or wanting to be able to use the language for study abroad.

(2) Once he is clear about his goals, he can set limits on what he makes himself responsible for. He probably does not have to learn every word in the textbook or be able to say everything his classmates can say.

(3) Alex can make a conscious effort to stop counting his mistakes and count the number of times he succeeds in getting someone else to understand what he is trying to say.

Figure 4.1

Performance anxiety

Closely related to foreign-language anxiety, and typically a subset of it, is performance anxiety. You may experience performance anxiety when you worry about answering questions, reciting, making presentations, or doing a role play in front of your peers. Some students are concerned that they sound silly. Other students worry that their accent will be strong or that their answers will be wrong. If you belong to either of these groups, you may be suffering from performance anxiety. It might help to understand that many of your peers feel the same way – and for naught because most students are too busy worrying about their own performance to judge the performance of their peers.

Performance anxiety can occur in study abroad and other in-country situations, as well. In a way, it is similar to stage fright when one has to perform a play or a musical score in front of an audience or the blank-brain syndrome that math competitions and spelling bees sometimes bring. For language learners, though, there is an additional element in that performance anxiety can result in the

---

CASE STUDY

Problem

Shawna is in Kazakhstan on a visit and wants to buy some bread from a bread cart. She feels very apprehensive because she has never done this before; this is not the place she buys bread at home nor are the interpersonal verbal exchanges required similar to ones that she uses in her own language for shopping. What can she do?

Possible solutions

(1) Shawna might use the strategy of rehearse: if she has role-played this situation in advance, once she takes a big breath and starts the conversation, she will probably find that the pieces will fall into place for her.

(2) Shawna might take a friend with her, at least the first time, so that she does not have to be alone when she makes these exchanges; having gone through the experience successfully once with a friend is likely to remove any anxiety for her in the future.

Figure 4.2

near-total loss of communicative ability – suddenly, you cannot buy the bread you need at the store, and the like. In addition to resulting in the language learner potentially going hungry, that performance failure makes some learners feel like little children, and this feeling may lead them to avoiding performing at all. One of our colleagues tells the following story.

> I remember vividly on my first study abroad visit to the USSR how stunning it was for me that a 3-year old child could communicate more effectively in Russian than I, although I had been studying intensively for two years – the child had had more immersion than I had in that time!!!   (B. Rifkin, personal communication, December 23, 2003)

Performance anxiety is probably best handled through preparedness. One of the reasons that teachers like to do role plays in the classroom is that they prepare students for performing outside the classroom. If performance anxiety strikes in the community, often the tongue will work automatically due to the classroom practice, and you will know that you dealt with the situation at least once already. If you have not had classroom practice, you can create your own practice by rehearsing the anticipated exchanges sufficient times in advance that your brain and tongue will be on automatic, regardless of what is happening with your nerves, when you have to make those exchanges for real. (For many, the situation of using your foreign language in the community is not all that unlike musicians and actors appearing in front of audiences – very few would ever consider doing so without a lot of rehearsals and repetition. For others, it is more like a jazz performance: part of the pleasure is the improvisation.)

Test anxiety

About test anxiety

For many of us, taking tests is one of the most anxiety-provoking situations we encounter as learners. Being judged is very difficult and arouses an enormous amount of anxiety. Far more energy can go into worrying about the test and your results than into learning and performing on the test. There are a number of reasons why you might feel anxious about taking a test. Here are some of them:

- previous conditioning;
- self-image;
- consequences;
- fear and frustration caused by limited language skills; and
- "facing the music."

Previous conditioning

Your previous experience with tests in school may have conditioned you to expect an unpleasant experience, filled with anxiety and fraught with heavy consequences. In some cases, much or even everything may depend on a single performance, and if you had a bad day, that is your bad luck. That need not be the case, however. If you had a bad day, see if you can negotiate a retest or other way of demonstrating your knowledge.

Self-image

You receive a rating, whether by a course or test grade or by assignment of a language proficiency level. A rating has an effect on our self-image, and we may end up labeling ourselves in ways that hurt our learning ability. For example, a learner may be tempted to think "I got a bad grade – I'm really a bad student." This is very destructive and to be avoided if at all possible; it is much better to think, "I got a bad grade this time. Next time I'll try to do better."

Consequences

When something concrete depends on the test, such as pay increases, a future job, or parents' willingness to continue to pay for coursework, the anxiety is compounded. If you are in this situation, try to keep the consequences out of your mind as much as possible. This is, of course, much easier to say than to do, but there are some techniques in the next section that you can use. Probably the most powerful is to think about something else – such as the content of what you are learning.

Fear and frustration

A test is a concentrated medium for kinds of anxiety we described in the previous sections, such as fear of making mistakes, frustration at difficulties communicating, or even the sense of interpersonal failure (if in an oral interview and you feel that you have let down the person you are talking with). In a class setting, the anxieties may be spread out over time and mixed with many successes, but in a test, they are distilled into an hour or two, so it is important for you to find ways to keep them at bay.

"Facing the music"

A test can force you to face up to what you do and don't know. You may have thought you knew all the Chinese characters you needed to read news articles about the weather, but you come across something you never saw before. (This will be easier for inductive learners, who use context to figure out what something means, than for deductive ones, who want to learn in advance and not figure out.) The prospect of failure, however it may be defined by the test-taker, is a heavy threat to emotional well-being. A test is designed and usually evaluated by someone else. That means someone else has the power to decide what you should know, whether it corresponds to your interests and purposes or not.

Coping with test anxiety

Test anxiety is not easy to manage, but there are some things you can do. Here are some examples with explanations that follow:

*   Manage your image of yourself.
*   Manage your learning before the test.
*   Managing yourself before the test (your feelings and your activities)
*   Manage yourself during the tests
*   Manage your relationships with those who evaluate you

You may notice that all the subheadings in this test anxiety section start with the word *managing*. There is a reason for this. Coping with the stresses that tests cause most of us is something only you can do. It therefore depends heavily on your self-regulation skills (there is more information on self-regulation in chapter 9); you need to manage your feelings, your thoughts, your activities before and during the test, and your relationships with people who rate you.

Managing self-image

Managing your self-image can contribute significantly to reducing your test anxiety. The first thing to do is to stop dwelling on your anxiety. Such negative thoughts can lead you to set up images of yourself failing, which in turn may create a negative self-fulfilling prophecy (that is, you may make yourself fail). Instead, use positive imaging of yourself. For example, imagine entering and taking the test in a cool, calm, self-confident way. That can help you build self-fulfilling prophecies in a positive direction. There is a good deal of psychological research on managing one's self-image and one's mood – mind over matter, so to speak; if you are interested, you might find many more suggestions on how to do this in the work of the neurolinguistic programmers (Dilts, 1979; Bandler, 1985).

Managing pre-test learning

Being prepared for a test may be the best defense against test anxiety. Managing pre-test learning consists of a number of steps. First, ensure that you are keeping up in class, and if you are not, seek help from your teacher – the earlier the better. This way, nothing on the test should be a surprise to you. Second, clarify what will be on the test. Your teacher will usually indicate what is important and what is not. If you are uncertain, it is always best to ask. Obviously, not everything covered in class is equally important. Paying attention to the most important things and letting the less important ones slide by if you do not have enough time for them is the best way to spend your study time. Third, study time is important; prepare for a test a little bit every day. Cramming the night before is very counterproductive and only causes greater test anxiety. Research shows that crammers do more poorly on tests in general than students who prepare well in advance and get a good night's sleep before the test, whether or not they feel they are ready for it (E. Leaver, 1999).

Managing yourself before the test

In general, self-management techniques include relaxation, distracting yourself, and rest. Everyone has different ways to relax. Some people might soak in a hot bath; others might meditate. Another way to relax is to distract yourself with a good book, a game, or other activity that engages your mind and takes it away from the test. We highly recommend escape literature like mysteries or other fiction, for example. Even if it means you lose a little time from studying, it will pay off, because a refreshed mind is a more receptive and productive mind.

Every list of strategies for coping with test anxiety suggests that students get a good night's sleep the night before. We follow suit because evidence (cite) indicates the importance of enough sleep to physical and mental well-being. It is something like getting your mind off of the task for a little while when you are awake. When you sleep, you refresh your abilities and push anxiety away. In fact, many people find that they do a lot of mental processing when they sleep, resulting in consolidated knowledge or new ideas.

Managing yourself during the test

While in the test, focus on the task, not on "what-if" thoughts. That is, think about how to do your best on the questions or tasks you have right now. Don't think about "What if I get this one wrong?" Instead, think about strategies to "beat" the test. For example, if something is too hard or taking too much time, move on to the next thing. Another example: random learners (who choose their own order to learn things) will normally look over the whole test (if it is written) to see what is there, and the random learners may well choose the easiest parts to

---

CASE STUDY

Problem

Taylor is doing well in her Chinese class. She has learned many of the written characters and can guess at meanings of texts even where she does not know all the character symbols. However, she makes use of context to learn – she is highly synoptic – and this test will focus on recognition of individual characters without any context. Taylor knows that this is a task at which she is less adept and is starting to spend increasing time stewing about the test. She knows that this is not helping her but is feeling stuck with it.

Possible solutions

(1) Taylor might first ensure that she has a solid base in recognizing the characters that could be in the test. Flashcards, if she is a visual verbalist learner (see chapter 3) might prove useful.

(2) She could also check with the teacher to find out if there are areas she does not need to study. That leaves time to study the things the teacher thinks are important.

(3) She could set aside a certain amount of time every day to let herself think about the test, but other than that, she should keep busy with things that block out the anxious thoughts.

Figure 4.3

do first. If you are a sequential learner (prefers to follow the set order), this is a good cross-style technique for you to use.

Managing your relationship with an interviewer

In an oral interview test, build a relationship with the interviewer, and show friendliness (but not obsequiousness). An interviewer who feels positive toward you is likely to be more helpful to you.

Also in interviews, be open about areas you don't find of interest. For example, if you don't pay attention to sports, you will have a hard time talking about them in any language, so let the interviewer know this isn't an area you have much to say about. Depending on the situation, you may be able to suggest another topic. For example, you might say something like, "I don't much like sports, so I don't know much about them, but I do know that Western music is very popular in your country. Do you like it?"

Motivation

Motivation refers to "why" – why you are studying a language in the first place, why you like reading better than listening (if you do), why you study rather than party or vice versa. When you come right down to it, motivation is behind all the choices you make and everything you do. Here we focus on motivation in language learning.

About motivation

In this section, we look at some different approaches to general motivation and at how people can lose their motivation (demotivation).

•   Some kinds of motivation
•   Motivation and choices
•   Losing motivation (demotivation)

Some kinds of motivation

The two best-known ways of looking at motivation are called intrinsic–extrinsic and integrative–instrumental. There is some overlap between the two approaches.

Intrinsic and extrinsic motivation have to do with whether the motivator is more inside you or outside of you (Deci and Ryan, 1985). Intrinsic motivation is about doing something because it makes you feel happy, more whole, or because it fits in some way with something important to who you are. Extrinsic motivation has to do with doing something for such 'outside' reasons as money, job requirements, or passing a test. The two kinds of motivation probably overlap to some degree when the job or test, for example, are part of a career that you care a lot about, or are part of a degree program in a subject you really like. Then your work for the test or assignment may be extrinsically motivated, but the program of which it is a part brings about intrinsic motivation, too.

Within the language learning field, the classic model is the distinction between instrumental and integrative motivation (Gardner and Lambert, 1972). If you are learning a language primarily for a purpose like getting a job or fulfilling an academic requirement you are affected by instrumental motivation. Integrative motivation has to do with wanting to be accepted by another community. You may have both kinds of motivation: you are instrumentally motivated to pass a test or meet a requirement, but at the same time, you might have fallen in love with, for example, Hindu culture and want to learn Hindi for the sake of getting to know Indians better and maybe participating in their culture to some degree.

Extrinsic and instrumental motivation are similar but not exactly alike – extrinsic focuses on the fact that the reason is outside of you, whereas instrumental is about the purpose of your learning. Intrinsic and integrative motivations are even more different: intrinsic motivation has to do with what makes you feel good or whole, whereas integrative motivation is about acceptance and some form of membership in a language community.

Motivation and choices

Motivation applies not only to why you are learning a language (see chapter 1), but also to why you make the choices you do while learning. Factors that influence that motivation and hence the choices include learning style and personality, anxiety, self-efficacy (discussed below), and personal history, among other things. For example, you might have taken a trip to Thailand recently and now want to learn Thai (personal history, intrinsic), be enrolled in a program in international relations (extrinsic and indirectly intrinsic if you really like the subject), enjoy learning by talking to others rather than in a classroom and thus seek to participate in immersion learning (learning style and personality).

Another place motivation can affect your choices is in the learning strategies you use. Some years ago, one of the authors needed to learn some Arabic for a two-week stay in the Middle East. What she wanted (her motivation) was to build friendships and get her basic needs met. She also wanted a base to keep learning while abroad. Knowing that she had only a few hours to devote to the language before her departure, she decided that what she would need most was a good understanding of foreign guest etiquette and very basic language for exchanging courtesies and getting around town on her own. That's what she worked on with her teacher. Discussions of culture and etiquette were in English, but she tried to make the most of her minimal Arabic during the rest of the time, with the result that she had a splendid visit, both socially and linguistically. This is an example of how her motivation determined what and how she chose to study.

Losing motivation (demotivation)

It is possible to lack or lose motivation. Some experiences can be demotivating for you, for example a classroom in which you cannot make the most of your learning style. If you are an inductive learner, for instance, and everything is pointed out by the teacher, you may feel frustration at not being able to make your own discoveries. On the other hand, this might be a more comfortable situation if you are a deductive learner, who would rather apply what is learned than discover it.

Another demotivating situation, depending on your personality, may be feeling rejected by a speaker of the language. One of the authors felt for some time that a teacher of one of the languages she was learning did not like her. She had to work very hard to overcome the discouragement she felt and even took to meditating to clear her mind before each session with that teacher. (The story had a happy ending; not only did she learn the language well, but the teacher became a good friend.)

Anxiety can be highly demotivating. After all, who wants to face constant threats and stress? You may be tempted to cope with your anxiety by avoiding the situation that makes you anxious and justify it to yourself as something you didn't want to do anyway (this is the "sour grapes" defense: the grapes turn out to be sour, so I didn't want them anyway). Avoiding learning and deciding you don't want it after all because it makes you anxious is unlikely to lead to success; it would be better to try some of the anxiety management techniques described above in the section on anxiety.

You can really get discouraged when you do poorly in an examination or feel that you are not as good as others in the class. As mentioned earlier in this chapter, changing your focus to doing better next time or to your own progress is a good way to cope with this kind of discouragement.

Sometimes you may have to learn the language because it is required. Some of you may find it hard to get motivated to work if you do not see any practical reason for learning the language. In this case you may need to find things that catch your interest, or better yet, make some friends from the country where the language is spoken.

Maintaining motivation

So what can you do if you are not feeling motivated to learn the language, do your homework, or speak with others in the language? Listed below are some suggestions.

- Review your goals.
- Have some fun with or through the language.
- Manage your feelings.
- Interact with other people.

Review your goals

You can review for yourself why you are learning the language. You may be able to get back to what got you into it in the first place. For example, even though you are meeting a university requirement to take a language, you chose to study Russian because you were thinking you would like to visit the cultural treasures in St. Petersburg and elsewhere in Russia. You had also met some Russians and liked them. Now you are having a hard time with Russian, and you're losing interest. Once you remind yourself of these reasons, some simple things you can do are to find a book with pictures of the great Russian museums. Go visit your friends if they are nearby. If they are farther away, try a phone call, just to renew your positive feelings and motivate yourself again.

Build in some pleasure

Find something you like related to the language and let it be your focus. For instance, you might get engaged by the culture of the people who speak the language, by the music, or by sports played by members of the culture. Then you can put some energy into learning words related to your topic of interest and into learning how to talk about it in the language. If you enjoy languages for their own sake, you might find that some of the concepts used in the language are interesting (new grammar categories, for example). You might like creating something new with the language such as a story or simple poem. A number of good language learners find fun in playing the kind of game described in the section on anxiety, where you see how much you can do in the language with what you know. A variation on that game is adding the task of seeing how well you can learn new things without having to go back into your native language. You can use any or all of these techniques to activate your interest in your study, and you will surely come up with some of your own. Additionally, you might keep a list of things in your head that you like (music and art, science and history) or are interested in about a culture and try to learn as much as you can about each. When you get demotivated or bored with one topic, move to another; you can come back to the original topic later.

Manage your feelings

Put failures in their place. Mistakes are not statements about you and your overall competence or value. They are only obstacles for you to overcome and from which you can learn.

Instead of avoiding necessary learning situations that make you anxious or using the "sour grapes" strategy (I didn't really want it anyway), make use of the suggestions made above for managing anxiety. Find things you enjoy doing, or find new ways to achieve the same result. For example, if you don't like memorizing verb forms, try reading texts in the language that use different tenses and aspects. Notice the verbs and their forms. Blank out the verbs, and then go through and try to fill them in right. This way you get exposure and a way to test yourself without having to use brute memorization, and you get a sense of gradual mastery as well.

One thing that might help is the fact that most native speakers (outside your classroom) are very tolerant of learner error and accent (albeit the French have a reputation, perhaps unfairly ascribed, for intolerance of the latter).

Interact with others

Relationships with other people can make a wonderful motivator. After all, language is communication, and communication is with other people. Sometimes we learn not only for our own purposes but because it will please someone else, such as a parent, teacher, or friend. In fact, one theory says that we often learn at first to please someone else, and then, by some mental magic, that love of the other person becomes love of the subject (Mishne, 1996). (Many good teachers know this, and they use the relationships they build with students to help them learn. You can use it in the reverse direction: you get an additional benefit from your relationships to help you learn.)

Perhaps the best way to build such relationships is to make friends who speak the language. It would be ideal to use the language with them to practice conversation, but even if you cannot for some reason, you will pick up a lot about the language and culture from them, and your friendship with them will support your motivation

---

CASE STUDY

Problem

Elena works for a foreign company whose managers speak English. She has found that she needs to improve her English to advance in the company. Although this is not her highest priority in how to have fun, she has enrolled in an English as a Second Language program. She has been in it for about two weeks and is thinking of quitting. The others in the class seem to know more English than she does, and she misses the time she spent dancing with friends. The subject matter is boring to her; it is all about sports and politics.

Possible solutions

(1) Elena could revisit her purpose in joining the class and visualize herself speaking with company managers and clients in much better English and succeeding in her projects.

(2) She could find some English speakers who like to dance and go dancing (and talking) with them.

(3) She could introduce some topics she likes into the class. Maybe a word with the teacher might help, if she cannot bring up the topics as part of the lesson.

Figure 4.4

to keep working on learning their language. A variation on this approach is to work out an exchange with them, where you spend some of the time with their language and some of the time with yours so that you both learn.

Sometimes it just helps to talk with a sympathetic person when you're frustrated or discouraged about the language learning. Teachers and friends are the obvious starting points, but you may have others you find helpful, such as the librarian or a relative. Some universities have language advisory services or language-learning skill centers; they are a good place to talk out what is going on, and they can give you advice tailored to your individual needs. Think about your social circle: perhaps there is someone you never thought of as a source of listening and possibly advice to whom you can turn.

Self-efficacy

About self-efficacy

Knowing what self-efficacy is can help you reach your goals successfully in many endeavors, not just in foreign language. To improve your sense of self-efficacy, two pieces of information will help:

- a definition of self-efficacy; and
- a description of the factors that affect self-efficacy.

Defining self-efficacy

Feelings of self-efficacy have to do with one's feeling that one can accomplish a task or project, such as learning a foreign language. It is not quite the same thing as self-confidence, which is more general. You may be generally self-confident in most settings, but you may or may not have a sense of self-efficacy as a language learner, on the playing field, or at cocktail parties, just to take a few examples. Self-efficacy is a close partner with motivation: if you think you can accomplish something, you are likely to want to try it. If you think you are likely to fail or not be very good at something, your motivation may suffer. Needless to say, lack of self-efficacy is likely to involve some anxiety, so the two concepts are related, and so are the ways to cope.

A sense of self-efficacy is normally the result of previous successful experience. If you have succeeded at the same or a similar task, you will enter the new project confident that you can do this one too. This is one of the reasons for practicing small tasks, like getting the verb at the end of the sentence in Turkish, and large ones, such as making contact with a customer or client. Once you have practiced it, you know that you have what it takes to do it when you need it.

For you and for teachers, building in success is extremely important. Experiences of success breed success, and too much failure can lead to discouragement and demotivation. If you are finding something difficult, break it down into parts, and tackle only one part at a time. You do not have to learn all the Arabic plural forms, for example. Instead, set your priorities, and select one or two of the most common categories to learn, listen for, and practice.

Factors that affect self-efficacy

Not only does self-efficacy vary by domain of activity (such as sports, political debate, or language learning), it also is influenced by what you are like (your personality and learning style), and by other people. Some important factors include:

* personality
* learning style
* relationships

Personality

Some personality characteristics increase or decrease feelings of self-efficacy, depending on the specific situation. One example is extraversion (tendency to seek stimulation from outside yourself, especially with other people), which is likely to promote a sense of self-efficacy in situations where you need to talk to a lot of people in the foreign language. (This is not to say that introverts, who tend to try to control external stimulation, lack self-efficacy in talking to people, but their strengths are likely to be in deeper discussions with one or two other people, rather than in crowds.) An introvert, on the other hand, might approach a writing task with more confidence than an extravert. (There will be a lot more about personality later in this chapter; we suggest that as you read it, you consider how it may affect your sense of language-learning self-efficacy.)

Learning style

Your learning style is likely to play a major role in your sense of self-efficacy in specific situations. Those learners who like dealing with the unpredictable, for example, may enter an unstructured learning situation like an immersion learning program with confidence or even pleasurable anticipation. Learners who prefer overt structure might feel at a loss without it.

Relationships

If being liked is important to you, your self-efficacy will probably be increased if you feel that the people you are talking with are "on your side" and are laughing *with* you when you make errors rather than *at* you. Good relationships can help. One of the authors has found that even when she is at the early language-learning stages, one way to build successful relationships is to let native speakers become her teachers. Most of them enjoy the role, especially because she is adept at letting the "teachers" know she is enjoying being taught. This technique works for her at all levels of proficiency.

Building and maintaining self-efficacy

When you enter a language-learning experience, you may be certain if the teaching style or situation will fit you. You may have learned foreign languages as a child just by growing up in a country where more than one language was spoken, so trying to learn a language in a classroom may be new for you. Or the opposite may be true: you may have had years of classroom Japanese, but this is the first time for you to try to speak Japanese in Japan. What can you do to help yourself build more confidence in your ability to learn Japanese? There are a number of strategies. Here a few of them; you can probably think of even more yourself:

- being self-aware;
- imaging;
- making friends;
- being realistic;
- checking your progress;
- improving your weak areas gradually;
- using positive self-talk; and
- chunking.

Self-awareness

The first step toward building self-confidence is self-awareness. If you know what your learning style and personality preferences are, you will have a better idea of the situations that enhance your self-efficacy and those which will detract from it. There is a great deal about learning style in chapter 3, and you will read about personality later in this chapter. If, for example, you learn that the class requires a lot of oral work – which you are not good at – but that there is also a textbook, which is more in keeping with your preferences for visual learning, you can plan on being able to manage the learning situation by reading the chapters before going to class rather than waiting for them to be assigned following oral work.

Imaging

Imaging, or imagining yourself in a situation, is not only a good technique for managing anxiety and enhancing motivation, it can help you with self-efficacy as well. For example, imagine yourself succeeding at speaking Indonesian in Jakarta and making friends with Indonesians or managing the Finnish cases so well that you are understood by Finns. If you are a visual learner, you might close your eyes and visualize future scenes where you are joking with a group of Indonesian friends or making a short presentation to a group of Finns. That feeling of success can carry over to your classroom and, later, even to the actual situation.

Making friends

Making friends who encourage you and help you see your uppermost potential and who "hold your hand" when you are feeling down can boost your feelings of self-efficacy. These friends can be speakers of your own language, but it is even better if they can come from the culture and country whose language you are learning. It may take some time to develop such friendships, but they can be worth a huge amount if you are patient. Language exchange (your language for theirs) is a good way to start.

Realism

Be realistic, neither too optimistic nor too pessimistic. Everyone has limitations. However, instead of focusing on the limitations, spend your efforts focusing on how you can overcome (and are overcoming) those limitations every day.

Checking your progress

If you are feeling some discouragement, take a look at material you learned earlier in your course and see how far you've come. There will always be a gap between what you are learning now and what you feel you have mastered, so it is a good idea to look at your increasingly solid base from time to time.

Look for what you're good at and emphasize it. For example, if you do well with making yourself understood despite your limitations, find opportunities to do that, and let yourself feel good about your successes at it.

CASE STUDY

Problem

Beth enjoys her class in Indonesian, but she is afraid she will not be able to talk to Indonesians in a way that will help her get her needs met and her work done. She is both anticipating and dreading her immersion study there – anticipating because she loves the language and culture, but dreading because she lacks confidence in her ability to manage Indonesian in an unstructured situation.

Possible solutions

(1) Beth could imagine herself in successful interactions in a variety of situations in Indonesia.

(2) She could pick some topics she likes to talk about and prepare herself to make conversation about them.

(3) She could make some Indonesian friends – maybe Beth's teacher can help her find some people to talk with outside of class. She can use the topics she has prepared.

Figure 4.5

Improving your weak areas gradually

While emphasizing your strengths, do not neglect the things you do not like as well or are not very good at doing. Get into these things gradually, and try to be sure that you do them in small enough steps that you build in more success than failure. Here's an example: instead of trying to learn all of the irregular verbs in French at once, learn the regular present first, then the future, then the compound past, etc.

Using positive self-talk

Give yourself a pep talk from time to time, saying such things as "I am a good learner. Sometimes I run into things that are hard, and then I find strategies to help myself. I'm smart about learning strategically." If you catch yourself saying things like "I'm no good at language learning," stop yourself as fast as you can. It may be a natural defense against the feeling of failure, but it is also likely to engender more failure that you can avoid. If necessary, start doing something other than language-learning tasks to distract yourself.

Chunking

Good teachers know that building in success is a key feature for lesson planning. When they have students who are having particular difficulty, they also design activities or lesson materials for those learners that move more slowly but ensure success at each step. If you are a learner, you can do some of the same thing for yourself in your learning plans. The kind of chunking where you break a large task into smaller ones is a good example of this.

Personality

Personality is closely intertwined with everything we have discussed already: memory, learning styles, learning strategies, learning aptitude, anxiety, motivation, and self-efficacy. What we pay attention to and remember, how we prefer to learn, what makes us anxious, what motivates us, and what we are confident at, all are linked to our personality preferences. It also makes a big difference in how we conduct our interpersonal relations, which are addressed in the next chapter.

Since personality is such a complex area, the maxim "The map is not the territory" is especially apt. Philosophers and psychologists have been trying to understand human personality since at least the time of the ancient Greeks, and there are a great many maps to explore. No one map completely covers the territory, and it is entirely possible that even if the maps were combined, there would still be unknown territory.

We will focus here on a few of the more widely used models of personality that have proved useful in language learning and teaching. They are

- the Jungian Myers–Briggs type indicator (MBTI),
- other Jungian personality models, and
- other personality models.

The Myers–Briggs type indicator

Personality typing, especially through the Myers–Briggs type indicator (MBTI) (Myers, McCaulley, et al., 1998), has become widespread. It is used in companies, schools, by counselors, and in research. While it is not the only personality typology in existence, it is the one that has been the most researched, especially for educational settings.

The MBTI is based on and adapted from the work of Swiss psychiatrist Carl Jung (1971). Jung described three aspects of psychological activity. These aspects are

- extraversion and introversion (direction of energy flow),
- sensing and intuition (mental function for taking in data), and
- thinking and feeling (mental function for coming to conclusions and making decisions).

One from each of these pairs is preferred and used most of the time in your conscious activity. The other member of each pair stays with you too, but it affects your unconscious functioning more (Jung, 1971).

Myers and Briggs (Myers with Myers, 1980; Myers, McCaulley, et al., 1998) added a fourth dimension, which we include here, as well:

*   judging-perceiving (how you prefer to deal with the world outside of you, especially how much structure you want from it).

Extraversion (E) vs. introversion (I)

You are probably familiar with these terms; they are widely used. Most people think of extraverts as outgoing and talkative, and introverts as reserved and quiet. These stereotypes are partially true, but not always. Introverts can be very outgoing and assertive (for example, one of the authors describes herself as a "noisy introvert" when in learning situations); extraverts also need "down time" and quiet to restore their balance. What Jung meant by extraversion is not the same as what is usually meant by the popular term: instead, he meant that the external world is attractive to the extravert and at the same time energizes him or her. Some of the traits like gregariousness and so on are often characteristic of extraverts, but they are not extraversion. The same is true of introverts: the internal world is attractive and energizing; introverts may be quiet and reserved, but those traits are not introversion.

Recent research suggests that extraversion-introversion is probably related to level of neural arousal (Revelle, Anderson, and Humphreys, 1987; Eysenck, 1991). Introversion appears to relate to a higher level of internal neural arousal and activity. As a result, it is easy for an introvert to get too much stimulation from the outside world and thus need to withdraw from stimulation to restore balance. On the other hand, extraverts appear to bring less neural arousal to their interactions with the outside world and thus may seek external stimulation. As a result, extraverts and introverts tend to behave differently. One good example is that extraverts tend to be impulsive and jump right into situations, whereas introverts need more time to process before acting. "Let me think about it" is a key phrase for introverts. If you are an extravert, you are more likely to talk a lot in the classroom and seek new acquaintance in non-classroom language-learning settings. If you are an introvert, you will also want to talk (some more than others – remember the "noisy introvert") in class but will probably want to think about it first, even if briefly. Outside the classroom, you, too, will make friends, but you will probably do it one person at a time and take more time to get to know native speakers.

Sensing (S) vs. intuition (I)

Sensing and intuition have to do with how you take in information and whether you focus more on the present or the future. If you prefer sensing, you probably like factual information more than speculation and more interested in the present than the future. You would rather focus on "what is" than on "what might be." On the other hand, if you prefer intuition, you are likely more interested in what the facts mean than in the facts themselves and are future-oriented, interested in possibilities. Sensing and intuition play a major role in interests and choices of subjects for study. Sensing types are likely to choose to concentrate in areas like accounting, surgery, and business, for example, whereas intuitives are more likely to be interested in areas like literature, psychology, and philosophy.

Not only does this dimension strongly influence your interests, it also affects how you go about learning: sensing types are more likely to prefer ectenic learning, and intuitives tend to prefer synoptic approaches (see chapter 3). In other words, in foreign-language classes, if you are a sensing type, you may want to have an explanation of rules before you are expected to apply them. If you are in a language class that does not approach language learning in this way, you can buy yourself a grammar reference book or a textbook with rules and read through the explanations as you come to the various grammar features in the classroom. Conversely, if you are an intuitive type in a classroom where you basically learn grammar rules and then practice applying them, you might do a lot of supplemental reading of literature of all sorts from the target culture.

Thinking (T) vs. feeling (F)

Once you have information from sensing or intuition, you are likely to want to do something with it, such as make decisions and choices. The thinking–feeling scale describes different ways to do this. Thinking individuals seek to deal with the world through logic and cause-effect; feeling individuals look more at right–wrong, good–bad, that is, values. All of us use thinking, and all of us use feeling, the issue is more which one you prefer to use and which tends to be more automatic for you. Your preference for thinking or feeling will also influence how much priority you give to task achievement (thinking) over interpersonal harmony (feeling), and vice versa. (Of course most of us want some of both, but sometimes when we must give priority, our thinking or feeling preference tips the balance.) In the classroom, thinking types tend to be more comfortable with competition and argument than feeling types; a class that consists largely of feeling types will generally feel more harmonious. In terms of learning strategies, thinking types tend to like analyzing language; feeling types tend to reject it.

If you are a thinking type who finds yourself in a classroom with many feeling types, or in which the norms seem to be more feeling than thinking, you need to try to be aware when you may be coming across as argumentative, even when you think you are engaging in simple debate. What seems like debate to you may feel like friction to feeling types. On the other hand, your bent for analyzing may be helpful to your feeling classmates, who find it much less congenial. Offer to help them. Building relationships through studying together is sometimes easier for thinking types than trying to establish interpersonal relations in other kinds of ways.

If you are a feeling type who finds yourself in what may feel like a competitive classroom, you can try to keep it in perspective. For most thinking types, argument and debate are not personal. If you find yourself taking things too personally, step back, think about it, and maybe even ask one or more classmates if they meant what they said personally if it really stings you. If you find yourself in a teaching program that focuses attention on analyzing grammar, you can of course use it as a chance to learn new skills. If it is really hard for you, see if you can get some help from the teacher or a classmate who seems to be good at helping others to learn how to do analysis better. And don't forget that you have other things to offer.

Judging (J) vs. perceiving (P)

In personality type theory, everyone has both inner worlds (most important to introverts) and outer worlds (primary for extraverts), but all of us have to deal with the outer world, whether or not it is preferred. Judging–perceiving indicates how you like to relate to your outer world, and how much structuring you want from it. Judgers generally like a planned and relatively predictable life; they want things decided so they can get on with the task (whatever the task may be). Perceivers prefer to keep their options open and maintain flexibility, and they often prefer to delay decisions so they can get more information. If you are a judger (structure and closure), you are likely to be good at getting things done on time and manage your time well. You turn in your homework in an orderly way. If you prefer perceiving, on the other hand, your time management may be less regular, with a lot of last-minute scrambles, but you are likely to be relatively tolerant of the ambiguity you encounter in language learning and relatively flexible in dealing with the inevitable surprises.

If you are a perceiver in classes with judging norms – which in fact is the case in most classes – you will probably find that you need to learn to adapt to those norms, because you will find them in most organizations after you leave your schooling, as well. (This paragraph is written by a perceiver, so it's not coming from judger bias.) That doesn't mean you can't continue to find ways to express your spontaneity and enjoyment of the unexpected, but you do need to learn to manage your time. One last minute paper is fine, but what if you end up with three things that all have to be done at the same time?

If you are a judger, you will probably find that most situations are relatively comfortable for you, because of the judging norms found in most institutions and organizations, as well as most Western cultures in general. However, you can still learn to enjoy the perceiver gift for spontaneity and even play in learning situations. Bear with the perceivers: their need for more data is likely to provide something you never thought of and may not even have known you needed to know.

The sixteen types

If you have one preference from each of these dimensions, you then have four characteristics, which are abbreviated by the first letter of the preference E for extraversion, I for introversion, and so forth (the exception is intuition, for which the abbreviation is N, since I is used for introversion). There are sixteen possible combinations of the four preferences; these combinations are called personality types. They are

ISTJ	INTJ
ESTJ	ENTJ
ISFJ	INFJ
ESFJ	ENFJ
ISTP	INTP
ESTP	ENTP
ISFP	INFP
ESFP	ENFP

None of these sixteen possible outcomes (types) is considered better than any of the others although there are likely to be environments that provide a better fit for some types than for others. For example, an extraverted teacher might expect more frequent and rapid class participation than some introverts find easy to achieve. Certainly, there will be good and bad matches between you and your instructors and with fellow students. Understanding such mismatches is the first step in preventing them from causing problems.

As an example of how the personality scales combine into personality types, let's look at the first type on the list, ISTJ (introverted–sensing–thinking–judging). This is one of the more common American personality types (Keirsey and Bates, 1988). A person of this personality type usually likes very clear-cut settings with few surprises and tends to be highly reliable, meticulous, and thorough when working. If you belong to the ISTJ personality group, you are apt to seek stability and maintain an orderly, structured life. Your interests may be quite down-to-earth and non-fanciful. As a student, you will usually want a so-called "structured" curriculum and program with objectives, lesson material that is minimally ambiguous, and frequent quizzes and tests on covered material covered, to ensure mastery. You are likely to need to develop skills at dealing with language as it is spoken naturally, with all its ambiguities, fluctuations, and volatility. ISTJs are likely to complain most about unpredictable, apparently disorganized programs and teachers.

Now, let's look at the last type on the list, ENFP (extraverted–intuiting–feeling–perceiving). This is the polar opposite of the ISTJ. ENFPs are outgoing people pleasers. They feel a strong need for freedom of choice in activity and time. For that reason, deadlines sometimes amuse, sometimes irritate them, and sometimes frighten them. Often, they simply ignore them, or will say (typically honestly) that they forgot that something was due. They tend to be happy people who gather friends around them. In the classroom, they love group work, and they are great team players – as long as they are not threatened with a restrictive curriculum, quizzes, and tight deadlines.

Each of the sixteen types can be described similarly, though there is insufficient space here for it. There are many books and websites available with descriptions of the sixteen types; we suggest that you use terms like *personality type*, *psychological type*, *MBTI*, or *Myers–Briggs* to find them through a search engine on the Internet.

The importance of understanding personality types for you is the recognition that most of the sixteen types will appear in your classroom. For example, sometimes classrooms are heavily balanced toward extraverts, which can make the class seem very noisy and overactive to you if you are an introvert. Sometimes they will be balanced toward introverts, which may make the classroom seem uncomfortably quiet if you are an extravert. If your teacher is a thinker, and you are a feeler, there is a strong chance that you will find difficulty from your side in establishing rapport with him or her because a T teacher simply does not, by nature, give the amounts and kinds of warm, personal support for feedback. Rather, the T teacher works on developing the intellectual capacity of students – and that is a sign that the teacher really cares. The problem is that if you are an F, you may not be looking for signs of your teacher's concern in the right places. In reverse, the F teacher may seem too friendly to you if you are a T student, and you might wish that the teacher spent more time dealing with your ideas than with your feelings. Classrooms work or do not work, to some extent, by how well the personality types in them mix. Any mixture is immediately improved when the students and teacher understand personality theory and make concessions and adaptations for the overall representation of personality types within their groups.

Other Jungian personality models

The Myers–Briggs model is widely used in the US, Britain, and Australia. However, it is not the only model that is based on Jung. Other derivatives from Jung's work include

- socionics,
- Jungian functions, and
- Jungian temperaments.

Socionics

Like the MBTI, socionics is a sixteen-type derivative of Jung's work. Unlike the MBTI, the socionics model, which is in wide use in Eastern and Western Europe, as well as throughout Eurasia, Central Asia, and the Baltic nations, strives to stay very close to the original descriptions and type labels suggested by Jung.

Jungian functions

The types can be subgrouped by combinations of the four component preferences. These frequently are important in learning situations. One common way of looking at subtypes is to pull out the two functions (the two middle letters in the type label). These are referred to as *function pairs* (Silver and Hanson, 1996). The function pairs are

- ST (sensing–thinking),
- NT (intuitive–thinking),
- SF (sensing–feeling), and
- NF (intuitive–feeling).

Sensing–thinking (ST). If you prefer the sensing and thinking combination, you probably are oriented toward facts and experience and want practical solutions to tangible, current problems. As a student, you are likely to want a stable, firm base of knowledge before moving on and usually appreciate information that is presented sequentially for you to process one step at a time. You may not respond well to approaches that seem overly theoretical, unrelated to the problem now, or ingenious at the expense of practicality. It is likely that you do not want to be involved in the design of your program – that is the teacher's job, and you want to learn in a logical sequence, not through the random access that some other students prefer. You may tend to reject appeals to your feelings.

If you find yourself in a non-ST classroom, there are ways you can help yourself. For example if you find yourself in situations where you are missing a logical sequence, you might ask for a backtrack, either in the class (there may be others who want it too) or, if you think that would be intrusive, privately with the teacher or other student. You can take the material you are getting and outline it later, to bring it into better order. If there seems to be little or no lesson plan, see if you can negotiate some time for more structured learning, and treat the rest of the time as practice for when you are in real language use situations, where you can expect a lot of unpredictability.

Intuition–thinking (NT). If you lean toward intuition and thinking, you are probably relatively oriented toward possibilities, future potential, strategy, theory, and systems thinking. If you are an NT, then, like the ST, you will probably be put off by things you consider to be "touchy-feely." You may get interested in the system or set of constructs underlying what you are learning, such as how the verbal system works, at the expense of using it (i.e. including a range of verbs in your speech), because you enjoy the intellectual challenge. NT learners want to feel that their program is designed by and in the hands of competent staff; if you are an NT, you may become cynical if you don't trust the competence of your teachers. If you prefer NT, you probably want more learning autonomy than many of your classmates and may like random-access, non-linear learning strategies.

If you find yourself in a non-NT classroom, keep in mind that there are a lot of ways to learn. Two of the authors are NT, and we both find learning through experiences like role plays and immersions to be extremely useful. Keep in mind that you can probably do the analyses and cognitive organization for yourself or with a reference of some sort. The experiential learning you get is something that you may not be able to manage on your own. If there seems to be too much mechanical drilling, bear with it, and see if you get anything out of it. If it really seems less than useful, you might negotiate with your teacher to do something else that is not disruptive to the rest of the class, such as self-study, working on reading, or the like.

Sensing–feeling (SF). If you like sensing and feeling (SF) best, you probably are fact-oriented, care about the everyday concerns of people (yourself and others), and gravitate toward providing practical help to others (teaching, health care, etc.). As a student, you are likely to prefer to learn carefully, systematically, and methodically, but you also enjoy the occasional people-related surprise, such as birthday parties and other social events. You probably enjoy field trips and other practical learning activities that involve other people. SFs frequently bring a kind of *joie de vivre* to their classrooms and learning. You may tolerate ambiguity somewhat more than your ST classmates, possibly because your orientation to people and people's needs leads to more flexibility in general.

Some ways that SFs can get into trouble in language classes are through lack of interest in abstractions that seem unrelated to people, boredom with what seems like dry information, or difficulties with setting priorities. If you find any of these to be the case for you, find some way to relate what you are learning to people (make up a story and keep adding to it as you get new language, for example, or find a pen-pal or friend on the Internet to get to know as an example of a speaker of the language who is real to you). As for priorities, there are good suggestions in chapters 2 and 3 of this book; see how they work for you if you apply them systematically.

Intuition–feeling (NF). The key for intuition and feeling is usually personal authenticity, expressing who you really are. If you are one of the NF types, you are likely to want to understand and communicate with others, so language is a natural medium for you and for your self-expression. Like the intuitive thinking types (NT), you are probably oriented toward possibilities. As students, you especially enjoy creativity both in how you are taught and in your learning activities. A real advantage for you as an NF language learner can be your natural interest in communication and your relative flexibility in learning activities. When you get into trouble, though, it is often because you may take in so much that you get inundated, and you may not make important distinctions (that is, you may level too much and not do necessary sharpening). If this happens, you might get your teacher or someone else to help you develop some sharpening exercises, starting gradually with relatively easy distinctions and working your way into harder or more complex ones. You can do some of this for yourself by finding a text passage with some synonyms in it. Try to see if you can make the distinctions in meaning. (You can do this in your native language or the foreign one.) Similarly, do the same thing with deciding what is most important for you. If you have been exposed to fifty words, choose the most important ten for right now, and don't worry about the ones that might be useful later.

Jungian temperaments

Another common way to subdivide the types is known as *temperament*, which differentiates among the SJs, SPs, NFs, and NTs (Keirsey and Bates, 1988; Keirsey, 1998). Since the NF and NT groups are the same as those for the function pairs described above, we only describe sensing–judging and sensing–perceiving here. One of the important aspects of temperaments is that it can serve as the basis of rapport (or lack of it) between a teacher and a student (Leaver, 2000). Keirsey and Bates give names to these. It is not important that you remember the names, but we give them below because some people find it easier to remember the temperaments that way.

Sensing–judging (SJ)

SJ learners have many of the same qualities as the ISTJ described above. If you prefer sensing and judging, you probably tend to be factual, practical, and interested in "reality." SJ personality types are also called *guardians* because they tend to be conservative and to pass down cultural values from one generation to the next. Responsible membership in a community and service to it is a deep motivator for you. As students, you will probably like rules, things (including language features) in their places, and you will want more predictability in activities and subject content than many other learners. This means that you are likely to appreciate program structure because you know that you can count on the structure to help you avoid being overwhelmed with information and choices.

If you find yourself in an unstructured program (though this is rather rare), you may need to build in some structure for yourself. Much of what was said above for STs will also apply to you, especially if you are an STJ. You may find it helpful to outline material, find organized references, and negotiate with the teacher for some more sequentially organized activities. Similarly, if you are an SFJ, much of what was written above about SFs will also apply to you, though you may be less bothered by the lack of formal structure than your STJ classmates. You will need to find ways to make the learning personal and people-related.

Sensing–perceiving (SP)

If you prefer sensing and perceiving, you probably like freedom of action – not that you need to be taking action all the time, but you want to be able to act immediately when it is needed. You may find outdoor or outdoor-related activities and occupations appealing. You also may find arts and crafts a mechanism for learning. For this reason, sensing–perceiving types are also called *artisans*. As a student, the chances are that you enjoy activities like hands-on experiments, creating various products (drawings, projects, musical pieces), and field trips, where you can move relatively freely and take action more readily as you see the need for it. Although you are usually comfortable with a moderately structured syllabus, you probably also enjoy surprises and diversions more than your SJ classmates.

If you find yourself in a highly structured or a highly intellectual classroom, you may feel dissatisfied. In this case, you can seek ways to bring in both some surprises and some concrete learning experience. Field trips and immersion are often a good way to do this (you would need to talk to your teacher about these). You can also suggest language learning games and try to find fun ways to use the language, like informal competitions, or go ahead and do some creative extra-credit work, such as making a craft item from the culture you are studying. The main thing for you is to avoid too much routine.

Other personality models: the Greek temperaments

There are many other models of personality type. They come and go with the fancy of the reading/using public. Among the more stable ones are the old Greek temperaments that have endured for centuries.

The four-temperament model of personality type proposed by Hippocrates and Galen (Itsines, 1996) in the days of Old Greece is still followed in many countries today. The model is not all that unlike contemporary theories of personality type. It describes four personality types: phlegmatic, sanguine, choleric, and melancholy.

The phlegmatic personality is that of a person who is slow to emotional arousal and, therefore, rarely moody. Impressions made upon him or her are not strong, and he or she is slow to take action or to react to situations that are positively or negatively exciting. The phlegmatic personality often prefers play to work. When he or she does work intensively, it is in a slow but sure way. To some extent, those who have a phlegmatic personality are unflappable. They are not often particularly ambitious. Individuals who test phlegmatic usually also test as introverts on questionnaires based on Jungian personality types. If you are a phlegmatic learner, you may find it helpful to have things repeated to you more often than your teacher is wont to do. In that case, you can repeat for yourself. Make a tape or buy one, and listen to it over and over. If you are more of a visual learner than an auditory one, read your textbook again and again, or even better, buy a novel and read that. (Most authors tend to use the same images over and over and even their word choices tend to repeat.)

Those with a sanguine personality are easily but not strongly excited. Their interests, like their tempers, are generally short-lived. They are quick to move from one interest to another, and their moods can change equally quickly. They are also more likely to be attracted to the external world – communicating with others, communing with nature – than the internal one – introspection. The processing strategies of the sanguine tend to be surface ones. Those who test as sanguine often exhibit sharpening skills, extraversion, and a preference for sensing (rather than intuition). Sanguine individuals are typically highly optimistic and outgoing. They tend to be of good humor. If you are a sanguine type of personality, you might want to spend some time in developing deep processing strategies, which may not come easily to you. You might also want to seek out foreign-language teachers who make extensive use of small-group instruction and cooperative learning.

Choleric individuals tend to be impetuous. They are quickly and strongly emotionally aroused by events and ideas that surround them. They want to excel and work hard to do so. They prefer to lead rather than follow, and are by nature extraverts and thinkers in the Jungian model of personality types. They are also often ambitious and perfectionists. Their impulsivity, however, often works against them since they miss important details in their haste. If you are a choleric personality and working in a cooperative classroom, you may find that your natural proclivities for leadership often cast you in the role of group leader, mentor, guide. On the other hand, you may find yourself annoyed with the plodding pace

---

CASE STUDY

Problem

Edgar is an intuitive-feeling (NF) type. He likes to have good, personal relations with his teachers and classmates, and he sees learning Swedish as a route to personal growth. His teacher, however, is an ISTJ, a well meaning man for whom overt demonstration of affection is highly uncomfortable, and who believes that lesson time is for lessons, not for relationships. Edgar has no problem with the content or structure of the lessons, but he feels alienated somewhat, because there is no attention to individuals at all. He is wondering how to make this class more satisfying, in light of the clash in psychological types between him and his teacher.

Possible solutions

(1) Edgar could build relationships with classmates by understanding their needs, as well as his own, and making compromises.

(2) He might suggest extracurricular activities using the language that both he and his classmates would find interesting.

(3) Edgar could use lesson materials in ways that support his personal interests.

(4) Edgar could start building relationships with Swedish speakers with whom he finds greater compatibility than he can with the individuals within his class.

Figure 4.6

of the group and need to restrain your tendency to show that annoyance. Like levelers on the E and L scale, cholerics may need to develop some sharpening skills in order to succeed in foreign-language classrooms.

The fourth temperament, melancholic, refers to individuals who are inclined to reflection. Generally introverted, individuals with a melancholic personality like silence and independent work. A classroom with whispering students can distract them, and cooperative-learning situations can sometimes overwhelm them until they acquire some skills for interacting in small or large groups – often through predicting activities ahead of time and rehearsing a role for themselves in them. If you are melancholic, you may find that you are sometimes confused when called upon by a teacher or slow in your response when compared to classmates who are not melancholic. For dealing with this characteristic, too, as well as with the melancholic's tendency to feel self-conscious, prediction and rehearsal can be of great advantage. Melancholics are rarely sharpeners, and learning to notice details can also be very important to their success in foreign-language learning.

Ego boundaries

Another important personality variable is that of ego boundaries (Hartmann, 1991). People vary with respect to their fluidity of mental categories, especially those that relate to one's identity and one's relation to other people and other ways of perceiving the world. There are two directions a personality can take, toward

- thin ego boundaries or
- thick ego boundaries.

Thin boundaries

Thin (relatively permeable) ego boundaries are associated with tolerance of ambiguity, flexible categories, and learning by osmosis (without being aware of the learning). What this means is that if you are a thin-boundary person, you will probably be able to accept the fact that in immersion and communicative classrooms there will be many words and much grammar that you do not understand, especially in the beginning, and that sometimes a word will have multiple meanings in a foreign language, some of which do not equate to the same range of meanings in English. You are relatively likely to "go with the flow" and try to figure out what you can as you go along. Sometimes, you may learn new things and not know for sure where they came from. So, if you have relatively thin boundaries, you have a good start for language learning, as long as you do not let yourself "drown" in all the input. Moreover, the flexibility of thin ego boundaries probably promotes empathy, which also helps with accepting and absorbing another language and culture.

Nonetheless, there are probably instances in which you run into difficulty in language learning precisely because of your thin boundaries. You may need to set up new categories to make sense of what you are taking in (Ehrman 1993, 1996, 1999; Ehrman and Oxford, 1995); otherwise, you may find yourself awash in data and not know what to do about it. For example, in watching a foreign-language film, you may encounter fifty new vocabulary items that you understand on the spot but cannot recall without some system for filing them in your memory. Field-independent learners tend to do this naturally. If you are not field independent, there are some things you can do to develop the techniques used instinctively by your field-independent peers. While you may experience some frustration with the task, you might spend time doing such things as crossword puzzles, word games (e.g. find a word in the middle of a bunch of letters), and the like. If you do these in the foreign language, so much the better. If you still find yourself at a loss, you might ask your teacher for some help in setting up a personalized dictionary that is divided into categories for keeping lists of new words that are important to you. Likewise, you might categorize lexical items by content topics. The idea is simply to get used to using the strategy of categorization in order to sort incoming information and to be able to locate it in your head later when you need it.

Thick boundaries

Thick (relatively impermeable) ego boundaries relate to a desire for clear categories, compartmentalization of information and lifestyle, and relative intolerance of ambiguity. What this means is that if you are a thick-boundary person, you may be irritated and confused when you cannot figure out clear rules for the grammar you encounter in class or clear meanings for the words you hear. Sometimes, thick-boundary students will try to translate words literally from their native language into the foreign language. It is understandable why they do this: they want everything to have a clear, predictable place in their mental organization. Generally, few teachers would recommend this as a helpful strategy; however, for some students, it does help them understand grammar better. For example, translating a Russian sentence with a participial structure that does not exist in English into literal English (e.g. *the walking-down-the-street man saw the just-opened-by-his-neighbor store*) can make the structure very clear to a thick-boundary learner in need of clarity.

The advantage to having thick boundaries is the ability to compartmentalize. After all, we all need some mental compartmentalization to keep from being overwhelmed by too much input. Learners with thick ego boundaries can learn languages well, especially in instructed settings. Once experienced at language learning, they do well in setting up their own kinds of instruction that take into account their own learning styles. Some thick-boundary learners are very good at independent study and at using native speakers for obtaining the language information they need and/or want. (If you are a thick-boundary learner, you might consider taking some courses in linguistics, especially field methods. Not only might courses in linguistics help you with your language learning endeavors, but also you may be fascinated by the ways in which they categorize languages, language features, and language change.) As a learner with thick ego boundaries, a major strength for you is your ability to ensure that you do not get lost in data, something that can be a problem for thin-boundary learners.

Nonetheless, there are some disadvantages to having thick boundaries. Effective communicative language learning can benefit from some lessening of the need to be always in control. If you cannot tolerate less-than-neat surroundings, you might also find frustration in languages, which are by nature not very neat. After you have found a number of the "systems" and "categories" in the language you are studying, try dealing with the exceptions by seeing in what ways they differ from "the system." When presented with confusing language elements, try to associate them with things you already know in the language, in another language, or, if you have studied linguistics, in linguistic theory.

There is another disadvantage to having thick boundaries; empathy may not be as well developed in thick-boundary people as in those at the other end of the scale. Try putting yourself in the place of a person from the culture you are studying. Before you can do that well, though, you may need to learn something about the cultural values and typical reactions to various situations. You may also want to watch some native speakers in action (in real life or in films) and discuss with your teachers the reactions that you noticed (and did not notice). After you have built up some of these insights (which may not come as intuitively to you as they do to thin-boundary individuals), you should be able to hold your own

---

CASE STUDY

Problem

Marsha has always believed that there is a place for everything and everything has its place. She has firm ideas about how organizational roles should be played out, believing that authorities should be respected because of their position. She wants a clear sequence and schedule in everything she does. In her communicative language class, she is frequently irritated when the teacher departs from the syllabus and responds to unexpected student questions by bringing in material that does not fit in with what Marsha has previously prepared for class. She has begun complaining to her classmates and is feeling an overall sense of anxiety.

Possible solutions

(1) Marsha can start practicing to be more tolerant of ambiguity, beginning with easy exercises like taking a short passage in which she knows most of the content and language and making guesses about unfamiliar material. As she develops her skill, she can increase the challenge for herself.

(2) She can work on seeing relationships and similarities among even very diverse things. Perhaps she can make this a game or a challenge for herself.

Figure 4.7

with your thin-boundary peers when it comes to understanding native speakers and being able to put yourself in their place.

Defense mechanisms

Emotional equilibrium and self-esteem are vital to all of us, and we employ a number of ways to protect them in ourselves. A term that is frequently used by psychologists for these activities is defense mechanisms (Vaillant, 1993). Everyone uses defense mechanisms, every day; they are part of normal life. Ehrman (1996, p. 151) writes:

> Defense mechanisms are essential for softening failures, protecting us from otherwise overwhelming anxiety, and maintaining our sense of personal worth . . . *every normal person uses all of them* – immature or mature – in greater or lesser degree all the time. Much of the time, we use defense mechanisms appropriately, but . . . [if] inappropriately used, they do not produce realistic adaptation, and sometimes they involve others in inappropriate ways.

What does this mean? It means that all students have ways of "defending" themselves against psychological discomfort. What these are will vary from student to student. One student may withdraw emotional energy; another might deflect attention onto socializing with students whose company enhances his sense of his worth. Yet another might refuse to invest emotional energy in language learning without intrinsic motivation (i.e. personal interest). Some students may avoid becoming involved with a new culture in order to avoid being disappointed. And so on.

There are a number of ways of categorizing all these kinds of behaviors. We suggest four principal categories, although other authors may suggest others. These are:

*   flight or withdrawal behaviors;
*   aggressive or "fight" behaviors;
*   group manipulation behaviors; and
*   compromise behaviors.

Flight/withdrawal behaviors

You have probably engaged in some of these behaviors at one time or another; nearly everyone does. These are the things that you do to avoid uncomfortable situations.

One example of these kinds of defense mechanisms is test preparation. Let us say that you have a test tomorrow, which will cover verbal forms, which you do not understand well. Instead of working at understanding these forms, you might spend more time with the meaning of the verbs and the various parts of the verbs (stems, suffixes, etc.) even though you already understand these things. In some cases, you might decide to put off studying and eat supper first. You might, in this way, add other activities and fritter away much of your study time.

Another example is "flight/withdrawal" reaction to a test score. Instead of trying to figure out what you did wrong, you may ignore a bad grade on a test. You might even blame the teacher for the grade if you think he or she does not like you or underrates your skills. Rather than learning why you made the grammar mistakes that you did, you might excuse the grade by saying that it is meaningless to you because the test was on grammar and what is most important to you is developing a large vocabulary.

The common element in these examples is that you are in all these instances walking about from the real issue – and in the long run, that is not helpful. (In the short run, it will make you feel better, which is why we call these behaviors defense mechanisms: they defend against our feeling bad about ourselves.)

Aggressive/fight behaviors

Aggressive/fight behaviors are just the opposite of flight/withdrawal behaviors. They meet the problem head-on, but not in a particularly rational way. You may have experienced some of these kinds of behaviors from your classmates. (Perhaps you have even engaged in them yourself.) Perhaps a classmate laughed at your pronunciation or complained that you hogged the speaking time. This is one example of aggressive/fight behaviors.

Perhaps a classmate tried to compete with the teacher for control of the class, whispering, making negative comments about the teacher, and the like. This is another example of this kind of defense mechanism.

CASE STUDY

Problem

Susan says: I need to try to say things more simply, and I just can't do it. Is the problem my attitude or the situation? I feel devalued when there is a change in teacher or I get feedback after a test. Sometimes I feel written off. When I'm doing drills, I don't learn much new, but in free conversation, I make mistakes and keep getting corrected. It leads to a lot of frustration. There isn't enough speaking or drilling time, and that's what I need. I hate drills – they're boring and mechanical, but I know I need them. When other students take a confrontation approach in debates, it gets in my learning space, and I don't function well (from Ehrman, 1996, p. 155).

Possible solutions

(1) These comments represent a number of ways of externalizing, because the student perceives her difficulties as coming from outside herself.

(2) Susan will be much better off if she can come to see how many of her difficulties come from choices she makes but attributes to others.

(3) Classmates and teachers need to immunize themselves so that they do not fall into the role of accepting the blame or arguing with Susan.

Figure 4.8

Here is a third example: perhaps a classmate has said bad things about the course, its structure, the teaching method, or even about his or her peers. Sometimes someone who feels defensive will argue with the teacher ("The textbook says A, so why are you telling us B?" or "I know a native speaker who uses a different word for that, so you must be wrong!") or barrage the teacher with questions to delay going over the homework, which he or she has not understood (or done).

Class clowns are often exhibiting defense mechanisms, but in good spirit, rather than a negative one. The common element is that these behaviors attack the symptom while ignoring the real problem.

Group manipulation behaviors

These behaviors are very typical in elementary and high school programs, in which students try to establish some kind of pecking order. Cliques form, and there are some students who are "in" and others who are "out." This same kind of behavior can continue into college although it is usually less overt at this level. Sometimes, though, when some students are not succeeding well at learning a foreign language, they will start to form subgroups within the class. They may pick on a particularly gifted or untalented learner, drawing attention away from their own lack of success. Or, they may become a support group for each other, but not in a positive sense; rather, they protect each other's right to

Table 4.1

Category	About me	Unproductive aspects	What to do
anxiety			
motivation			
self-efficacy			
personality type			
etc.			

do poorly and not feel badly about it. These kinds of defense mechanisms are not helpful.

Compromise behaviors

Compromise behaviors are a mature form of defense mechanisms. Some are anticipating difficulties and preparing for them. If you think you did poorly on the test, be prepared for a low grade and make plans to learn from the experience – and to learn whatever language points you missed. If you make a funny mistake and people instinctively laugh, laugh along with them; they cannot laugh *at* you if you are laughing along *with* them. Rather than picking on a slower learner in the class, you and your classmates could tutor the learner. Thinking of the class as a whole needing to perform well can contribute to your own better performance.

Practice what you have learned!

1. Review the various categories discussed in this chapter and apply them to yourself. For example, do you get anxious when you have to speak in class? Do you think you are more like a thick-boundary learner or a thin-boundary one? You can make a table like the example above and start by filling in the first two columns (Category and About me).
2. Evaluate whether the behavior and feelings you have noted in column 2 (About me) are helpful or not. If they are not helpful, or not helpful enough, make a note in column 3 (What to change). For example, if you are anxious about speaking in class, and it's inhibiting you, make a note that you need to find a way to control or prevent the anxiety.
3. Now go through and think of some steps you can take to increase your success. For example, one person might meditate before class, whereas another might practice a few key phrases to try to use in class, so the focus is on the phrases and not on the anxiety.
4. Examine your strategies. Did they work? Take the satisfying step of crossing off the section where you have reduced your difficulties substantially.

Review

In this chapter, you considered a number of themes. The content of these themes can be summarized as follows:

- Foreign-language anxiety is often caused by the amount of material to be learned, the difficulties of communicating at lower levels of proficiency, self-consciousness about errors, and the foreignness of the language. Foreign-language anxiety can be coped with successfully through simplification, using islands, focusing on the known, reframing, accepting the fact that anxiety is normal, goal-setting, and game playing.
- Performance anxiety is related to foreign-language anxiety and is felt when you are anxious about answering questions, reciting, making presentations, or doing role-plays in front of your peers. You can manage performance anxiety by preparing in advance.
- Test anxiety comes from previous conditioning, self-image, consequences, fear and frustration from limited language skills, and "facing the music." It can be managed by asking for a retest, resolving to do better the next time, putting the consequences out of mind as much as possible and focusing on something more helpful, managing your image of yourself, preparing well in advance, managing your time actively and effectively during the test, and maintaining a good relationship with those who test you.
- Motivation comes in various types: extrinsic (e.g. rewards), intrinsic (e.g. interest in languages), instrumental (e.g. learning the language for a job), and integrative (e.g. learning the language in order to become better friends with native speakers of the language).
- Self-efficacy can be promoted through success (success breeds success). Personality, learning styles, and relationships all affect self-efficacy positively or negatively.
- Personality types abound (in the Jungian model, there are sixteen of them); understanding the various personality types can improve teacher–student and student–student relationships and explain why one classroom and its activities are more comfortable for you than another. In addition, some people have thick ego boundaries (and others thin ego boundaries); these, too, affect the way they go about relating to native speakers and to cross-cultural experiences.
- Defense mechanisms are part of everyday life; everyone uses them even though they can sometimes get in the way of effective learning; some defenses are more mature responses than others.

If you want to learn more about the topics in this chapter, check out the following references: Bandura (1993); Dörnyei (2001); Ehrman (1996); Ehrman (1999); Horwitz and Young (1991); Keirsey (1998); Myers with Myers (1980); Vaillant (1993).

5 Interpersonal dynamics in the learning process

Preview

This chapter introduces you to the interpersonal dimension of learning – your relationships with others involved in your learning process such as teachers and other students. Topics that this chapter will address include:

- Levels of interaction: individual, pairs, groups, and between groups.
- The importance of group cohesion.
- Individual differences and group dynamics.
- Teachers' attributes and needs.
- Teacher–student relations.
- Student–student relations.

Your personality and your feelings are both influenced by your relationships with others, and in turn they influence how you play out those relationships. To continue our example of a learner with a strong need for orderliness, that learner might want to interact only with other students who make few mistakes. That could be because the learner does not want to have to sort out what is right and wrong, but would rather put energy into learning the vocabulary that is so hard to retain. We will talk about some ways learners interact with teachers, other students, and with themselves.

Levels of interaction

In a foreign-language classroom, there can be a number of ways of interrelating. We call these levels of interaction. While not all levels of interaction that exist in real life are present in the foreign-language classroom, at least three are. These include:

- Within the individual (intrapersonal processes)
- Between two individuals (processes or relations)
- Among members of a group (group dynamics)

Interaction within the individual

Individual dynamics are reactions to outside stimuli that you experience but do not share with or express to others. These show up as likes and dislikes, tension, anxiety, and other emotions. You may find yourself feeling sick when you need to open your textbook or go to class. There are positive aspects of individual dynamics, as well. These are when you can hardly wait to open your textbook and feel a sense of belonging in class and a feeling of euphoria after class. If you are not experiencing the positive forms of intrapersonal processes, you might want to analyze what is missing – and add that to your experiences. If you are experiencing the negative forms of intrapersonal processes, you might want to find the source (often your teacher or a counselor can help you with that) – and eliminate that.

Interactions between two individuals

Interpersonal dynamics are quite different. When two people interact, they influence each other in many ways, and are normally unaware of most of those ways. For example, in a pair with different talents and interests, one may become the "social" member of the pair, and the other the "practical" one. Then consciously, the "social" one takes over most of the arrangements with friends, whereas the other looks after the practicalities like paying bills or getting the furnace fixed. At the unconscious level, though, the individuals may come to identify with these roles and eventually believe that they do not have the capacity to take the other role. In the classroom, this can often happen with teachers and students. Students can come to believe that the teacher has all the skill, because the teacher's role is to know and inform. You can work to avoid this by keeping aware of all your abilities and knowledge. There are almost certainly things you know better than the teacher: one of them is what you need and what you know and don't know.

Interactions within the group

Intragroup dynamics are very important to your feeling comfortable in your foreign language classroom. Intragroup dynamics can take at least three forms that can create dysfunctional classrooms: division into subgroups, scape-goating, and group reaction to the teacher.

Note that any behavior has multiple functions and at multiple levels. For example, when you make a joke, you may be attempting to establish a connection with another person, or you may be expressing veiled hostility. Your joke may serve as a defense against anxiety; or it could function as a bid for group leadership. Furthermore, for members of a group or pair, multiple perspectives can be a source of conflict. If two subgroups view the same situation differently, achievement of cohesion can be more difficult.

Subgroups

There can be subgroups within your class (this is not desirable, but it does happen) that have positive, or, more likely, negative, feelings toward each other. Perhaps several of the students in your class come from the same city or the same high school and are used to working together; without knowing it they could be excluding the other students from their relationships. You might talk with them about the importance of whole-group cohesion and how you can help each other with your learning efforts. It may be that they are not even aware of their subgroup. Even better, you might ask your teacher to explain group dynamics to your class, emphasizing the importance of harmony and cohesion to the language-learning process.

Scapegoating

Sometimes the subgroup is only one person, and that person is uniformly disliked. In these cases, the students in your class might make fun of that student. This is called "scapegoating," and it is very detrimental to the development of group cohesion and to the ability of any one in the class to learn well and comfortably. If you find that you have a scapegoat in the class, talk to your classmates about how this is not helpful to your learning process. If you have, for some reason, become the scapegoat, talk to your classmates and explain how they make you feel. If you feel that you need some support in doing this, enlist your teacher's help.

Group reaction to the teacher

A third kind of group dynamic is the relationship between the teacher and the class. This can be positive or negative. On the positive side, students like the teacher and a bond forms. In some cases, this bond can last years. You probably have elementary school teachers of whom you are fond to this day. On the negative side, you may have been in situations where no one liked the teacher and perhaps the class as a whole formed an opposition to the teacher. You may well remember teachers who fell into this group, too, and if you analyze the kinds of learning that went on and what you took away from the classroom, you may find that this kind of relationship was dysfunctional and impeded your learning.

The importance of group cohesion

The term *cohesion* literally means "sticking together." A cohesive group is one that holds together; its members usually like each other and jointly

Problem

Adam has a number of difficulties with his Hausa class.

(1) He does not like the topics that come up in class: they are boring and sometimes offensive to him; they are often associated with negative experiences of individual students.

(2) One of the other students has confided in Adam that she feels the same way and is thinking of dropping the course because the class atmosphere is so bad.

(3) In fact, almost everyone is very anxious when they have to speak and no one ever volunteers.

(4) The students are somewhat cohesive in that most of them do not like the teacher and so have formed a kind of anti-teacher coalition.

Possible solutions

(1) Adam has problems at all three levels of interaction. It may not be possible to solve all these problems within the course of a single semester. He might, then, decide what is the most important problem to tackle (i.e. what makes his learning experience least palatable) and work on that first, and he may have to settle for some improvement, not total change, and keep himself going with the thought that most groups are together only for a semester and not let himself let one unhappy group spoil his overall language-learning experience.

(2) At the individual level, Adam describes his dislike for the class and the topics that came up in it. Even though the class dislikes the teacher, he might nonetheless approach the teacher about the issue of topics. After all, nothing venture, nothing gained. He may be surprised that the teacher is not aware of his dislikes and may subsequently make an effort to find more interesting and comfortable topics for him.

(3) At the interpersonal level, an inhibited student told Adam about her fear of speaking up. Adam might share his own concerns and work out, with her, a common approach to overcoming their inhibitions.

(4) At the group level, Adam is trapped in a group that is anxious and unfriendly. Further, the only thing that is holding the group together is its dislike of the teacher. Fixing this problem is a big chore for Adam to take on. He might start by talking to his group about their dislike of the teacher and brainstorming ways to approach the teacher and ask him or her to change specific behaviors. (Some teachers are very receptive to this kind of feedback although not all are.) In working on this kind of task together, the class might turn their negative bonding into a more positive one. If the teacher turns out to be sensitive to class concerns, then there is a possibility that he or she can handle the group dynamics issues among the students – but that is a very idealistic hope and not likely to occur given the current class.

Figure 5.1

identify as members of their groups. You can probably think of a number of cohesive groups that you belong to, ranging from athletic teams to religious denominations.

Groups that suffer from friction and fragmentation are less likely to promote learning than cohesive ones. Lack of cohesion increases the potential for subgrouping, where some members form a kind of alliance that is often in adversarial relation with other members and subgroups. A person who is not a member of a subgroup may end up as a scapegoat, vulnerable to attack from any subgroup. This kind of behavior is most blatant on the playground, but in fact it plays out constantly (though often with more subtlety) in adult organizations of any sort, including classrooms. In-group and out-group phenomena arouse anxiety and thus increase defensive behavior; energy is deflected from learning.

The cohesion of the classroom group is thus an important factor in our willingness as students to take risks and to invest ourselves in the learning task. When our learning group is cohesive, most of us feel encouraged to take speaking risks and enjoy the company of our classmates both in and out of class. We may feel a sense of solidarity with the teacher, who is perceived to be on the side of the students. Adam's class is an example of the opposite situation: students avoided even small risks in class, did not much enjoy each other's company, and shunned class. They perceived classroom topics as "contaminated" when outside class, and the class suffered from an adversarial relationship with the teacher, who became an enemy.

The levels apply to cohesion. Between individuals a cohesive group can promote cooperation that enhances both individuals' efforts. On the other hand, lack of cohesion can bring about interpersonal friction and demotivation. At the group level, a cohesive, effective group can enhance self-efficacy among its members. Effective cooperation in a cohesive group makes use of member diversity for the benefit of all. As a result of poor group functioning, members may experience apathy, inefficient learning, or even destructive psychological effects on the members that result in intense aversion to further learning. Like within-group effects, between-group interactions can be positive, promoting increased receptivity to the people and culture of the new language, or negative, potentially leading to rejection and negative stereotyping of the target language group. For more about interpersonal dynamics in second language education, see Ehrman and Dörnyei (1998a).

Cohesion does not mean the enforcement of conformity and "group think" on members. It is a sense of affiliation and to some degree identification with other group members. An effective group, however, has a great deal of room for individuality and diverse points of view among its members. In the groups that you feel positive in, you probably also feel considerable freedom to be yourself.

CASE STUDY

Problem

Shandra wishes her class would do more together, such as field trips and excursions, which she finds fun and easy ways of learning language. What can she do?

Possible solutions

(1) She can analyze the situation, thinking about why the group seems not to do much together. Might it be that they feel competitive? Are they adults with families who cannot take time away from their spouses and children? In analyzing the situation, she can ask her classmates about their thoughts on the matter. Do they even like each other? If the answer to that question is yes, they could perhaps develop some ideas for joint activities on their own and propose them to the teacher. An example might be a language picnic at which family members would be welcome. If the answer is no, they do not like each other or want to be involved in group activities, Shandra might need to find another class or wait for another semester.

(2) She might also talk to her teacher about this desire. Perhaps there are excursions that she can join with other classes or even ones that are meant for native speakers at local museums. Her teacher might be able to help her meet her interests and learning needs without necessarily involving the whole class.

(3) She could compromise with the students in the class on other possible group activities that are less involved, such as class parties, special projects, watching movies together, playing soccer or volleyball together, developing a class website, and the like.

Figure 5.2

Individual differences and group dynamics

Individual differences are important to group dynamics. Like other domains of human life, social relationships are affected by selective attention and different ways of perceiving experience. For example, if you are the kind of person who is aware of details, you may well relate to others differently from people who take a more holistic view of interactions, viewing them in generalities.

Group culture is the product of the individuals who are members of the group. Your learning experiences and the effectiveness of your teachers are influenced by cultures of the groups to which you belong. Examples of groups are girls vs. boys, older students vs. younger students, one learning style vs. another learning style, conservative vs. liberal values, and so on. Every one of your attributes will put you into a group of students with like attributes and out of groups without those attributes. In your language class, your group is the full set of your classmates, even though each of you may belong to different groups outside of class, and your teacher.

CASE STUDY

Problem

Wanda's class is lively and cohesive. Only one thing makes her uncomfortable: everyone seems to pick on one person as the butt of sometimes hostile humor. Not only does it feel wrong to Wanda, but if the scapegoat were to leave for some reason, she fears that she might end up filling the role. What can she do?

Possible solutions

(1) She should be aware of her temptation to join in, as a way of ensuring her membership in the group and her safety. There is no denying that teasing can be fun, at least for the teasers, even if it is destructive. Wanda should resist the temptation.

(2) Wanda can make a point of befriending the scapegoat and of finding things to like and admire about him or her.

(3) If she feels secure enough about doing it, Wanda can talk to her classmates about the situation and why and how it makes her uncomfortable and what she finds unfair and offensive about it.

(4) Wanda can try to redirect the action when hostile humor emerges.

(5) If the situation does not improve, Wanda might turn to the teacher for help.

Figure 5.3

How well your class works together as a group depends a lot on you and every member of the class. If you like some members and not others and let that show, you will be creating a subgroup within your class – and this is harmful to learning. If you are a quick learner and together with other quick learners look down on learners who need more explanation or take longer to give a response, you will be creating a different kind of subgroup within your class, and ultimately this will not help either you or the class. Watch out as well for individual students becoming scapegoats. This sometimes happens because students are afraid to express their own learning anxieties and "take them out" on a specific student. To the extent that each member of the class can help each other, be supportive to each other, and learn together as a harmonious group, your learning experience will be more effective and pleasant.

Teachers

Your teachers, no less than you and your classmates, have personal styles, needs, fears, and motivations that affect their effectiveness and the quality of their relations with you. Their work is made more complicated by the fact that they usually act as group leaders as well as teaching.

CASE STUDY

Problem

Nell has had a history of difficulty in learning languages and is now convinced that she can't do it. Her new teacher is surprised to hear this, because Nell shows considerable ability in class, especially in using the language for communication. Nell seems eager to please and to build a relationship with the teacher and her classmates. The teacher has observed Nell, and sees that Nell does not respond well when she is taught *about* the language, though. Nell's lack of self-confidence is clearly standing in her way.

Possible solutions

(1) The teacher can make use of Nell's tendency to build attachments with others by showing her warmth and indicating interest in Nell's success. It will be important, though, for the teacher and Nell both to be sure that this does not become favoritism (or be perceived that way). Both have a responsibility to ensure fairness.

(2) Nell can become aware of how she may well learn at first because of the relationship with the teacher but eventually become more independent and self-confident. If both are aware of the dynamics of the "learning alliance," they can make better use of it.

Figure 5.4

Ehrman (1998) and Ehrman and Dörnyei (1998a) describe a "learning alliance" (see also Wool, 1989) based on unconscious communications between teacher and students that allow both to take risks and to suspend ordinary power relationships. The teacher contributes to the alliance by building a "frame" that promotes a sense of safety. Reliability, stability of time and place, and maintenance of appropriate interpersonal boundaries are parts of that frame. The student participates by becoming open to learning, and admitting flaws and lacks in the safe place the effective teacher provides.

Fortunately, teachers, teacher supervisors, trainers, and students who understand what is going on in a classroom can substantially enhance learning effectiveness by adroit application of interpersonal and group dynamics. And by changing the culture of dysfunctional groups they benefit not only the current members of the group but also future members.

Teacher–student

It is fortunate that most teachers and students like each other. This bond is one of the motivators of learning. In fact, some methodologies, such as counseling–learning, are built on the teacher and student relationship. The motivating force of the student–teacher relationship is extremely powerful; it taps deep unconscious needs on the part of both participants. One term for this relationship is the "learning alliance" (Ehrman, 1998b). This term refers to the psychological contract between teacher and student, in which the teacher provides a safe, stable structure for learning, and the student works to learn and can feel free to take risks. The safety and stability are emotional as well as physical and intellectual, as are the risks.

This is to say that there is a substantial emotional investment between teacher and student. When the relationship is working well, it enhances the learning process: the students are (usually unconsciously) working because they care about the teacher as well as for the intrinsic, extrinsic, integrative, and instrumental reasons described above. Teachers, in turn, hope to nurture their students and receive gratification from their successes.

Think for a moment about your favorite teachers. Do you feel a certain bond with them and hope to please them (and not just for a grade)? Sometimes, of course, things do not go quite so well. Teacher and student needs can operate at cross-purposes. For example, a student may want a teacher who provides a great deal of overt emotional support, with lots of encouragement. In a class with a teacher whose style is more subject-matter focused, such a student could become frustrated. The frustration could show up as one of the behaviors described above under defense mechanisms, which the teacher might find disruptive. The friction could grow, and neither one would understand the underlying disappointment on the part of the student and pressure the teacher was feeling to get closer, the paradoxical result of which might be that the teacher pulls away.

Many students idealize teachers they like or those who provide the kind of good support that a functional learning alliance involves. This can be quite uncomfortable for the teacher, because with idealization comes the risk of disappointment. A student who feels let down by a teacher who was once idealized can end up devaluing the teacher. This is a very difficult situation for both student and teacher and can end up interfering with the success of their work together.

Student–student

In the same way as teachers and students can either enhance each other's work or can interfere with it through their interpersonal dynamics, student–student relationships can be helpful or destructive. You can probably think of good examples of both possibilities based on your experience.

In a preceding section of this chapter, we talked about cohesion. When a group is cohesive, it and its members can accomplish a great deal, often more than any individual could achieve alone. Your fellow learners can help you in concrete and emotional ways. They can take notes when you are absent, study with you, and join you in projects. At least as important, they can also encourage you, share your more difficult moments, and provide a sense of belonging that is the essence of a secure base from which to take learning risks. If you feel that your classmates are on your side, mistakes sting much less.

There is a less pleasant side of student–student dynamics, of course. The first thing that comes to mind is competition. Some level of competition is useful, just

CASE STUDY

Problem

Ragheb is in a class in which the teacher tries to be friendly with all of the students. He sometimes find her too friendly – he would prefer to concentrate on learning Romanian. This is not to say that he dislikes the teacher – in fact he finds her fun and lively in class, but he would prefer that she be less personal. What can he do without confronting the teacher?

Possible solutions

(1) He can be aware of style differences between the teacher and himself (she may well be an extraverted feeling type, and he might be an introverted thinking type).

(2) He can use that awareness to look at the good points and bad points of the teacher and of the relationship: what does he like about her?

(3) He can manage his expectations of the teacher and focus on what he likes. It is probably a waste of time to expect her to change, so he may need to think about how to manage the boundaries between the two of them so both benefit and avoid being hurt.

Figure 5.5

CASE STUDY

Problem

Teddy is amusing – the trouble is, he is amusing all the time, even when Donna would like to study. She does not want to hurt his feelings, and in fact she really does think his jokes are funny. On the other hand, she cannot afford the amount of time his stories are taking from her homework. What can she do?

Possible solutions

(1) She can recognize that you cannot really control Teddy's behavior; the only behavior she can change is her own.

(2) She can find another place to study and be firmer about refusing invitations.

(3) She can try to set a time when she can spend time with Teddy and give him more attention (and feel less uncomfortable herself about the work not getting done).

Figure 5.6

Table 5.1

Individual	Dyad	Group	Between groups	Comment
Was praised by teacher				
	Peter passed me a note with an explanation			
		Some of the class got frustrated with the assignment, but others didn't		
			There was some rivalry expressed with another class section of this language	

as is a low level of anxiety. Both promote action. You have probably seen much more destructive competition, whether in the language classroom, in the drama club, or on the playing field. If you feel that to be accepted you have to be the best, or if you are always having to watch out in case someone needs to make you look bad so they can look good, you will probably become anxious. Anxiety can detract from effective learning because it uses cognitive and emotional resources that would otherwise go into learning.

Other students can also undermine your efforts by distracting you or keeping you off task. They may have a wide range of motivations for this, ranging from their own disinclination to work to an active desire to put you behind in a competition of which only they might be aware. A common motivation is guilt: the sight of the other person working may result in your feeling uncomfortable because you are not. Then you try to ease the discomfort by pulling the other person away from their work.

Practice what you have learned!

1. Look at the description of Adam's class in the introduction to this chapter again. Which of these things have happened to you? How did you deal with them? Which defense mechanisms did you use? What do your best classes look like with respect to relations among the group members (including the teacher)?

2. Discuss the following questions with your classmates:

How do you help other students work harder and better? How do they help you?

Table 5.2

Individual	Dyad	Group	Between groups	Comment
Was praised by teacher				Made me feel good but distracted me a bit.
	Peter passed me a note with an explanation			Helpful to our pair relationship and to my study. Be careful of threats to group cohesion.

Think about your relationship with a favored teacher. What makes it a "learning alliance"? How does your teacher enhance your motivation?

Have you had less than satisfactory experiences with some teachers, where you felt the relationship had broken down? If so, what do you think was the cause?

3.   Observe ten minutes of a class you are in. Note down the behaviors that seem to occur at each of the four levels. Don't forget to include yourself in all the columns as relevant. The chart above (Table 5.1) might help.

4.   After you have finished observing, review the completed chart and comment on each entry. Did the interaction enhance cohesion? Did it help the group learn better? Samples are given above (Table 5.2).

5.   Does your classroom group help you take learning risks? If so, how? If not, why not; what is happening to lead to your feeling inhibited?

6.   How does your teacher interact with the class? Which of the following is the closest? (You can select more than one.)

   a. Is always in strict control, dictates all activities, and works with a tight syllabus.
   b. Acts like part of the classroom group.
   c. Moves in and out of direct control, often assigning work for smaller groups.
   d. Encourages learner independence.
   e. Aloof from the class group.
   f. Focuses primarily on task
   g. Focuses primarily on relationships

What effect does this behavior have on the cohesion of your class?

If you want to learn more about the topics in this chapter, please consult the following sources: Dörnyei and Malderez (1997); Ehrman (1996); Ehrman (1998b); Ehrman and Dörnyei (1998); Stevick (1980); Wool (1989).

Review

In this chapter, you considered these themes:

- Levels of interaction: individual, pairs, groups.
- The importance of group cohesion.
- Individual differences and group dynamics.
- Teachers.
- Teacher–student relations.
- Student–student relations.

Levels of interaction

(1) **Individual**. Intrapersonal interaction consists of one's nonverbalized reactions to others.
(2) **Between two individuals**. Interpersonal interaction is what goes on between you and someone else.
(3) **Within groups**. Group dynamics includes such things as subgroup formation, scapegoating, and developing opposition to or support of the teacher.

The importance of group cohesion

(1) Group members stick together and support each other.
(2) Lack of cohesion can cause subgrouping, fragmenting the group further.
(3) Group cohesion makes it easier for individuals to take risks.
(4) A cohesive group can make use of the skills of all the members.

Individual differences and group dynamics

This topic includes:
(1) How we perceive and react to experience affects our relationships.
(2) Task orientation vs. social orientation.
(3) Group culture is a product of the individuals in the group.

Teachers

(1) Teacher styles, needs, and motivations differ.
(2) There is a learning alliance between teacher and student.
(3) Teachers can have a large effect on group atmosphere in the classroom.

Teacher–student relations

(1) Teachers and students usually invest a great deal in each other.
(2) The teacher's investment in the student can be a powerful motivator for the student.
(3) Student–teacher friction can occur, to the detriment of learning.
(4) Idealization of teachers can result in disappointment.

Student–student relations

(1) Relations among students can support or interfere with effective learning.
(2) Other learners can help in a wide variety of ways.
(3) Competition can be helpful or hurtful, depending on how you handle it.
(4) Defensive behavior (yours and/or that of others) can prevent you from staying on task.

Part II

Language

6 Verbal language

Preview

This chapter introduces you to verbal language. Topics that this chapter will address include:

- Structure: parts of speech; finding meaning through word order, word changes, or particle use
- Pronunciation: sounds, word stress, word boundaries, sentence stress, pitch, tone, intonation
- Vocabulary: word building, using cognates, using context, using memory strategies, extensive reading

This chapter is written for those learners who have not had any previous opportunity to learn the terminology associated with talking about language – grammar and vocabulary. If you have had a good grounding in English grammar, this will be a review for you, but it might be interesting to learn about aspects of the grammatical systems of some other languages. In studying a foreign language, you may frequently find yourself in the position of comparing the structure of your foreign language to that of English. Knowing the English system well will help you. (We cannot present the entire overview of English grammar here; if you find that this is an area of weakness for you, you might seek out a reference book on English grammar to use as a guide. Some are listed at the end of this chapter.)

Structure

Parts of speech

All languages differentiate among kinds, or classes, of words, or, rather the functions that words have. These different kinds of words are classified into parts of speech. In English, we have eight parts of speech: nouns, pronouns, adjectives, verbs, adverbs, conjunctions, prepositions, and exclamations. Most Indo-European languages are similar in the presence of these parts but not necessarily in their forms. Some languages will have other parts of speech. All languages will have to account for these various categories, even if they do it in ways that differ very much from English. We will use English here as the common language for looking at language structure in general.

Nouns

Nouns, as you probably learned in your English classes in elementary school, are the names of people, places, things, and ideas. In English, there are common nouns (those begin with lower-case letters; they are the "common" words for people, places, and things) or proper nouns (those begin with upper case letters; they are the titles for people, places, and things). Thus, we talk about a *doctor* (common noun) or *Doctor Zhivago* (proper noun). We need to know the difference in English so that we use the proper spelling. Some other languages follow the same convention. Others do not. In German, for example, all nouns are capitalized, whether they are common nouns or proper nouns. In French, personal names are capitalized, but the titles that go with them are not: *le docteur Aibobo* "Dr. Doolittle."

Nouns in English can be singular or plural: *the doctor* or *the doctors*, *the bush* or *the bushes*. We usually form the plural in English by adding an ending, but sometimes we use a different word altogether: *child, children*; *mouse, mice*. Many languages do something similar: add an ending to make a singular noun plural. Some languages, such as Russian and Czech, where nouns in the singular also have endings, change the endings in the plural. In some Asian languages, such as Thai, Vietnamese, and Cambodian, nouns are not differentiated by singular and plural. If this seems strange, think of collective nouns in English, such as *sheep* and *deer*. We say *one sheep, five sheep, few deer, many deer*. We do not say **five sheeps* or **many deers*, although that is a common mistake of learners of English as a second language who overgeneralize the more common rule – add *-s* to make plural – to all categories of nouns, including, erroneously, to collective nouns. (You will very likely do similar things in the language you are studying; overgeneralization is quite natural, especially for synoptic levelers.)

Nouns in English are not marked for gender, but they are in some languages. In French and Spanish, for example, nouns can be either feminine or masculine. The article (the words *a, an,* or *the*) that goes with them will change depending on the gender of the noun. In German, the article also changes, depending on the gender of the noun, but in this case, there are three choices: masculine, feminine, and neuter. Slavic languages, such as Polish and Serbian, also have the three genders – masculine, feminine, and neuter – but in these cases, there is no article in the language at all and gender is indicated by the ending on the singular noun. This is another area in which learners make mistakes in grammar: if they come from a language without gender markings on nouns, such as English, it is often difficult for them to remember whether a noun is masculine, feminine, or neuter. Moreover, if the learner has studied more than one foreign language, the confusion can be stronger. The word *problem*, for example, has no gender in

English, is masculine in gender French, and is feminine in Russian. Typically, native speakers of Russian and speakers of other languages who have learned Russian are influenced by the Russian word *problema* (feminine), when speaking French and use *la*, instead of *le*, as the article.

In some languages, nouns are marked for case. That is, the function of the noun in the sentence can change the article that is used with it or the form of the noun itself. Some languages, such as Finnish, have more than twelve cases. Here are some examples of case:

*   *The boy went to school.*
*   *The teacher saw the boy.*
*   *The teacher gave the boy a book.*

In each of these sentences, the role of *the boy* is different. In English, that does not matter, and you will find out why in the section below about locus of meaning. In other languages, that does matter. So, let us look at each of those sentences. In the first sentence, the boy is doing the action; that makes the boy the subject of the sentence. In German, that would require the use of the article *der*. In Russian, that would require a bare stem (i.e. no ending): *mal'chik*. In the second sentence, the boy is the recipient of the action. In German, that would require use of the article *den*. In Russian, that would require the ending *-a*: *mal'chika*. In the third sentence, the boy is indirectly the recipient of the action, the book being the direct recipient. In German, that would require the use of the article *dem*. In Russian, that would require the use of the ending *-u*: *mal'chiku*. There are, of course, many more cases. You will learn what these are, if they are a part of the grammatical system of your language, in your textbook.

Pronouns

Pronouns take the place of nouns. In English, we have pronouns for first person (i.e. the person doing the talking: *I*, *we*), second person (i.e. the person we are talking to: *you*), and third person (i.e. the person we are talking about: *he*, *she*, *it*, *they*). Only in the case of the third person singular (*he*, *she*, *it*) do we indicate gender of pronouns. However, other languages can indicate gender in all three persons, plural and singular. Each language has rules for how this is done, and you will learn these rules when you learn your language.

In some languages, pronouns will change depending on the function they have in the sentence. If they are the subject (see discussion below about case), they may have one form, and if they are the object (see discussion below about case), they may have another form. That is what happens in English:

subject pronoun: *He* went to the store.
objective pronoun: *I saw him* at the store.

A number of languages do the same thing. Most of the Asian languages, on the other hand, do not do this.

Adjectives

Adjectives are the words that modify nouns. i.e. they tell the reader or listener more about the noun. Thus, we might have *pretty* deer or *tall* men. In English, adjectives come before the noun. In other languages, however, they can be placed in other locations. In French, for example, some specific adjectives, e.g. *la jeune fille* (the girl, lit. the young girl), come before the noun, but most come after it, as in *le livre intéressant* (the interesting book, lit. the book interesting). In other languages, the adjective can be even farther away from the noun.

Adjectives in English have one form for use with all the nouns they modify: *the big man, the big woman, the big tree, the big tables*, and so on. In some languages, however, adjectives will take on different endings based on gender and number (singular or plural) of the noun and even case of the noun.

Verbs

Verbs are the action elements in a sentence. They tell you what is happening. Verbs can have many characteristics, depending on the language.

Verbs in English are conjugated (change their forms), depending on person and tense. Let's stay with person for a minute. We can say *I eat*, but we cannot say **he eat*. We have to say *he eats*. That is what we mean by conjugation. In English, endings change, depending on whether we are using the first, second, or third person. In some languages, this does not happen.

Verbs in English also have tense. The tense shows the time that something is happening, has happened, or will happen. In English, we have six of these tenses (present, past, future, present perfect, past perfect, future perfect). Tense changes can be shown by endings or by stem changes (changes in the word itself). An example of the former is the verb *to touch* (*every day I touch my toes*; *yesterday I touched my toes*; *tomorrow I will touch my toes, now I have touched my toes*; *yesterday I had already touched my toes when I saw you*; *by tomorrow I will have touched my toes when I see you*). An example of the latter is *ring* (*every day I ring the bell, yesterday I rang the bell, tomorrow I will ring the bell, now I have rung the bell, yesterday I had already rung the bell when I saw you, by tomorrow I will have rung the bell when I see you*). English also has continuous forms of all these tenses, as in *I am ringing the bell, I was ringing the bell*, and so on. A few other languages also have continuous tenses, but many do not. One form serves to mean *I ring* and *I am ringing*. In the same way, not all languages have six tenses. Some have three (e.g. Russian), some have more (e.g. Czech). Some Southeast Asian languages do not have tense; they mark time with adverbs. All languages, however, do have a way of indicating the time of an action; you may just have to look for that information in a different place and a different way than in English.

Many languages, including English, have something called voice. In English, there is active voice – *a lady opened the door* – and passive voice – *the door was opened by a lady*. There is a parallel phenomenon in many other languages, although some languages do not make this distinction. In English and related languages, word order and verb forms tell us whether a sentence is active or passive. In other languages, both noun forms (case) and verb forms change to indicate passive, and word order may or may not be the same. In yet other languages, such as Thai and Cambodian, passive is indicated by a particle.

Some verb forms change according to mood. Depending on the language, you may encounter indicative, imperative, subjunctive, or conditional mood. Indicative mood reflects simple statements of fact: *He opened the window*. Imperative mood is the command form: *Open the window*! Subjunctive, in English, refers to statements contrary to fact: *If he were you* (he is *not* you), *he would open the window*. Conditional mood refers to fact that is accompanied by, as the name suggests, a condition: *If it is hot, he will open the window*. Some languages are similar to English; they have all these moods, and they use changes in verb forms to indicate the moods. Some languages have fewer moods. Others do not use changes in verb forms, but a particle or something similar in the case of some moods (Russian, for example, uses the particle *by* to indicate subjunctive mood.) Some languages, such as French and Spanish, use subjunctive mood far more often than English, and it is often the verb in the main clause (the main part of the sentence) that determines the mood in the subordinate clause, as in *I wish that he would open the window*. In French, after verbs of wishing in the main clause (*I wish*), one must use a subjunctive form of the verb in the subordinate clause (*that he would open the window*).

Some languages have aspect. This is not something that we have in contemporary English, and it can take some time to get used to. In Swahili, for example, one might say *alikufa* or *amekufa*. Both of these expressions mean "died." The first one, though, is imperfective and is used in a descriptive sense: something happened and this something is that he died. The second expression, perfective, shows a change of state, as in he died so he is now dead. The closest we can come to the second one in English is something like "he has died." In Russian, use of aspect is similar but not identical to Swahili. We can take, for example, the situation in which someone has read a book. We can say it in one of two ways: *on chital knigu* or *on prochital knigu*. The first expression, which is imperfective, means something took place and that something was a reading of the book. It is a pure description of a fact. There are several ways of translating this sample sentence, depending on the context: (1) "he was reading the book" (as in "he was in the process of reading the book" when something happened); (2) "he read the book" (as in "he spent some time reading the book"), among others. In the second, perfective, expression, we have more information: he read the book in its entirety at a specific point in time and now is in the state of knowing the content. Another use of the perfective as matter completed can be part of a sequence: "After he had read the book, he went to bed." These are only two examples of the use of aspect. There are many more; they vary by language. You will become acquainted with them, if they occur in your language, at various levels of proficiency.

Some languages, and English is among them, have compound verb forms. For example, in English we can say *I go* (present tense) and *I am going* (present progressive or present continuous). The latter is a compound verb form. Spanish has compound verb forms like English. Many other languages do not. One form serves for both the regular tenses and the progressive tenses.

Many, but not all, languages have auxiliary verbs. These are sometimes called helping verbs and are used in compound tenses. For example, in English the word *have* can be used both as a stand-alone verb and as a helper: *I **have** a ball* (verb) and *I **have** seen the ball* (auxiliary). In French, there is a choice between *avoir* and *être* as the auxiliary verbs: *il a vu le bois* ("he saw the forest," using *avoir*) and *il est allé au bois* ("he has gone to the forest," using *être*). Other Romance languages have a similar phenomenon, as does German (*haben* vs. *sein*).

Some languages, e.g. German and English, have modals. Examples of modals are *must* and *should*. In German, one says, "*Ich **muss** gehen*" and in English "*I **must** go*."

English also has a phenomenon in which verbs can be used as nouns by simply adding an *-ing* ending to the verb. This form of verbal noun is called a gerund. One can say *I like to run* (verb) or *Running* (gerund) *is fun for me*. Some languages have gerunds; others do not. Some use a change in the form of the verb, as English does. Others substitute something else, for example the infinitive (*to* do, *to* be, *to* X) form of the verb, as in *To run is fun for me*.

In addition to verbal nouns, English has verbal adjectives. These are called participles, and they look very much like adjectives, except that they are verbs with endings in *-ing* (present participles) or *-ed* (past participles). Thus, we can have *a cleaning lady* and *a cleaned house*. Some languages also have active and passive participles. (Remember what we said about voice? Voice, in some languages, can be reflected in participial forms, as well as verbal forms.)

There is another verb combination that can be made. That is verbal adverbs. English does not have this phenomenon, but some other languages do. English would be more likely to express the verbal adverb with a participle, as in *Having read the book* (past verbal adverb in some languages), *the man went to bed* or *While reading the book* (present verbal adverb in some languages), *the man fell asleep*. Where a language has a verbal adverb, it is usually formed by making some ending change to the verb.

Adverbs

Adverbs modify verbs, i.e. they give us more information about the action that is going on in the sentence. In English, most, but not all, adverbs end in *-ly*. Here are some examples: *the boy walked slowly to school, the girl skipped happily about the room*. Most languages use adverbs. Where they are placed in the sentence and how they are formed depends on the language. In many languages, adverbs are formed as they are in English, by adding an ending to the stem of the word (the stem being everything except the ending). In such cases, very often if you know the adjective, you can figure or guess how to make the adverb, and vice versa. That can be very helpful in understanding or in speaking/writing.

Conjunctions

Conjunctions are words that connect words or clauses. Typical conjunctions are *and* and *but*. There is, of course, a long list of conjunctions, and you can probably think of a lot of these – or find them quickly by looking at any article or book.

There are rules of using conjunctions that differ among languages. For example, in English, in formal discourse, one is not supposed to start a sentence with a coordinating conjunction, such as *and* or *but*. However, in other languages, that is not only accepted, it is expected.

Meaning of conjunctions might differ also among languages. For example, in Russian, there is a conjunction, *a*, which can mean either "and" or "but," depending on the situation. Your textbook will familiarize you with these situations. What you will need to do is develop new ways of thinking about these words to match the categories that are used in the language you are studying.

Conjunctions not only have the function of making sentences smoother and more informative because they allow the embedding and connecting of additional words and clauses, but they also make them longer for the same reason. In English, we permit a moderate amount of conjunction use so that we can have sentences that may be anywhere from 1 to 4 lines long. Much longer than that, though, we tend to get lost in the sentence structure because English is not set up for paragraph-length sentence use. Some other languages, such as Russian, are.

Numbers

One of the most difficult parts of speech to acquire in a foreign language is numbers, even though on the surface it would appear that it is simply a matter of learning a set of new words. The fact of the matter is that languages treat numbers in all sorts of unpredictable ways. It is not just a matter of counting (cardinal numbers): *five tables*. It is also a matter of modifying nouns (ordinal numbers): *the fifth table*. Some languages decline numbers (i.e. change the ending, depending on case). In some languages, the number determines the ending on the noun. There are languages in which numbers can be singular and plural. Others have singular, dual, and plural. There are far more systems for numbers than we can include here. Suffice it to say two things: (1) you will quickly encounter numbers in your textbook, and (2) learning numbers will be something you work on for a long time. Numbers are a very good way to differentiate between native speakers and non-native speakers. Native speakers use them without thinking twice, and non-native speakers, even those at high levels of proficiency, can get tripped up by the more complicated forms of them or unusual applications of them (as in counting backwards).

Numbers are not only important by themselves. They are also embedded into other expressions. For example, it is impossible to talk about dates, time, and age without being able to use numbers. In many languages, numbers in time expressions will have different forms from numbers used for counting.

Interjections

Interjections are such words as *oh*, *ouch*, *geez*, and the like. They do exist in most languages and are simply parts of speech to be memorized in most cases. They are generally highly idiomatic and change with the popular culture. Skillful use of interjections can make you sound quite fluent, even if you are not (Shekhtman, 2003a).

Word order and locus of meaning

All languages have some way of showing how the words in a sentence relate to each other. In other words, sentences typically tell us who (the subject) did what (the direct object) to whom (the indirect object). In English, it is easy to figure who or what is the subject, direct object, or indirect object because the order of words in the sentence (otherwise known as syntax) makes that clear. We can see that in the following sentences:

(1)   *John gave Mary roses.*
(2)   *Mary sent the book to Sam.*
(3)   *The men saw the women.*

In the first sentence, we know that *John* is the subject, i.e. it is *John* who takes the action, because John's name is at the beginning of the sentence. The same is true for sentences 2 and 3. The first word or phrase in each sentence – *Mary*, *the men* – are the actors, or subjects. We do not have to look at anything except word order to know this.

Likewise, in the first sentence we know that what Mary received was roses. *Roses* is the direct object. We know this because it follows the verb. There are actually two nouns that follow the verb in the first sentence: *Mary* and *roses*. When this happens, the first one is generally the indirect object (in this case, *Mary*) and the second is the direct object (in this case, *roses*). If you flip the words around, i.e. change the word order, you get a different meaning: *Mary gave John roses.*

Sentence 2 contains a variation of this basic English word structure. In this case, the direct object, *book*, immediately follows the verb, and the indirect object comes after that. In this instance, though, the indirect object, *Sam*, is preceded by the preposition *to*. We could also have said *Mary sent Sam the book*. In this case, the meaning would have been the same as it is in sentence 2, but the word order rule would have been the same as in sentence 1.

In sentence 3 we know it is *the men* (subject) who did the seeing because the reference to them comes first in the sentence, and we know that what they saw were the women.

English word order provides meaning. That is why it is important to put words in the right order and why order in English is very inflexible. This sometimes poses a difficulty for students from other language families, who are learning English. Other languages can show meaning in a different way (not through word order alone); they can also have rather fixed word order (even more so than English) or very flexible word order. Let us take a look at some examples.

In Russian, word order is very flexible. Subject–verb–object (SVO) word order is common; this parallels English and is somewhat easier for English speakers to understand than other word orders. SOV, though, is also common, as is VSO and OVS. In other words, it is not the word order that is providing meaning in Russian, it is something else. That something else is case, i.e. the endings on the nouns (structural elements collectively known as morphology – which is discussed a little later). Thus, two sentences can have the same word order but quite different meaning, as in *Ivan dal Mashe rozy*, "Ivan gave Masha roses" versus *Ivanu dala Masha rozy*, "Masha gave Ivan roses."

Word order in some other languages is fixed as in English, but fixed differently. In German, for example, the verb has to be the second element of the sentence: *Ich siehe das Buch* (I see the book). In the case of perfect tenses, then the auxiliary verb, "have" or "is," is the second element, but the participle goes at the end: *Ich habe das Buch gesehen*, "I saw / have seen the book," or literally, "I have the book seen." Pashto also has fixed word order but in a different way: SOV. In this case, the verb is always at the end of the sentence, literally "I the book see."

Japanese word order is somewhat flexible, too, although the verb is normally at the end. The locus of meaning here, though, is determined neither through case ending nor order in the sentence but through the use of such particles as *wa*, *ga*, and *o* that indicate subject or object.

Pronunciation

Sounds

Acquiring a second language well depends on acquiring the sound system of that language. What "acquisition" in this case means is knowing what sounds are possible and what sounds are not possible in your foreign/second language (Gass and Selinker, 2001).

The basic unit of meaningful sound is called a phoneme. When a change of sound causes a change of meaning, that sound is "phonemic" in the language. For example, there is a sound in English represented by the letter *t*. If we substitute a different sound for *t* in a word that otherwise has the same sequence of sounds and the resulting word differs in meaning, for example, *ten/den* or *tin/thin*, then *t*, *d*, and *th* are all phonemic in English.

A phoneme may be pronounced in different ways, depending on its position within the word or larger unit, without causing meaning to change. For example, *t* can be pronounced in many different ways. It can be pronounced with a little

CASE STUDY

Problem
Robert cannot seem to remember case endings in Russian, no matter what he does. They simply do not make sense to him. What can he do?

Possible solutions
Robert's learning style will have a lot to do with effective ways of learning these small pieces of important information. Here are some of the many possibilities:

(1) If Robert is a visual, synoptic learner, he might stop trying to remember endings as discrete pieces of information and start reading newspapers, novels, and anything else authentic that is easy for him to read. (This is not the time to be working on new vocabulary.) As he sees more and more case endings in action in meaningful environments, he may remember them through association with these environments.

(2) If Robert is an auditory, ectenic learner, he might learn the endings in the same way he would memorize a piece of music (one does not have to understand Italian, for example, to sing opera). Thus, he could make a musical scale or a chant out of the endings and sing it to himself several times a day until the endings are instinctive.

(3) If Robert is a mechanical, synoptic learner, he might start writing short stories or essays, putting them away for a day, then going back and correcting them. He can use similar stories in the Russian press or Russian literature as models. When done, he can ask his teacher to correct the grammar in them, after which he can rewrite the essay (maybe even more than once) correctly.

Figure 6.1

puff of air (we call that aspiration), as in *ten*. It can be unaspirated (no puff of air), as in *pet*. It can be pronounced with a tapping of the tongue, like in *batter* or, in some dialects, *winter*. All these different ways of pronouncing *t* do not change its meaning. We could aspirate the *t* in *batter* or *pet* or not aspirate the *t* in *ten*. All these different ways of pronouncing *t* do not change the meaning of these words. In English, then, all these varying pronunciations of *t* are called allophones of the phoneme *t*. However, if we take the same phoneme, *t*, and add the feature of voicing (air vibrating in our vocal cords) to it, we get *d*, which is a different phoneme: *ten* vs. *den*. So, voicing in English is phonemic: it changes meaning; but tapping and aspirating are allophonic, not phonemic. Your foreign language may well differ from English. In some languages, aspiration and lack of aspiration are phonemic differences, tapped and untapped sounds are phonemic differences, and so on. In some languages, voiced and unvoiced sounds may not make any difference in meaning. Getting used to these differences takes developing a good ear for differences you have not been used to listening for – and time/exposure.

To deal with these differences, you will need first to develop an ear for them, so that you can hear them. Then, you will need to develop the ability to make them. Here is where the language laboratory and use of a mirror can come in handy. Not learning to hear and make phonemic differences will mean that you will sound foreign at best and not be understood at worst. Not hearing these differences can mean that you will interpret one word to be another, incorrect word.

Word boundaries

In many languages, we easily see where one word stops and the next one starts when we read. That is not as easy when we listen. Sometimes, we can fail to understand a spoken sentence even though we know every word and can understand the sentence when we read it. That is because word boundaries (where one word stops and the next starts) can become blurred in normal speech. For learners of English, the sentence *Did you eat yet?* is quite infamous for the difficulty it causes foreigners when spoken rapidly by a native speaker. That sentence typically sounds like: *"Djeat yet?"* The same thing happens in longer sentences. Try out any sentence and say it as if you were talking to your best friend. You will hear how sounds get distorted or dropped, as words are run together in normal discourse.

The same thing happens in foreign languages, and sometimes there are even different ways of combining sounds. In French, for example, "silent" letters sometimes become "vocal" because of elision. Here is one example (and there are many more): *Je suis* "I am" is pronounced /*zh' sui*/. However, when combined with any following word that starts with a vowel, the final *s* of *suis* is pronounced (as *z*): *je suis étonnée* "I (f) am surprised" is pronounced /*zh'suizétonnée*/. Here is another example from French: *Je ne sais pas* can often sound like one word, *zhnspa*, or even truncated to *spa*.

In some languages, the beginning of one word can have an influence on the sound of a preceding word. This is called regressive assimilation, but it is not important that you know the term for this, just that you are aware of the phenomenon and get used to interpreting sounds correctly when you hear them spoken in ways that might seem unexpected. Here is an example from Russian. The word *v*, "in", is pronounced, in general, just like it looks: *Shkola v gorode* "the school is in town" is pronounced just like it looks, with the exception that *v gorode* "in town" is usually pronounced as one word, *vgorode*. However, in the sentence, *uchitel' v shkole* "the teacher is at school", *v* is pronounced like *f*, *fshkole* "at/in school," because the unvoiced sound, *sh*, assimilates backward to influence the *v*. We have regressive assimilation in English, too: *in person* ➔ *imperson*.

Learning to hear the word boundaries where words have been run together or elided is only half the task that the language learner faces. There is also the need to be able to reproduce these same elisions when speaking in order to make speech more natural-sounding. To hear the word boundaries may be accomplished better, especially if you are a visual learner, by reading a script as you listen to an oral text. When you "see" how the words are run together, it is both easier to understand them and easier to make them.

It is also important to notice what happens to word boundaries in everyday speech (as opposed to well articulated, formal speech). When people speak rapidly and/or colloquially, word boundaries become even more blurred, and whole parts of words drop out, as in *I wa'n't gonna do it* (New England dialect of English for "I was not going to do it"), the well known *round tuit*, as in "I will do it when I get around to it," or the mind-bender for foreign speakers of English that asks *djeet 'day?* ("Did you eat today?").

Word stress

In addition to boundaries (or sometimes, the seeming lack of them), spoken words also have stress. Stress is the emphasizing of one part of a word over the rest of the word. In English, sometimes we talk humorously about putting the stress on the wrong syl-L A B-le. English is a very difficult language to learn in respect to word stress. Why do we say R E-lative, but re-L A-tion? O B-ject but ob-J E C T-ive? In addition, stress is phonemic in English as it can change meaning, as in *OB-ject* (noun) vs. *ob-JECT* (verb).

Stress in English is somewhat unpredictable, although there are patterns that native speakers seem to have acquired. We know this because experiments with nonsense words show that most native speakers will stress them in the same way. The same is true for Russian. Stress is not predictable, but native speakers generally have internalized a system that we have not yet figured out for teaching to foreigners. Vast amounts of listening to the language will help you acquire the same kinds of intuitions, but that takes much time and many years – part of a lifelong approach to learning foreign language. In the interim, paying attention to stress and to any patterns of stress that you can ferret out will be helpful.

Some languages, on the other hand, will make learning stress easier for you. That is because they have fairly consistent patterns of stress. In some languages, stress is nearly always on the first syllable, in others on the penultimate (next to last) syllable. Czech is one of the former. Polish is one of the latter.

Sentence stress

Not only do words have stress, so do sentences in many languages. Most sentences have one, occasionally two, words that are stressed. The stressed word in most languages – and English is one of them – is directly related to the message of the sentence. As each word in the same sentence can be differently stressed (one at a time), so does the meaning of that sentence change, in terms of varying contrast or emphasis. Let us take an example in English:

What did you sell at the fair, Sandy?

This sentence can have six different contextualized meanings, depending upon which word is stressed or emphasized. Try it out:

1. *What did you sell at the fair, Sandy?* (This is pretty clear and probably the most common stress pattern. The speaker wants to know just what item Sandy took to the fair and sold.)

2. *What did you sell at the fair, Sandy?* (This stress pattern implies that the speaker has heard about something bad or weird coming from Sandy's selling at the fair and wants to make a statement to this effect. Sometimes it can be a remonstration. There is also another way to interpret this stress: perhaps Sandy took lots of items to the fair and brought most of them home. Or perhaps Sandy returned home with much more money than her items were worth! We do not know for sure which meaning is intended unless we know the context.)

3. *What did you sell at the fair, Sandy?* (This stress pattern would be used if a group of people were selling things at the fair, and the speaker wants to know Sandy's role in this group.)

4. *What did you sell at the fair, Sandy?* (This stress pattern is a bit humorous. Perhaps Sandy bought a lot of things at the fair, and the speaker wants to know whether she spent any time at all on selling. Or perhaps Sandy proudly told her friends that she gave away a lot of her items, as well as selling some.)

5. *What did you sell at the fair, Sandy?* (This stress pattern indicates that Sandy sold things on the fairgrounds before the fair started and the speaker would like to know what, if anything, was sold during the fair itself.)

6. *What did you sell at the fair, Sandy?* (This somewhat rare stress pattern would be used if there were several fairs but one, this one, was pretty special. Sandy might have been selling things at all the fairs, but the speaker is only interested in this special one.)

7. *What did you sell at the fair, Sandy?* (This stress pattern assumes that Sandy goes from one sales venue to another. One of those venues is the fair, and the speaker wants to know which items were sold at the fair, rather than at another venue.)

8. *What did you sell at the fair, Sandy?* (This stress pattern is quite humorous and implies that Sandy was sold at the fair. In this case, unlike in the previous sentences, the "you" of the discourse is not Sandy. There is another interpretation, as well, which would require a longer break before the word *Sandy* than the first interpretation. In this case, perhaps a teacher is trying to get Sandy's attention.)

Some languages use stress in very similar ways, and the stress patterns of those should not be difficult to acquire. Other languages use more subtle ways of doing the same things, such as changing word order. It is important for you to learn how sentence stress is managed in the language you are studying because, as you have seen, wrong sentence stress (or wrong word order in those languages where "stress" or emphasis is accomplished in this way) can radically change the meaning of a sentence. Your textbook will very likely describe sentence stress in your language; however, knowing the stress patterns and using them are two different things and a matter of much practice.

Pitch

Languages use changes in "pitch" (phonetic changes in the "fundamental frequency" of the voice) in various ways: to emphasize particular syllables for contrast (called "contrastive pitch," which often accompanies word or sentence stress); to differentiate the meaning of one word from one another (called "tone"); or to signal meaningful changes in types of phrases or sentences, as in differentiating a statement from a question (called "intonation").

Tone

In some languages, a monosyllabic word with a high pitch may have a totally different meaning from the same syllable pronounced with a low or falling pitch. Such pitch differences are called "tone" differences. Tones are phonemic in those languages in exactly the same way that a change in a consonant or vowel phoneme can change the meaning of a word. Such languages are known as tone languages or languages with tonal systems. In tone languages, the tones themselves may be steady or flat (such as high, mid, low) or contour (such as rising, falling, low-rising, or mid-falling). Tone languages typically have a combination of these two types in their tonal systems. English is not a tone language.

Many Asian and African languages are tone languages. Among the tonal languages are Thai, Chinese, Burmese, Yoruba, and Vietnamese. In Mandarin Chinese, there are four tones; Thai has five. Some dialects of these tonal languages have even more tones. Let's take Thai as an example of a tonal language. The four tones are flat, rising, falling-rising, and falling. The use of the wrong tone can change the meaning of a word in Thai (or any tonal language, for that matter). In Thai, the word *khaj* spoken with a mid tone means dried sweat, with a rising tone unlock, high tone scoop out, low tone egg, and falling tone fever. Another example, in Mandarin, is the verb *wen*, which in tone 4 means ask (*wo wen ni* – I ask you). However, there is also a verb *wen* in tone 3 that means kiss and in tone 2 that means smell. (Teachers of Chinese say that their students very often tell them, through a mistake in tone, "I smell you" or "I kiss you," when they really mean "I ask you!")

Since tones do not exist in English, it will take some practice to learn to hear and to make them. However, it should be clear from the description above why learning tones is important.

Intonation

Intonation is a change in pitch usually used over a larger unit than the word, such as the phrase or sentence, to convey or modify meaning. You probably instinctively recognize both your native language and any language you have studied, even from afar when the words themselves are indistinguishable, from the intonation contours and sounds alone.

Different intonation patterns (or intonation contours) are what can make a difference to a simple sentence such as *He went to the store*. This can be interpreted as a statement when using a falling intonation or as a question when using a rising intonation. Intonation contours may affect the entire pitch of the phrase or sentence, or just the pitch of certain words in the sentence. The word *store* in the statement has a falling pitch, whereas it has a rising pitch in the question. Even in an utterance that consists of only a single word, intonation still applies. The word *good* can be said with different intonation contours to convey different shades of meaning.

The same holds true of tonal languages when they interact with intonation. For example, in the Hausa sentences *Ya tafi Kano* and *Ya tafi Kano?* ("He went to Kano" as statement vs. question), the entire pitch of the question is more elevated than the statement. In addition, the final word *Kano* (with high-low tones) itself has a much higher relative pitch with question intonation than with statement intonation. The tonal identities of the words are retained but "riding along," as it were, on the crest of "waves" of intonation.

All languages have patterns of intonation but they are not the same. In some languages, of which Russian is an example, falling intonation can be used for asking questions. When native speakers of these languages speak English, they can often sound peremptory, when in reality they are only asking a question.

It is important to learn how intonation is used in your foreign language. That way, you will avoid making the wrong impression, or worse, saying the wrong thing. Think of the difference in these two sentences in English: *He did it?* (rising intonation) and *He did it!* (falling intonation). The first is a question, possibly even questioning the person's ability to do it; the second states a fact, possibly triumphantly recognizing his accomplishment. What a difference in meaning the same string of words can make, all because of different intonation patterns!

It has been said that intonation may even vary between speakers of the same language. Among American English speakers, it has been found that some people, more often women than men, use rising intonation very broadly. Rising intonation with statements, however, implies uncertainty or tentativeness, even shyness, and according to some sociolinguistic research (Tannen, 1987, 1996, 2001a, 2001b), women who use rising intonation as their normal manner of making statements are often viewed as insecure or unknowledgeable – an attribute that holds some of them back at work. On the other hand, sometimes women who use a strongly falling intonation in such sentences are perceived negatively.

Intonational contours often have expressive functions in language, such as indicating an attitude or a state of emotion. For English, these include, but are not limited, to:

- stating a fact
- asking a question with a question word (*what, when*, etc.)
- asking a question without a question word
- complaining
- upbraiding
- pleading
- exclaiming
- expressing surprise
- making a suggestion
- expressing fear
- calling for help
- making an announcement

Vocabulary

Vocabulary has been called the building blocks of language learning. There are even some teaching approaches (e.g. the Natural Approach) in which the proponents suggest that *the* most important thing in acquiring a language is vocabulary. Whether you agree with that point of view or not, there is no one who will say that vocabulary is unimportant. The more vocabulary you know, the more things you will be able to talk about, read about, write about, and listen to well. The more vocabulary you know, the more options you have in selecting the kinds of grammar to use in speaking and writing. More important, sometimes just knowing the words will get you past a difficult point in grammar; even if you do not understand the grammar of something that is being said or that you are reading, you may be able to get the gist of it if you know all the words.

Certainly, one could seek to gain a large vocabulary by memorizing the dictionary. There have been a few folks who have done well with that approach. This is a surface strategy, however, and very likely to make the language-learning process slower and more arduous than using deep strategies for word building. What are some of these strategies? They are:

- word-building
- using cognates
- using context
- using memory strategies
- extensive reading

CASE STUDY

Problem

Farah has a very definite English accent when she speaks Farsi. It is so strong that native speakers often do not understand her, and if they speak English, they switch to English. She is certain that if she were to improve her accent, she would get more practice in Farsi because more people would be comfortable speaking with her. What can she do?

Possible solutions

(1) Farah should first have someone assess her pronunciation and list where she makes mistakes in either intonation or sounds. That way, she will know where to begin and what to concentrate on.

(2) If Farah has problems with intonation, she should first concentrate on getting this right. Even good sounds, with bad intonation, can be so irritating or confusing to a native speaker that the conversation will be impaired or switched to English. (In the authors' experience, improper intonation is far more debilitating than mispronunciation of individual sounds.)

(3) After acquiring good intonation, Farah can turn her attention to individual sounds, concentrating first on the ones that are most important for communication and where her pronunciation is the furthest from the norm. Her teacher or a native speaker-linguist can help her make those determinations. In practicing them, she might use tapes or the language lab, and when she says the sounds, saying them very loud will help feel and hear them better – and learn them faster.

(4) Most important, Farah needs to have patience. She has undoubtedly developed some ingrained mispronunciations, and it will take some time to replace them with correct versions. Keeping a record of her progress can help tame Farah's impatience and stave off any impending despair.

Figure 6.2

Word-building

One key to acquiring a large vocabulary reserve is to understand how words are composed or come into being in the language you are studying. There are at least two ways of word building that can be very helpful to you and speed up the process of acquiring a vocabulary beyond what you could possibly learn through intensive reading and textbook vocabulary lists: borrowing words from other languages and building words from their parts.

Borrowing words from other languages, of course, is only possible where your language has a common heritage. Thus, if you know that French has had a strong influence on your language, as it has had on Russian and English, you could try a French word, adapted to the typical word structure of your language. An example

Table 6.1 *Affixes for converting among grammar categories*

If you know . . .	noun	verb	adjective	adverb
real	real**ism** real**ity** real**istic**	real**ize**	real**istic**	real**istically**
create	creat**or** creat**ion** creat**ionism** recreat**ion** **mis**creant	**mis**create **re**create	creat**ive** recreat**ional**	creat**ively**
love	lov**er** lov**ing**	(love)	lov**ed** **un**loved **be**loved	lovingly **un**lov**ingly** lov**erly**

would be the word *liberté* "freedom" in French, which becomes *liberatsiya* in Russian and *liberty* in English. Often, taking and adapting words from another language in this way will provide you with a word that, if not accurate, will be understood. Borrowing words is even more reliable in languages that are linguistically related. Thus, if you know a word in French but are studying Spanish, you can take the word and adapt it to the Spanish patterns. E.g. *information* (French) and *información* (Spanish).

Another option is the learning of the pieces that make up the building blocks of language – the roots and stems. The root is the smallest indivisible meaningful part of a word, and the stems are related words that are built on the root by the addition of various affixes (usually prefixes and suffixes). For example, in the word, *antidisestablishmentarianism, establish* is the root; *disestablish, antidisestablishment, antidisestablishmentarian*, etc. are its stems. If you know roots and stems of words and the typical prefixes (parts of words that can be added in the beginning) and suffixes (endings) that can be used, you can make new words that will be understandable – and you will not have to wait until you meet them in your textbook or elsewhere. For example, if you know the word *comfort*, plus the typical prefixes and suffixes in your language, you can "know" many more words immediately: *comfortable, comfortably, comforting, comforted* (and all other forms of the verb), *discomfort, discomforting, uncomfortable, uncomfortably*, and so on. Table 6.1 gives a list of the affixes (prefixes and suffixes) that can be used to create nouns from verbs, adverbs from adjectives, etc. The examples are for English, but your foreign language will probably have similar things – and knowing these kinds of suffixes can help you deconstruct new words you encounter to determine their meaning as well as to come close in guessing at how a word should look like on your own. Even if you pick the wrong affix (one with a synonymous meaning to the right one), you

Table 6.2 *Productive and nonproductive affixes in English*

affix	sample words
-ize/-ise (verb)	finalize, realize, concretize
-er (noun)	painter, drawer, lover
-ist (noun	plagiarist, pianist, machinist
de- (any category)	destabilize, derailment, demonstrably
*-ology/-ologism (noun)	theology, syllogism
*-ate (adjective)	consummate
*-ac (noun/adj.)	maniac, cardiac

will be understood – and, in fact, native speakers make these kinds of mistakes not all that infrequently and other native speakers generally have no problems with this.

Some affixes are productive; they can be used with new words that appear in the language to make other new words. Some affixes are non-productive. You can use them to figure out words, but you cannot make new words with them. Table 6.2 provides a list of productive and nonproductive affixes (nonproductive ones are marked with an asterisk) for English.

Cognates

Cognates are words in two different languages that come from the same origin, either through common ancestry or through borrowing. For example, German *drei* and English *three* are cognates because the languages are members of the same language family. Cognates are words that are very easy to "borrow" in learning languages. Cognates can also be international words. For example, in contemporary times, many languages have adopted technical words from English, such as *computer* and *dividi*, "DVD." These cognates will help you in reading and listening; watch for them carefully because they may be spelled a little differently or their pronunciation may make them not readily recognized. In speaking and writing, cognates can get you through many topics.

In using cognates, it is possible to overgeneralize. Make sure that you really know what a seeming cognate is before using it because in nearly any language you will run into "false friends." For example, *embarrassada* in Spanish has nothing to do with being embarrassed; rather, it refers to someone who is pregnant!

Context

In reading and listening, context can help you build much vocabulary rapidly. Use induction to figure out a word from context, and very often you will remember that word from having made the effort. If, for example, you do not know the word *trunk*, but you are reading a paragraph about forests and see the phrase, all the other words of which you know, *the dark brown trunks of the trees, topped with green branches, stretched toward the sun*, it is pretty clear that the dark brown anything of a tree that stretches toward the sun must be the trunk.

Memory strategies

There are a number of memory strategies you can use for recalling new vocabulary. These include:

* using mnemonics
* writing the word many times
* associating the word with one that you already know

Each of these strategies takes advantage of different aspects of memory, as discussed in chapter 2.

Using mnemonics involves finding other things that sound like the word you want to remember. Let's say, for example, in English, you want to remember the word *libation*; you might think of the word *liberty*, and consider that some people think that a drink can provide freedom (liberty) from stress. Alternatively, you might make it part of a series of words that sound alike: *libation, mutation, nation*, and remember it as part of a "mantra" in alphabetical order. There is no end to the number of alternative ways you can find to use mnemonics.

Writing the word many times appeals to rote memory. While it is somewhat laborious, much of what you learned in your native language you learned through extensive repetition.

Faster than repetition is to learn something through associating it with something you already know. Since one piece of information is already in memory, it is easier to put a second piece of information together with it. Thus, you could associate the word *kangaroo* with the words *kick* and *jump*, maybe even using the alliteration of the *k* in *kangaroo* and *kick* to help you; or if you have read A. A. Milne's *Winnie the Pooh* and know the characters, *Kanga* and *Roo*, use them.

Extensive reading

You have heard it before, but we will repeat it here (and probably in many other places in this book because it is so important): one of the most effective ways to build a large vocabulary is to read voraciously. *Read, read, read* is a mantra that will serve you in good stead throughout your language learning days.

CASE STUDY

Problem

Jana's teacher will be giving her a test, using newspaper articles that she has not seen before but on topics that the class has studied. Jana is worried that she will get a poor mark. She is used to studying for tests by reviewing materials from class and memorizing information from the textbook, and there is no way to study for this test.

Possible solutions

Jana is wrong in thinking that there is no way to study for this test. There are a number of things she might do, and focusing on her knowledge of vocabulary may be the most helpful. Here are some ways she can prepare for the test:

(1) Just as she reviews other kinds of classroom materials, she can review the texts that the class has studied. She should make certain that she understands everything in the text that the class spent time discussing.

(2) If she is more comfortable memorizing discrete pieces of information than in letting osmosis from extensive reading take care of her vocabulary needs, she can comb the articles from class for common vocabulary, make sure that she understands all the words, perhaps sort them into related categories, and then use memorization strategies, such as mnemonics, to remember them. It is very likely that the new newspaper articles, if they are on the same topics as they have studied in class, will have much of the same vocabulary.

(3) Similarly, she can find the common grammar features, organize them, and use memory strategies to remember them.

(4) If she is willing to let osmosis do its deed, she might also find articles on her own on the same topics as she read in class and try to understand them as much as she can, using inductive strategies, the dictionary (if necessary), articles on the same topics in English, her notes from class, and other aids.

Figure 6.3

Practice what you have learned!

1.   Use the list of productive affixes to make up at least a dozen new words in English. Can you think of other productive affixes in English? Try for another dozen new words. Now, find out what the productive affixes are in your language and make up a dozen new words in it. See if your classmates can figure out what they mean. Look them up in the dictionary and see if you came close to any words that really do exist.

2.   Randomly select two dozen words from your foreign-language dictionary. Can you figure out what they mean by looking at their parts?

If you cannot figure out the meaning, can you figure out the function (grammatical category)? Understanding functions, even when you do not know meaning, can help you in reading. Now, take some newspaper articles and do the same things with words you do not know in them.

3. Do what has been recommended for Farah. Have someone assess your pronunciation and find out what sounds or intonation patterns mark you the most strongly as a foreign speaker and pick one of these to improve this semester. Work on it every day, and at the end of the semester do another pronunciation test and pick another feature to work on for the next semester.

4. For the following activities, you will need to learn a few words and structures from an artificial language that we will call Bovish. You will learn this language as you complete the activities, so in this chapter you will need to do all the activities in sequence.

   a. Read the following sentences and determine what word order is typical for Bovish.

   Botran kranu mon goboni pribi.
   The boy hit the ball with the bat.

   Botrin kranu min botranis jika.
   The girl took the ball from the boy.

   Motrin kranu a gobonu min botrinis jika.
   The mother took the ball and bat from the girl.

   Motran botranu a botrinu min motrinis riki.
   The father picked up the boy and girl from the mother.

   b. Based on the sentences above, tell someone the following:

   The boy took the ball from the girl.
   The father hit the ball with the bat.
   The boy took the ball and bat from the father.
   The mother picked up the girl and boy from the father.
   The boy picked up the ball and bat from the father.

   What other things can you say?

   c. Take a look at word building in this language. Can you see patterns? Use these patterns to answer the following questions:

   If the word for *grandfather* is *datran*, what would be the word for *grandmother*?
   If the word for sister is *fratrin*, what would be the word for brother?
   If the stem for the word "kick" is *lak-*, how would you say *the father kicked the ball*? Would there be any change if you wanted to say that the grandmother kicked the ball?

d. Fill in the proper form of the word for "ball" and "bat" in the following sentences. Don't worry about the other words in the sentence. Just think about the function that the word *ball* or *bat* plays in the sentence (subject, direct object, object of [a specific] preposition).

The ball (_____) is here.
The bat (_____) is here.
I saw the ball (_____).
I saw the bat (_____).
He played with the ball (_____).
The wood came from the bat (_____).

5.   Can you help John? He is studying a language called Puyon, and he wants to get ready to tell his teacher that he left his homework at home but he cannot figure out how to do that. He knows only the word *I*, which is *wawo*, and the following:

1. The dictionary gives the following information:

to leave = *tropir* or *afpir*
home = *craipin*
work = *trapin*
at = *pon*

2. The rule for past tense for regular verbs in his textbook is: repeat the stem, adding no ending for male subjects, an *-a* ending for female subjects, whether singular or plural.

3. He has seen the following sentences in his grammar-translation textbook:

- *Kitabin mespinpon.* The book is on the table.
- *Virapin kitalinabinpon.* The man is at the library.
- *Virapin kitabinu kitalinabinpon oglogl.* The man saw the book at the library.
- *Wawo virapinikitabinu mespinponkitalinabinpon oglogl.* I saw the man's book on the table at the library.
- *Virapinova wawirabuikitabinu mespinpon oglogla.* The lady saw my geography book on the table.

Now, speaking for John, how would you say "I left my homework at home"?

- Speaking for yourself (keep in mind your own gender), how would you say "I left my homework at home"?
- And, if you know the word *ano*, meaning "he," how would you tell the teacher that John left his geography homework at home?
- If you have trouble helping John, take a peek at Appendix A which provides some hints.

6.   For fun, make up your own language, as we did with Bovish and
            Puyon, and see if your classmates can figure it out. (Be sure to include
            enough similar sentences that it is possible to do this.) Make it as
            different from English as you can, or base it on some language you
            already know that is not the one you are studying and see if your
            classmates can figure out which language it is from the grammar or
            word stems.

Review

In this chapter, you learned about three important aspects of language: structure,
pronunciation, and vocabulary. The content of this chapter can be summarized as
follows.

Structure

(1) *Parts of speech*

  • **Nouns** are the names of persons, places, or things: man, city, book.
  • **Pronouns** replace nouns in a sentence: he, she, it, they, one, etc.
  • **Adjectives** modify nouns: pretty, tall, etc.
  • **Verbs** are the action elements in a sentence: go, do, run, etc.
  • **Adverbs** modify verbs: slowly, quickly, etc.
  • **Conjunctions** connect parts of sentences: but, and, or, etc.
  • **Numbers**
  • **Interjections** are emotional phrases that are added to a sentence: Oh!, Yikes!,
    etc.

(2) *Word order and locus of meaning*
    Languages can follow a variety of word orders: SVO is the word order of
    English, but other languages can differ. In some languages (English, German),
    word order is very strict. In other languages (Russian, Polish), it is much less
    so. Some languages express meaning not through word order but by changing
    words (often the endings on words are changed). Some languages show
    meaning by the use of particles, rather than word order.

Pronunciation

(1) *Sounds*
The smallest meaningful sound is a phoneme. A variation on a sound that does not
change meaning is an allophone. What is a phoneme in one language can be an
allophone in another and vice versa.

(2) *Word boundaries*
Most languages run words together; words are not pronounced in isolation. At the
junction of word boundaries, sounds can change under the influence of other
sounds, or they can be reduced to the point that they are barely heard, if heard at all.

(3) *Word stress*
Most languages differentiate among syllables, stressing one or another syllable in a
given word. In some languages, word stress is predictable; in others, it is not.

(4) *Sentence stress*

Many language have sentence stress. The stress that is placed on one word or another will change the meaning of the sentence. Some languages will use special word order instead of sentence stress to accomplish the same thing.

(5) *Pitch*

Pitch is the rising and falling of the voice. Changes in pitch can make a difference meaning at the word level (where it is called "tone") or in a larger sentential unit (where it is called "intonation").

(6) *Tone*

Tones are characteristic pitches that occur on one syllable of a word. Different tones on the same combination of sounds indicate different words.

(7) *Intonation*

Intonation is the combination of sentence stress and pitch. It is the melody of language and is often what causes people to sound foreign.

Vocabulary

(1) *Word building*

Many languages are very synthetic – there are identifiable patterns behind the formation of words. If you identify the patterns, you can make your own words pretty successfully and you can better figure out new words when you meet them.

(2) *Cognates*

Many languages, especially today and especially in such fields as science and technology, adopt words from English. Noticing and remembering cognates can increase vocabulary quickly.

(3) *Using context*

Figuring out new words can be easier if you use the context in which they occur to determine their likely meaning.

(4) *Using memory strategies*

There are many different memory strategies that can be used for recalling new vocabulary. These include but are not limited to mnemonics, repetition, and association.

(5) *Extensive reading*

One of the most effective ways of acquiring new vocabulary is through reading extensively.

If you want to learn more about the linguistic aspects of language, check out the following resources: Adorni and Primorac (1995); Brown and Attardo (2000); Bybee, Perkins, and Pagliuca (1994); Comrie (1989); Cruise (1993); Crystal (1985); Crystal (1997); Forsythe (1970); Franke with Rinere (1999); Gass and Selinker (2001); Goldman and Szymanski (1993); Golinkoff and Hirsh-Pasek, eds. (2000); Hudson (1994); Morton (2002); O'Grady, Archibald, Aronoff, and Rees-Miller (1997); Spinelli (2003); Zorach and Melin (2001). See also www. Lsadc.org, under About Linguistics, under Field of Linguistics.

7 Sociolinguistics: the right expression

Preview

This chapter introduces you to what linguists call sociolinguistic competence. Topics that this chapter will address include:

- Tailoring language.
- Turn-taking.
- The use of silence.

Tailoring language

Tailoring language means that you speak differently (choose different words, tone of voice, and even grammar) to different audiences. Your friends would be one kind of audience. Think about how you speak to them. Do you speak to your parents in the same way? Do you speak to your teachers the way you speak to your parents? You probably have a number of different audiences to whom you speak in your native language – and you probably intuitively talk to each of them differently. This is called tailoring language. While you won't need this skill at lower levels of proficiency, if you want to reach near-native proficiency you will need to be able to tailor your language to specific groups. Conversely, as you gain in proficiency, you will notice the tailoring that has gone on in the articles you read, the movies you watch, and the conversations in which you are involved.

Register

Register is a sociolinguistic term and concept that deals with the relationship between social identity and manner of speaking. Specifically, it refers to the modification of speech to the status of the speakers. One uses a different way of speaking (or different register) depending on whether one is talking to a child, an animal, a spouse, a boss, a teacher, a salesperson, or a conference audience. For example, think about how you would explain how to play "Monopoly" to a 9-year-old child in the culture you are studying. Now compare that to how, at a black-tie reception, you would explain the importance of board games in American culture to the child's mother who is the minister of culture in that country.

Register choice can be very powerful. For example, one might deliberately change register from familiar to polite forms (in those languages that differentiate) to express anger (in this case, one is distancing oneself from a friend or relative – and the message can, indeed, be strong without any particular words being used). Another example might be using baby talk to an infant or small animal, slang to communicate with teenagers, or very formal speech in dealing with a clerk or other official with whom you are angry and want to impress (or the equivalent mechanisms in the language you are studying).

At lower levels of proficiency, i.e. in beginning and intermediate classes, you will not be expected to exhibit sophisticated examples of register because sensitivity to register requires a lot of knowledge about the culture. However, you will learn to use such differences as formal and informal pronouns in the appropriate registers in those languages that make these grammatical differences. It might take you some time to "feel" these differences, although knowing the conditions under which each is used will help you to make the correct choices whether or not you feel them.

There can be many registers in a language and many different ways of expressing register. Here are some that we will discuss in some detail below:

- forms of address
- grammatical forms
- word choice

There are also non-verbal behaviors that sometimes and in some languages accompany register choice. These will be discussed in the next chapter.

Forms of address

Some languages have more than one form of the pronoun *you*. One form is formal/polite (in languages, such as French and Russian, this pronoun also doubles as the plural of *you*); the other form is informal (and in languages like French and Russian, it doubles as the singular form).

Some languages also have different ways of referring to individuals politely and/or formally. In Arabic, one says Dr. Mohammed, using the first name. In English, we say Dr. Smith, using the last name. In Russian, one uses the first name and patronymic (Ivan Viktorovich, literally, "Ivan son-of-Viktor") for polite forms of address.

Another form of address is the use of honorifics (or titles). These are traditionally used in Japanese society to show differences in age, seniority, or social status – in using these honorifics, called *keigo*, one chooses to elevate someone, humble oneself, etc. However, they seem to be fading out just a little in the twenty-first century; part of this is the result of more emphasis in businesses on performance over seniority for promotion, placement, and retention decisions (Onishi, 2003). On the other hand, they are still widely used in Taiwan and other places. Asian societies, however, are not the only ones to use honorifics. In Czech, one might say *Pany Dikanka* "Mrs. Dean" when referring to the dean of a school. Even English has an example: in court, one addresses the judge as *Your Honor*. When an older man refers to a waitress as *honey* or *doll*, there is a clear statement of social distance. *Yes, ma'am* as a response shows the opposite relationship – a statement of social distance in which the respondent considers the person to whom he or she is speaking to be superior in some way (perhaps a boss).

In some cultures, neighbors and friends of parents are referred to by children as *aunt* and *uncle* even though they are not relatives. It used to be this way in the United States several decades ago and still is in some isolated places. Mostly, though, nowadays this custom has disappeared from the United States and would sound quaint to most contemporary teenagers or their parents.

There are many variants in possible forms of address. You will need to learn the ones for your language.

Grammatical forms

In some languages, such as Japanese and Korean, not only is register and relationship expressed by titles and forms of address, but by grammatical forms, as well. Verb endings, adjectives, and entire words shift according to the circumstances. We have a little "taste" of this in English. There is, indeed, a difference in register, as well as grammatical form, between the expressions *Would you please do it for me?* and *How 'bout doin' it f'r me?* If these are important in your language, you will very likely encounter them early on.

Word choice

Register also refers to such things as use of slang, as well as the use of contractions (*gonna, wanna*). The choice of vocabulary, especially for sensitive topics like parts of the body, toilet and grooming, and referring to women and men (*guy, lad*) all have register implications.

Audience

As mentioned earlier, audiences are the people you are addressing, either in person or in writing. Every audience will have its idiosyncrasies. Being able to choose the words and expressions you need to engage an audience is an example of professional language use – in either your native language or your acquired one. Pay attention to how authors tailor their language; analyze the differences between academic texts, children's books, comic books, and newspapers. Listen to how presenters tailor their language. (This is an activity you can do in your own language, as well as in a foreign language, in order to develop your understanding of tailoring.) There are a number of characteristics, beyond register alone, to keep in mind when addressing an audience (and this can be an audience of one or of many). Some of these, which we will discuss in some detail below, are:

- age;
- gender;
- social status;
- genre expectations;
- educational background; and
- specialization.

Age

You will very likely change your choice of words, as well as the length and complexity of your sentences, depending on the age of your listener. With a child, you might use the word *doggy*; with an adult, the word *dog*. You might tell a child not to *lie*, but ask a peer not to *prevaricate*. As we grow up, our language changes – and this happens in all cultures.

Gender

Gender can also require differing treatments. Depending on the society, there will be larger or smaller differences between the genders. In English, we refer to "girl talk" and "boy talk." This reference is not only to topics of interest but also to the kinds of words we use. Boys tend to use more active words and expletives and girls more affiliative words, according to some researchers of the English language. In some languages, e.g. Russian, there are differences in male and female forms of grammar (e.g. adjectives, participles, and past tense of verbs); in Russian, continuing with our example, women are much more likely to use diminutive forms than men. In both English and Russian (as well as some other languages), the intonation patterns of men and women tend to differ.

Social status

If you are talking to a high-society audience, composed of local political leaders, medical professionals, wealthy individuals, and whoever else in the culture is considered to be of "high status," you will choose different words and grammar than if you are talking to a group of youngsters in the ghetto. If you use "high-falutin'" expressions with ghetto youngsters, you will find that they do not listen because you do not fit in, you "do not understand" them. Similarly, if you use ghetto speech in addressing a group of socialites, you will also be dismissed. If you want to fit in and be accepted, as well as listened to, you will need to learn the kinds of language that are used by the various social levels in the culture you are studying.

Genre expectations

Writing differs in the kinds of words, structures, style, discourse mechanisms, and text organization that are used for various categories of production. These categories of differences are called different genres. Let us take some specific examples. If you are writing your opinion about a current event in a letter to a pen-pal your own age, you will need to use a different kind of organization than you will if you write a letter to the editor. The former can be pretty informal in how you address the reader and pretty flexible in how you present your arguments. The latter will expect a formal level of address and a culturally appropriate logical development of thought and argument. Articles, conference presentations, and other written and oral genres have structures that differ one from another and that differ, depending on the language. Books for native speakers on how to write can provide some of these genre expectations. So can extensive reading in each of the genres. Using an authentic text as a model is often the best guide in preparing your own text.

Educational background

If you will be talking to a group of people, either formally or informally, it is somewhat important to know their educational background. You will want to pick different words for delivering a conference paper at a professional association to a group of individuals who, in general, appreciate erudition and use bigger words themselves than you would choose for, say, a mixed group of parents in speaking about a school project at a Parent–Teacher Association.

Specialization

The kind of vocabulary you use depends very much on the level of specialization of your listener, as well as on your own level of specialization. Two pet owners talking together will probably refer to *cats* and *dogs*, but two veterinarians might refer to *canines* and *felines*. Specialists share a considerable amount of jargon. This jargon can only be used with other specialists. With lay people, it creates confusion and misunderstanding. When you learn new words in your foreign language – whether in class or through independent reading – make an assessment of whether these are specialized or lay words, so that you will have a range of synonyms to use, as the circumstances require.

Position in a relationship

Closely related to register is the tailoring of language to reflect personal relationships. The choice of formal and informal forms of address, as well as the use of honorifics, depending on the language and culture involved, are all an important part of tailoring language to reflect personal relationship. On a more individual, personalized basis, with some people you may feel free to use rather loose, vivid language (even "four-letter words" – although you should always be aware that these words carry powerful emotions that may not feel as weighty to you as a foreign speaker of the language as they do to a native speaker of the language). With other people, you will feel more circumspect and choose a different set of words. You do this naturally in your own language; learning to do it in the foreign language will take some time, experience, observation, and the acquisition of a large set of synonymous expressions.

CASE STUDY

Problem

Shenan had the opportunity, for the first time after nearly three years of language study at a rural university, to talk to a native speaker of Russian. The conversation seemed to be going okay, until suddenly the elderly lady stopped, looked at him strangely, and asked why he was treating her so rudely.

Possible solutions

Clearly, Shenan has misjudged his audience in some way. He needs to determine what went wrong. Was he supposed to use a different form of address because of her age or gender? Had he chosen grammatical forms or vocabulary that were less than literate, inappropriately slang, or not observing her educational background (whatever it might have been)? Shenan should, of course, apologize and explain that he had not meant any offense. Then, there are some other things that he can do to prevent making the same mistake again.

(1) He can ask the lady to explain why she thought he was rude. This is not only the most expedient way to determine his error but also the most likely method to give him the information he needs not to continue insulting her once he has apologized!

(2) He can ask his teacher about the lady's reaction. She should have some good insights into what might have happened.

(3) He can learn about and practice tailoring his speech – this is something he probably should have done in advance and certainly should do now.

Figure 7.1

Turn-taking

Different cultures use differing approaches to turn-taking in interpersonal communication, formal communication, and on the telephone. Not following the rules of turn-taking for the culture(s) associated with your foreign language can mark you as rude and can highlight your foreignness, no matter how good your language skills really are. Sometimes one set of "rules" applies to all three of these situations. More often, though, each kind of communication has a different set of rules. It will be important for you to find out what kinds of rules apply to your foreign culture(s). Here we can provide only some generalities to show the scope of the differences.

Informal or interpersonal communication

Informal communication is the everyday conversations that you have with friends and neighbors. The rules for informal conversation will differ from the rules of formal conversation. (Strategies for managing informal or interpersonal communication are given in chapter 10.)

Tannen (1985) says in some cultures that when you're done talking, you start repeating yourself. This is a signal that your turn is done and it is okay to interrupt. Other cultures, of course, find this technique horribly rude – and individuals cannot get a word in edgewise when confronted with this wall of sound. A colleague of ours once supervised two team members who could not take turns. The Algerian man would wait for the Japanese woman to interrupt, and she would wait for him to be quiet (S. Flank, personal communication, December 6, 2003).

Formal communication

Formal communication includes such things as negotiation, presentation, and publication. These kinds of communications tend to have formulaic discourse. Such formulas differ among languages. Yamada (2002) points out that not knowing these "rules" can lead individuals from one culture to misunderstand very seriously individuals from another culture even when both understand all the words and grammar.

Becoming familiar with the formulas used in your foreign language will be very important to developing formal communication ability. As you gain in proficiency, you may find that your best source of information on formal communication is not a dictionary or a textbook but full-length authentic texts. They can serve as models for your own speaking and writing. (Strategies for managing formal communication are in chapter 10.)

Telephone communication

Telephone conversations are other forms of communication that differ among languages. In addition to the words used for greeting and parting, there are usually specific ways that are appropriate for starting and ending a conversation. There are also phrases and turn-taking behaviors that are requisite for interrupting a speaker. These behaviors and phraseologies are important to know in order to speak comfortably on the phone. For example, Americans often consider Russians rude because they simply hang up the phone when they are done talking. In the United States, by contrast, people typically say goodbye more than once and in more than one way. Telephone etiquette in Dutch can lead to amusing miscommunication. When you telephone someone, the person answering asks the question *Met vie?* "With/to whom (am I speaking)?" to which the right response is your name. However, a learner might interpret that phrase as "With whom do you want to speak?" and thus likely give the name of the person answering the phone!

CASE STUDY

Problem

Felicity was talking on the phone with a native speaker who, in her opinion, ended the conversation in a strange and abrupt way, in essence, hanging up on her. She was absolutely stunned and did not know what she did wrong. Now she feels angry with the native speaker. What should she do next?

Possible solutions

(1) The first thing that Felicity should do is what she should have done *before* making the phone call: learn phone courtesy for the culture she is studying. If she is learning English, then she should be angry because hanging up the phone without going through a parting ritual is discourteous in the United States. If she is learning Russian, on the other hand, a parting ritual is unusual. When the "business" that inspired the telephone conversation has been completed, it is logical simply to hang up the phone; there is no rudeness implied.

(2) In the case of English, Felicity should call the person back and ask what she said or did wrong to make the person hang up on her. She might be surprised: perhaps there was a technical problem in the phone line.

(3) In the case of Russian, Felicity should not only feel better but she should also adopt the same habit since it is culturally appropriate.

Figure 7.2

The use of silence

While it might seem that silence is not communicative, it certainly is, and it is part of what we call sociolinguistic competence. Knowing when to talk and when not to talk is a very important part of any culture. What is acceptable in some cultures is considered rude, unduly diffident, or otherwise unacceptable in other cultures. Let us look at some ways in which silence is used in English:

- To show respect (e.g. in class, listening to speakers)
- When confused or embarrassed
- When no answer is at hand or expected

Silence as respect (English)

Speakers of English tend to use silence to show respect. In a classroom, whispering is considered to be impolite, regardless of content or reason. The same is true if one is listening to a public lecture or is being addressed in a group by one's boss at a staff meeting or larger gathering.

CASE STUDY

Problem

Sheila was talking to a native speaker when he fell silent. In fact, he met a couple of questions with silence. This made her feel awkward. What should she have done?

Possible solutions

Sheila was lost because she had not learned the meaning of silence in the culture she was studying. There are some things she could have done.

(1) Beforehand, she should have learned the meaning of silence in the culture. Then, she would have known how to feel and how to react – and might not have caused the silence in the first place. After all, perhaps the kinds of questions she was asking were interpreted as rhetorical by her interlocutor. Or perhaps something she said had shocked him.

(2) At the moment that she encountered the silence, she had several choices: (a) to become silent herself – this would probably have made the situation worse, (b) to repeat the last question – perhaps it was not understood to be a question because of her intonation, (c) to try a different intonation or tell her interlocutor that she was asking a question, (d) to ask a different question or ask the question in a different way – perhaps the question had not been understood because of the way she had phrased it, (e) to change the topic of the conversation – perhaps she had chosen an uncomfortable topic for her interlocutor for personal or cultural reasons, or (f) to ask her interlocutor why he had fallen silent – if none of the other solutions worked, this might be the only way to find out what, if anything, had gone wrong.

(3) She should find out now how silence is used in the culture she is studying, so that she will not repeat her mistakes, if any, in the future.

Figure 7.3

This attitude toward or requirement for silence in these kinds of situations, however, is not typical of all cultures. Russian students, for example, whisper frequently while their teachers are lecturing, and Russian employees whisper frequently while their bosses are addressing large groups of them. Most would be surprised to learn that this behavior is considered rude in some other cultures. Generally, they whisper to clarify something that they did not understand, and this is perceived by speakers in their own culture as perfectly normal. Rather than whispering to a neighbor for help with clarification, English speakers are more likely to raise a hand to make a query (which is not a routine behavior in whispering cultures). In fact, in some whispering cultures, interrupting a teacher with a question because you did not understand or hear something can get you labeled as rude or stupid, whereas in western cultures this is perfectly normal and expected. (At the same time, some students in a variety of cultures, including western ones, while knowing that silence shows respect, still feel uncomfortable when the classroom is too quiet; this is more an issue of personality type.)

Table 7.1

person	English	your language
parents		
neighbor		
boss		
teacher		
person you just met		
doctor		
legislator		
child		
older colleague at work		

Confusion and embarrassment

Silence is one way in which people can react to confusion and embarrassment. Alternatives include displaying anger or excusing oneself. Some of how one reacts is highly individualized. However, there are cultural norms. Reacting in anger in the United States, for example, would be considered inappropriate. Excusing oneself, if one has not done anything wrong, can raise eyebrows, as well, although excusing oneself is, indeed, called for if one *has* done something wrong. Whether being silent if confused or embarrassed is appropriate or inappropriate is something you will need to ascertain for your culture.

No expected answer

Sometimes we are presented, in English, with ultimatums or with rhetorical questions. In both cases, an answer is usually not expected. If one is given, it is often viewed as argumentative or rude. In other cultures, this may not be the case. Further, there may be other circumstances in which no answer is expected. These are important pieces of information that your teacher – or a cross-culturally savvy native speaker – can provide.

Practice what you have learned!

1. What forms of address do you know for the culture/language you are studying? Fill out the chart by comparing how you personally would address each of the following people.
2. Find out the telephone etiquette for our culture. How does it differ from English? Fill out Table 7.1, then role play phone conversations on various topics with your classmates until all of you are comfortable with this etiquette.

3.   This chapter provides several instances in which silence would be appropriate in English. Make a similar list of when silence would be inappropriate in English. Then, for each of these instances (both the appropriate and inappropriate), find out what is (in)appropriate in the foreign language that you are studying.

Review

In this chapter, you considered a number of themes. The content of these themes can be summarized as follows:

- Tailoring language.
- Turn-taking.
- The use of silence.

Tailoring language

Register is the tailoring of language in accordance with social identity and includes forms of address, grammatical forms, and word choice.

Audience is important to consider in tailoring language and means that you need to adapt your speech depending on your listener(s)' age, gender, social status, genre expectations, education, and specialization.

Interpersonal relationships will also determine the words and expressions that you use in communication.

Turn-taking

Different cultures use differing approaches to turn-taking in interpersonal communication, formal communication, and on the telephone.

The use of silence

Silence has communicative power. It is used in different ways in different cultures.

If you want to learn more about the topics in this chapter, you might check out the following references: Ager (1999); Bergen (1990); Tannen (1985); Tannen (1987); Tannen (1996); Tannen (2001); Tannen (2001a); Trudgill (2001b); Wardhaugh (2001); Wennerstrom (2003).

8 Unspoken communication

Preview

Communication between two or more individuals is accomplished in many ways. Words are only one of these ways. This chapter addresses nonverbal means of communication. Topics that this chapter will address include:

- Greetings and partings
- Gestures.
- Taboos.
- Personal space.
- Body language.
- Touch.
- Facial expression.
- Clothing and coverage.

Communication between two or more individuals is accomplished in many ways. Words are only one of these ways. Gestures and body language are often even more important than words and can sometimes convey the opposite meaning to one's words – making understanding difficult. Unfortunately, these topics are addressed only in passing in textbooks, so you will need to make some effort to find out about them.

Greetings and partings

All foreign-language textbooks will teach you very early in the program the words used to greet people and to take leave of them. You may, in fact, already know these in the language you are studying. Words, however, are only part of the equation. What you do when greeting (and parting) is just as important as what you say – and accepted practices vary widely among cultures. Here is some possible non-verbal language you may encounter, followed by a short discussion of each item:

- handshake
- bow
- hug
- kiss
- order of introductions

Handshake

In the western world, the handshake is the typical non-verbal part of a greeting (and parting). A firm handshake is held in higher esteem than a weak one although, in general, men tend to have firmer handshakes than women. In some cultures, a weak handshake is the norm (e.g. native American cultures, a number of Asian cultures).

Handshakes can take many forms. In the United States, a handshake is usually done with the right hand extended at arm's length. In Italy, a handshake can include grasping the arm with the other hand. A two-handed handshake is common in Turkey. In Malayan culture, both parties stretch their arms and touch each other's hand(s) lightly, then put their hand(s) over their heart. In Uzbekistan, a slight bow, accompanied by the hand over the heart, is the typical greeting and parting. In Nicaragua and El Salvador, men shake hands, but women generally pat each other on the arm or shoulder (and hugging and kissing among friends is accepted).

In some countries, gender plays an important role. In Muslim countries, for example, men shake hands with each other, but they do not, except on rare occasion, shake hands with a woman (and those rare occasions involve foreign women and Muslims who have been exposed to foreign cultures). In these countries, women usually do not shake hands with women, nor do they typically touch in greeting. In India, the Hindus shake hands only with the same sex, unless they are Westernized. Likewise, in the Philippines, cross-gender handshaking is not culturally appropriate.

Bow

In some countries, for example, in Japan and Thailand, a bow is used in greeting and parting. The depth of the bow reflects the status between the two individuals (see the discussion of register and relationship in chapter 7). If you are bowing to a senior person or a person of higher status, then you should bow more deeply than that person bows. In bowing, lower your eyes and keep your palms flat against your thighs.

The bow can take other forms, too. In Sri Lanka, for example, the bow is very slight and is accomplished with hands placed together at chin level.

Hug

In many countries, a hug is a typical greeting, especially among friends. As with handshakes, hugs can take a number of forms. In Russia, a hug (and subsequent conversation) may be accompanied by the interlocutor patting or rubbing your arm. In Pakistan, men hug men and women women, but there is no cross-gender hugging.

CASE STUDY

Problem

Jamie was invited to a reception in Bahrain. Upon arrival, she immediately approached her host and extended her hand. He did not take it, and that made her feel very awkward. What should she have done?

Possible solutions

Jamie had clearly made a faux pas. What should she have done? Avoided it to begin with. Here are some things to think about:

(1) Jamie should have studied the customs before going to the reception. While westernized Bahrainis will shake hands in a cross-gender fashion, the indigenous men will not shake a woman's hand. Jamie should have waited for her host to extend his hand before she extended hers.

(2) Caught in this awkward situation, about all that Jamie could do would be to let her hand drop and focus on the conversation, rather than dwelling on the situation or feeling awkward about it.

Figure 8.1

In some countries, hugging and kissing are considered public displays of emotion and are frowned upon. India is one such country.

Kiss

In some countries, kissing, including kissing total strangers, is permitted and/or expected. Gender may or may not play a role. In Russia, friends greet by kissing three times on alternating cheeks; men kiss men, women kiss women – which might seem odd to a westerner. Close friends and relatives kiss on the lips, and strangers usually shake hands. By way of contrast, in Italy women kiss each other on each cheek, whereas men embrace or slap each other on the back. In Brazil and France, cheeks touch and lips kiss the air.

Hand-kissing is no longer very common, but it can still be found in some countries among the older population. Poland is an example.

Order of introductions

In some countries, the order of introductions is pre-established. In Italy, for example, the most senior people present are accorded deference. In Pakistan, you won't have to worry about order of introductions: all introductions will be done by the host. If you will be attending an event, it would be wise to find out how the introductions are carried out (beyond just the words).

Gestures

Every culture has its own set of distinct features. Sometimes, a gesture that is perfectly fine in one culture is meaningless, negative, funny, or even obscene in another. Smacking one's fist into one's hand is a casual gesture in the United States that many people, especially men, use while talking. In Latin American cultures, by way of contrast, this gesture is considered obscene. Russians snap their fingers against their neck to indicate that they would like to drink; to an American, that gesture means nothing and, in fact, looks rather weird. However, the Russian custom of pointing with the middle finger, rather than the index finger, can really confuse an American who ascribes other meanings to the use of the middle finger.

As your language proficiency improves, native speakers will increasingly expect you to use gestures that fit with the culture and with your level of proficiency. Textbooks are not usually very helpful at teaching the wide range of gestures that is used in any culture. However, for most languages and cultures, books and articles about culture-specific gestures are available. You can find these in bookstores and on the Internet. Observing native speakers carefully will teach you others. For starters, here are some of the many kinds of gestures you might watch for followed by some examples of differences among countries:

- hand movements
- finger movements
- head movements
- leg movements

Hand movements

To beckon to someone in the United States, one makes a crook of one's index finger and wiggles it toward oneself. Not so in Spain. In Spain, one turns the palm down and waves all the fingers or the whole hand. In Norway, one does not use the hand at all for beckoning, but the head.

In some cultures, hands have different values. In Indonesia and Middle Eastern countries, for example, the left hand is considered unclean and is not used to touch anything.

Finger movements

In some countries, pointing is quite normal, as in the United States. In many countries, however, it is considered rude. In Indonesia, it is impolite to point with the forefinger, but pointing with the thumb (and a closed fist) is normal. Likewise, the "thumbs up" gesture is accepted in the West but considered rude in many places in the East.

Also some finger movements have different meanings, depending on the culture. The thumb and forefinger formed into an "O" means OK in the United States, refers to money in Japan, and is considered obscene in Guatemala!

CASE STUDY

Problem

Robert was a new program manager for a group of people from Latin America. They spoke excellent English and had been in the United States for varying periods of time, although they mostly associated with other members of the Latin American community locally. As Robert waxed eloquent in his introductory speech to his employees, he dwelled on the importance of respect for each other. In doing so, he emphasized the words through gesture, hitting one fist against the palm of his hand. At first, his audience giggled, then they broke into full laughter. Robert was baffled and did not know how to proceed. What should he have done?

Possible solutions

(1) The first thing Robert should have done was to determine in advance the significance to his audience of any gestures he planned to use in his speech. He would have found out before making that particular gesture what one of his employees told him afterward: in Latin American culture his gesture had pretty much the same significance as showing the middle finger to someone in the United States – a sexual obscenity. So, Robert was sending a very mixed message. He was saying "let us respect each other" and indicating by gesture just the opposite. Of course, it was funny to his audience – who knew that he meant the words but did not understand the meaning of the gesture for them.

(2) Robert could have changed the topic and stopped the gesture. Obviously, something he did not understand was going on, and he was not achieving his goal. It does not matter whether the words are wrong, the gesture is wrong, or the combination is wrong. When in doubt, don't. Go on to the next point and find out afterward what the issue is – which is exactly what Robert did in this particular case.

Figure 8.2

Head movements

In Norway, as mentioned earlier, a toss of the head is used to beckon someone. (This is also done informally by some people in the United States.) In India, pointing is done with the chin.

Nodding and shaking of the head can be confusing, too. A nod in most western countries means *yes*, but it means *no* in Turkey and Greece. A shake of the head means *no* in western countries and *yes* in Turkey and Greece. Want to be more confused? Some Grecians have adopted the western customs – so it is sometimes not possible to tell whether someone means *yes* or *no*!

Leg movements

The feet, in some countries (e.g. Indonesia and the Middle East), are considered unclean. Showing the sole of one's foot to someone is considered rude, so crossing legs must be done carefully. Likewise, in these countries, nothing is touched or moved with the foot.

Taboos

Some words and behaviors are perceived as negative. Predicting them is not always possible. You will need to learn about them in advance. There are books that can help you. So can your teacher and any native speakers you know. Being observant and asking questions will also keep you out of trouble.

Taboo words

You can probably make quite a list of taboo words in English. Some teachers shy away from teaching these words to students because the same negative feelings and sense of restraint usually does not accompany these words in a foreign language as in a native language. Whether or not your teacher teaches them to you, you are very likely to hear them in-country and to pick them up on the street. Be careful how you use them – and better yet, do not use them until your proficiency level is very, very high.

Sometimes the lack of certain words is construed as negative. For example, when making a request in English, it is considered polite to include the word *please*. To omit it is often seen as rude, although the request would have been uttered in a form that was grammatically correct. Likewise, in most Arabic-speaking countries, the future tense is always followed by *in shaa' Allah* (God willing). If you do not include that phrase, your interlocutor, if a native speaker, will undoubtedly fill it in for you.

Taboo behaviors

Superstitions abound in nearly every culture. For example, in American culture, it is bad luck to walk under a ladder, step on a crack, or break a mirror, and people tend to avoid doing any of these things. In Russia, an even number of flowers is bad luck, and people will not present you with a bouquet (nor will vendors sell a bouquet) that has an even number of flowers in it. Most superstitions in most cultures will have some form of taboo or frowned-upon behavior associated with them.

Personal space

Personal space – the amount that is needed between interlocutors – differs considerably from culture to culture. While it is not associated specifically

CASE STUDY

Problem

Janet is living in St. Petersburg this year in a foreign-exchange program and has become very friendly with a young woman who lives in the same apartment

building. The woman will be delivering a baby soon, and Janet would like to organize a baby shower for her. How should Janet go about doing this?

Solution

Janet should stop – immediately. She should forget about giving a shower, and she should forget about giving a present. This is considered bad luck in Russia and would be very poorly received. How could Janet know this? Before undertaking any action that involves another person that Janet has not seen a native speaker do, she should research how that action will be interpreted and received. In this and other cases, she can "research" by:

(1) reading information about cultural behaviors in books by sociologists, language teachers, and the like;

(2) watching what others do in reaction to particular events and how they react to others' actions – i.e. learn what is the range of expected behavior for each life event (such as pregnancy and childbirth);

(3) checking the possible reaction with a friend who is a native speaker.

Figure 8.3

with linguistics or language itself, nonetheless maintaining an improper spacing between you and your native-speaker interlocutor can lead to labeling you as a foreigner and even to feeling a fair amount of discomfort in the interaction.

A rule of thumb that can be followed is that Americans and Europeans need an arm's distance between speakers. Russians need very little space, by comparison, whereas native speakers of Japanese want bowing distance between interlocutors. Other cultures will generally be similar to one or another of these three. You will need to determine what is the comfortable and expected distance for native speakers in the countries in which your foreign language is spoken. Good observation skills will tell you this without asking.

Body language and nonverbal behavior

As has been noted throughout this chapter, communication depends on more than just words. Body language can be every bit as important as verbal language. There are a number of body actions that differ among nations. Some of these are described below.

CASE STUDY

Problem

Mark was attending a reception at the American Embassy in Russia and was quite surprised by the "dance" that developed throughout the evening. Everyone started out around the food table, but by the end of the evening, all the Americans, including himself, were "plastered" against the walls and the Russians were facing them, talking to them, and while the conversation was pleasant enough, he felt very uncomfortable. What was going on and what could he have done about it?

Possible solution

Mark was caught in a personal-space difference. Russians like being up close, and Americans like to be at arm's length. So, every time the Russians got too close, the Americans stepped back in order to maintain the arm's length. That made the Russians come closer – and the Americans back away again. Over time, the Russians backed the Americans into the wall. Had Mark realized what was happening, he could have stood his ground – not taken that step backward. Being comfortable with such proximity, however, would not have happened on the spot. Mark, and anyone from an arm's-length or bowing-distance society, needs time to develop comfort in a different amount of personal space. (The same is the other way around; it takes time, too, to get used to a greater personal distance.) So, Mark should practice standing still and not moving away with his native-speaker friends and on any other occasions he can. Over time, he will develop a level of comfort with the smaller personal distance; after all, his current comfort level comes from a lifetime of experiencing the greater distance.

Figure 8.4

Posture

Accepted posture varies from culture to culture, and interpretation of posture varies, depending on culture. What is expected in one culture may be surprising in another. What is polite in one may be rude in another. Observation, study, and native speakers will help you become aware of these differences if you watch, ask, and learn.

Sitting back-to-back

In some cultures, sitting back-to-back, as westerners sometimes do on public transportation or in playing some kinds of games, is not accepted. It is considered to be the same as turning one's back on one's "brother." Qatar, in the Persian (Arabic) Gulf area, is one such country where the majority culture believes this.

Crossing legs

Crossing legs is done differently in different cultures. Some cultures expect legs to be crossed at the ankles. Other cultures accept legs crossed at the knees from men but not from women. In yet other cultures, crossing the legs at the knees is fine.

There is another matter to be aware of in crossing your legs, and this is what happens to your feet – how and where they are pointing. In most Islamic cultures, it is rude to show the sole of your shoe (or your foot) to an interlocutor. In some other cultures, e.g. mainstream American culture, no one would probably even notice – unless you happened to have a hole in your shoe!

Crossing arms

Crossing arms in some cultures can be seen as a way of shutting out the interlocutor. The body is closed to them, wrapped up for safety in the speaker's arms. In other cultures, people cross their arms all the time, and nothing is meant or perceived by this.

Entering and exiting theater aisles

Here again cultural differences are important. What is polite in one culture is rude in another. Entering theater rows in the United States, for example, people are expected to pass by those already seated by facing forward, i.e. by showing their backs to them. In some other cultures, e.g. in Russia, this would be considered rude. There one should get to one's seat by passing those already seated, facing them. Knowing the difference is important to making sure that people perceive your actions as they are intended.

Manners

Body language is also an important part of manners. Good manners in some cultures are very different from what are considered good manners in your culture. Western cultures, for example, consider the use of napkins part of good manners; some cultures do not. There is such a concept as "finger food" (fried chicken and the like) which one is permitted to eat with one's fingers and still be considered to be displaying proper manners in the United States. In some European countries, this would not be the case. In other countries, most food is finger food. Whether one moves the fork from one hand to another after cutting meat or not depends on culture. Whether one washes one hands before eating and whether one uses the washroom or a finger bowl will vary by culture. Who does the ordering of food in a restaurant is culture-dependent as is who can speak for a group. Nearly every interaction with another being reflects to some extent one's manners. Displaying good manners is very dependent upon knowing what is considered good manners in your target culture. Your teacher will know, and there are many books dedicated to this topic. Some of them are listed at the end of this chapter.

CASE STUDY

Problem

Suzanna will be going to Indonesia on an exchange program, and she does not want to offend anyone inadvertently with her body language or manners. What can she do to prepare?

Possible solutions

(1) She can ask her teacher to give her some pointers.

(2) She can read some books on the subject.

(3) She can watch films from there and pay attention both to the body language of the speaker and to the reaction of the listener.

(4) If she finds that some of her typical body language may be offensive, she can practice altering it – with friends, classmates, her teacher, native speakers, or alone at home.

Figure 8.5

Differences in gender

Body language and behavior will differ, depending upon culture. In the West, there is very little difference in expectations between the genders although there are still pockets of society where it is considered good manners for a man to pull out a chair at a table so that a woman can sit or hold open the door for a woman. Some cultures, e.g. that of Saudi Arabia, require women to be covered head (with a scarf and perhaps even a veil) and body (with an "abaya" or long-sleeved, floor-ankle-length black robe) when out in public. In some cultures, men and women do not shake hands with each other, while in others they share nude saunas. Learning about these differences in advance of travel or study abroad can be very important to a successful experience.

Touch

Some cultures expect members of their society to touch each other. Others expect people to refrain from touching each other. Knowing what amount of touch is appropriate and what kinds of touch to give and permit can make an important difference both in how you are perceived and in what happens to you! Appropriate greetings can be very important if you want to complete the mission you set out to accomplish in the foreign land (Morrison, Conaway, and Borden, 1994).

There are many kinds of culturally appropriate touches (and inappropriate ones). Some of these have been discussed already: handshakes, hugs, and kisses. Other kinds of touches include:

- patting and/or rubbing
- hand- or arm-holding
- head-touching

Patting and rubbing

In some cultures, people, especially women, "pat" each other in greeting or while talking. In Russia, women especially touch each other's heads, rub each other's hair and arms, and the like. If you come from a western culture, where this behavior is quite uncommon, you might initially experience some sense of "intrusion" with patting and touching behavior. It is not meant, however, as an intrusion but simply as a way of relating, of gaining and holding your attention, and of showing interest and solidarity. There is usually no other implication than that. Whether or not to touch in return will depend on your growing level of comfort with this cultural communication behavior if you are studying the language of a touching culture. The better your language and the greater your interaction with the people, the more likely you are not only to accept the touches but also to give them appropriately. (Our advice: never touch unless you know that it is appropriate and unless you are also very comfortable doing it. An inappropriate or awkward touch is worse than no touch at all. Moreover, in some other countries, e.g. Indonesia, the head is considered the seat of the soul and should never be touched.)

Holding hands

In some cultures, it is appropriate to hold the hand of someone of the same gender while working. This can be true of adults and even truer of children. In other cultures, two women or two men might walk down the street arm-in-arm (a custom that can make a very wrong impression in some parts of the western world).

Head touching

In some cultures, in talking, to show affection or happiness, two women might touch their heads or foreheads together.

Facial expression

Smiling

Everyone likes a smile, right? That is certainly an American concept, and most Americans would be surprised to learn how their meaningless

---

CASE STUDY

Problem
Roseann, an exchange student from Chicago, was sitting in a classroom in Moscow, taught by a native speaker of Russian, when that teacher suddenly stroked her head. She was shocked and did not know how to respond. How could she have responded?

Possible solutions
What Roseann did not know is that this is an affectionate gesture. The teacher, an older lady, was very pleased with her performance. Not knowing this:

(1) Roseann could probably safely assume that this is a custom to which she is not accustomed but that it is not a negative thing – especially if nothing has happened to lead her to believe that anything negative is going on. She can confirm her observation/assumption based on how well she had answered the question, the teacher's words, and the expressions on the faces of other students who might be more familiar with this action than she is. After class, she can ask someone how to interpret that behavior and how she should have responded. This is not the last time that Roseann is likely to experience an action that she does not know how to interpret. In these cases, her best choice of response is probably to assume that the actions are harmless and neutral (or positive) until she can find out what they really mean;

or

(2) Roseann could ask the teacher why she was stroking her hair; in this case, she could probably ask directly since the teacher is likely used to working with foreigners who do not always understand local customs, or, perhaps better, indirectly ("Am I doing okay?").

Figure 8.6

but friendly smiles are interpreted in some other countries. First, it is often the very first thing that gives away their nationality. Second, in some cultures (e.g. in Russia), the smile itself, when meaningless, can be interpreted as the person being brainless (light-minded), not as the person being friendly. Third, a smile shows friendliness and happiness, right? Not always so in Greece where a smile can be used to show anger!

Eye direction

How one looks or does not look at others often says more than words. Cultural differences here can cause you to send subliminal messages that you do not intend if you do not know the rules of facial expressions in that country. For example, looking down when someone is talking to you in the United States is considered rude. The same expression is considered polite in Japan, and it is expected if there is any difference in status, age, or relationship.

CASE STUDY

Problem

Barbara is an exchange student in Tokyo. She heard through one of her Japanese friends that a number of people consider her rude and imperious. She is shocked because at home she is considered somewhat self-effacing, even shy. She asked if she had used inappropriate language, and the answer was no, that it was her "attitude." What might be going on and what might Barbara do about it?

Possible solution

Barbara might well consider and pay attention to how she uses her eyes. In the United States, she probably has become used to looking someone straight in the eye. This is not accepted in Japan, especially when dealing with people senior to you or in a higher position (e.g. teachers). She needs to look down, and she will probably need to monitor her behavior consciously until it has become habit.

Figure 8.7

Likewise, in some cultures, looking a stranger in the eye is fine and even considered friendly and normal. Looking away can mark one as rude and anti-social. This is pretty typical in the United States. However, take those same behaviors to Russia, and you will be surprised. Looking someone directly in the eye, especially someone of the opposite sex about your own age, could be considered flirtatious – more than just a friendly face. With anyone else in that country, it might be considered rude and anti-social.

Clothing and coverage

Some cultures feel the need to cover more of the body than other cultures. Some Latin cultures accept a good deal of body exposure, including the stomachs of pregnant women. Such exposure would be less readily accepted in the United States or Europe. More conservatively, Muslim women in many Middle Eastern cultures are expected to cover nearly the whole body except feet and eyes.

At the opposite extreme, some cultures accept nudity as natural. In some cases, bath houses and saunas are places of nude gatherings (even, in a few cases, of mixed genders). Other countries have nude beaches.

If you want to be able to interact freely with members of the culture of the language you are studying, it is important to find out the clothing expectations – not just what kinds of clothes are worn (which may not be expected of you as a foreigner), but how much of the body may be exposed (which will be expected of you, foreign or otherwise).

It is not really strange that clothing should be a matter of cultural importance. Consider the range of acceptable clothing within US social contexts. It is not appropriate, for example, to go into a restaurant with bare feet, but it is certainly acceptable to do so at the beach. (Even some conservative cultures allow greater

---

CASE STUDY

Problem

Sean was excited about his first visit to a Finnish sauna. He met his new friends in front of the sauna, even showing up early, with a new bathing suit and towel in hand. His friends looked at him oddly and asked what those things were for. Slowly, it dawned on Sean that saunas were totally nude places.

Possible solutions

Sean should have researched the sauna situation before he agreed to come and certainly before he arrived. Now, he is in an awkward situation. How he handles it will depend very much on how much tolerance he has for nudity and how much cultural stretching he is capable of doing. There are really only two choices, depending upon what he is willing to handle.

(1) He can simply remove his clothes and enjoy the sauna; this takes some cultural flexing but many people flex like this all the time – and one of this book's authors "enjoyed" a nude staff meeting in a sauna at one point.

(2) He can politely explain that this much nudity is not something he is accustomed to – it does not happen in his culture – and ask to be excused from his agreement to participate in the bathing session, perhaps suggesting that he get together with them for a post-sauna drink and/or meal.

Figure 8.8

body exposure at the beach than elsewhere.) Similarly, it would not be considered appropriate to wear shorts to a church, mosque, or synagogue in the US, but one is certainly expected to wear them on the tennis court.

Practice what you have learned!

1. Interview native speakers (if they are available) and ask them to give you a list of gestures in their culture. (If you interview more than one native speaker, you will get a wider assortment of gestures because some people will think of one set and some will think of another.) List the gestures and find equivalents, if you can, in your own culture. Where do the same gestures mean different things? Where are different gestures used to express the same idea?

2. Research the clothing that is typical for people in your foreign culture. What are the ranges? What is acceptable? What is tolerated? What is looked at askance?

3. Find out what space and touch behavior is in your foreign country. Once you know, practice maintaining these distances and using these touches with your classmates or with native speakers whom you may meet.

4.   Find out at least four behaviors that are different in the country whose language you are studying and in your own. What would be considered good manners in each case and how will you need to adapt your typical behavior?

5.   Are there any differences between genders in the country whose language you are studying? If yes, how do you feel about that?

Review

In this chapter, you considered a number of themes. The content of these themes can be summarized as follows:

- greetings
- gestures
- taboos
- personal space
- body language and nonverbal behavior
- touch
- facial expression
- clothing

Greetings and partings

Every culture has its own rituals for greeting and parting. Some of these include handshaking, bowing, hugging, and kissing, depending on the culture. Order of introductions at receptions and the like can be strictly regulated in some societies.

Gestures

Gestures involve hand, finger, head, and leg movements, or combinations of these. The same gesture can mean two different things, depending upon the culture. An everyday gesture in one culture can sometimes be considered impolite or obscene in another culture. The same emotion can be expressed by differing gestures, depending upon the culture.

Taboos

Each culture has its own set of taboos. Words can be taboo; so can some behaviors.

Personal space

Cultures treat person space differently. People in some cultures like to be "up close and personal," in others, "at arm's length," and still others need "bowing distance."

Body language and nonverbal behavior

Body language, too, has different meaning, depending upon culture. What one does with one's arms, posture, and the like has many implicit meanings, but these meanings will differ by culture. What is considered good manners in one culture may be considered poor manners in another. Further, the "rules" may not be the same for both genders, depending upon the culture.

Touch

Cultures allow (or expect) varying amounts of touching. Some cultures are "hands on;" others are "hands off."

Facial expression
Interpreting facial expressions will be done differently in different cultures. A smile indicates friendliness in one culture, light-mindedness in another. Eyes down show respect in one culture and disrespect, diffidence, or prevarication in another.

Clothing and coverage
Some cultures "cover up;" others "bare it all." Most are somewhere in between and what gets covered and what gets bared will depend upon the culture.

If you want to learn more about the topics in this chapter, you might find the following sources helpful: Axtell (1990); Axtell (1993); Calbris, Doyle, and Fonagy (1999); Campbell (2000); Cole (1997); Costantino and Gambella (1996); Curry (1998); Curry and Nguyen (1997); Dabars and Vokhmina (2002); Daun and Cooperman (1996); El-Omari (2003); Engel and Murakami (2000); Flamini and Szerlip (1997); Flippo (1996); Foster (2000); Francia (1997); Gioseffi (1996); Herrington (n.d.); Joseph (1996); Joshi (1997); Keating (1998); Kevane (2004); Kissel (2000); Li (2000); Malat (2003); Micheloud (2001); Mitchell (1998a); Mitchell (1998b); Monahan (1984); Morrison, Conaway, and Borden (1994); Novas and Silva (1997); Redmond (1998); Rosenthal (1997); Seligman (2003); Shekhtman and Lord (1986); Tada (2003); Wilson Learning Corporation (1999); Wise and Whitney (1998).

Part III

Independence

Preview

Language learning – if one is to reach high levels of language proficiency – is a long-term commitment. After formal language study, many learners find themselves working independently. The topics in this chapter are related to working independently; they are also of benefit in the classroom since knowing about them can help with pacing and setting priorities. The topics in this chapter are about learning autonomy (taking control of one's own learning) and learner self-regulation (managing priorities, time, and feeling) and include:

- Myths about self-direction.
- Cognition in self-regulation.
- Affect in self-regulation.
- Interpersonal dimensions of learner autonomy.
- Teacher's role in self-regulated learning

It is an ideal and frequent goal in language teaching that learners will be able to manage their own learning when they leave the classroom and get into the real world of native speakers, newspapers, and films. There is much validity to this goal. The more you can manage your own learning while benefiting from formal instruction, the more likely it is that you will have tools for learning in unstructured settings too. Autonomous learning is influenced by all of the cognitive and affective factors we described in chapters 3, 4 and 5; here we pull together a number of those themes to describe how you can take more control of your own learning.

We have grouped self-regulation and autonomy together in this chapter because learner autonomy depends on effective self-regulation. In Part I (Learning), we looked at both cognitive and affective matters; both of these play important roles in self-regulation and learner autonomy, as do the interpersonal and group phenomena also described in Part I.

Some myths about self-directed learning

Many people hold some beliefs about learning on one's own, or directing one's own learning. Some of the most common are discussed below.

Adults are naturally self-directed learners

This belief has a corollary: children must be taught. The truth is that both children and adults sometimes learn on their own and sometimes require learning support. Everyone relies on instruction (though it may be informal, like guidance from a friend on a craft) some of the time and learns independently at other times (e.g. looking up a topic of interest in the library or on the Internet). Some personalities and cognitive styles are likely to insist on more autonomy than others; for example, inductive and random learners may tend to want relatively more independence than deductive or sequential ones.

Self-direction is all-or-nothing

This is, in fact, pure myth. Clearly, as indicated above, we all vary our learning approaches depending on what is being learned, our previous knowledge and self-confidence with it, and how energetic we are feeling, among other things. At earlier stages of learning something, we are more likely to want outside support (instruction, syllabus) than later. Even in later stages of learning, when there is something very new to master, we may cycle back to wanting more direct support.

Self-directed learning is done in isolation

As we shall see later in this chapter, self-direction is normally done in the context of other people and in social settings. Other people are frequently an important part of an independently developed learning plan. Important theorists like Vygotsky (1962) emphasize the importance of interactions with more knowledgeable others in an unconscious process of increasing knowledge and skill.

Cognition in self-regulation

Factors involved in self-regulation reflect emotional and cognitive development. This level of development is characterized by:

- the ability to function within a social unit;
- the possession of good metacognitive skills;
- trust in self and others; and the ability to
- set and pursue goals, tolerate frustration and compromise with reality, manage the multiple demands of life (work, interpersonal relations, value formation), and think abstractly.

The social unit

Being able to work independently while also accepting direction is an important part of self-regulation. This does not at all contradict the need to take initiative for your own learning, which is an important part of learner autonomy. You do need to come up with ideas of your own and ways to implement them, but you also need to keep in mind that you are probably part of social units, too. These social units are likely to require that you modify and even withhold your initiatives and that you be aware of your social obligations. Autonomy is decidedly not isolation.

Good metacognitive skills

Self-direction is impossible without good metacognitive skills (see chapter 2). Much of self-direction takes the form of "thinking about thinking." Skills in planning, monitoring yourself (either at the time or afterwards), assessing effectiveness of strategies, and even making up strategies for yourself are both metacognitive and important for self-regulation.

So setting and pursuing your goals form essential elements of self-regulation. You have to be able to decide what you want to learn and find ways to do so. At the same time, you need to remember that you will not always meet with success. Coping with the frustration of delayed or even failed plans is as important as making them in the first place. Self-regulation requires a "Plan B."

Trust in self and others

Self-regulation is a kind of balancing act. You need to believe in your own capacity to cope with difficulties, and yet you also need to trust others enough to let them (or ask them to) help you when you realize you cannot do everything on your own. Similarly, you need to be able to balance independent work planned, executed, and evaluated by you, with direction from outside, as in a classroom. Although you are responsible for learning and for knowing what you are learning for, the teacher is responsible for orchestrating events in the classroom. Further, you need to compromise with reality: you will not get everything you want when you want it (and maybe not at all), and yet you need to seek what you need and want in spite of the fact that you may not get it.

Abstract thinking

To self-regulate well, you need to think abstractly. This includes such mental activities as shifting your focus from one aspect of a situation to another while keeping several aspects in mind at the same time. You must both grasp the whole picture and analyze its components, synthesizing new with old

---

The self-regulated learner

When they begin to study, self-regulated learners set goals for extending knowledge and sustaining motivation. They are aware of what they know, what they believe, and what the differences between these kinds of information imply for approaching tasks. They understand their motivation, are aware of their affect, and plan how to manage the interplay between these as they engage with a task. They also deliberate about small-grain tactics [strategies for handling specific, narrow tasks and situations] and overall strategies, selecting some instead of others based on predictions about how each is able to support progress toward chosen goals. Or on rational grounds, they may abandon the task entirely. (Winne, 1995, p. 173)

Figure 9.1

and apparently disparate elements, forming hierarchic concepts, planning ahead, envisaging possibilities, and making use of symbols (Wolfe and Kolb, 1984).

These are complex tasks. For example goal setting entails awareness, expectation of success, psychological safety, goals that can be measured, self-controlled evaluation, and the belief that one can exercise at least some control in a situation (Kolb and Boyatzis, 1984).

A description of a self-regulated learner is presented in figure 9.1. It reminds us that knowing when to persist and when to quit in the face of impossible odds is another key to effective regulation of your own learning.

Tricks of the trade

Those who self-regulate well do a number of things that make them successful. You can apply these same "tricks" in your own learning. Some of them are discussed below. These include:

- setting achievable goals;
- staying aware of your feelings;
- keeping aware of your options;
- anticipating difficulties;
- prioritizing;
- increasing versatility;
- being realistic;
- depending on others;
- being independent where you can.

Setting achievable goals

It is easy to get overwhelmed by the sheer vastness of a foreign language, especially if you set vague goals like "learn the language in two weeks." Instead, set multiple small, near-term goals, rather than single, large, and more distant ones (Winne, 1995). Not only do you maintain some control over yourself and your learning, you also can get quicker and better targeted feedback on whether what you have tried is working.

Staying aware of your feelings

Try to stay aware of your feelings, both positive and negative. Use some of the feeling management tactics described in chapter 4. If you are aware that something "turns you off," you can try to find ways to work around it. (This is, in fact, a cognitive tactic even though you are dealing with feelings, because you are noticing and thinking about your feelings and how to handle them.)

Keep aware of your options

Keep aware of your options and avoid closing them off prematurely. It is possible that lack of success in one of your efforts might have a simple cause that you can fix easily.

Anticipate difficulties

Anticipate difficulties and prepare to meet them with a good action plan or a set of practical options. That is to say, if Plan A does not work, it's useful to have a Plan B and Plan C. They need not be fully formed, but some kind of backup ideas will maintain options and will provide the feeling that you are unlikely to fail because you have multiple paths.

Prioritizing

You can't do everything all at once, so do what matters most at the time. Set priorities. For example, you can pick and choose words to learn, grammar to focus on, and learning strategies, based on your current state of knowledge, your interests, and your learning style.

Increasing your versatility

Try some things that are outside your learning style to increase your versatility. If you tend toward impulsivity, for instance, try slowing down, counting to ten (or at least five) before acting, or checking your work. On the contrary, if you are more comfortable thinking things through, try doing a timed task: set a timer and when it goes off, the task should be complete. If it is not, try again and again, until your speed matches the timer. (Yes, your accuracy will likely go down; that is okay.)

Being realistic

Check your beliefs. One of the most damaging things you can believe is that learning should be rapid and knowledge without ambiguities. Experienced and effective learners understand that *learning can be slow, uneven, and gradual*, and they know that most of life is colored in shades of grey.

CASE STUDY

Problem

Valerie is beginning to feel completely lost in her Arabic class. Her teacher keeps telling her that she can figure out grammar rules for herself. She knows that she cannot do that. Not only is Arabic grammar very complicated for her, but in general she prefers someone to explain things to her before she tries to use them. So, how can she survive?

Possible solutions

Valerie can approach taking charge of her own learning in several ways:

(1) She can learn more about her learning style. Her teacher is trying to help her become more autonomous, but she is probably a deductive learner and would work better if she got the rules first. She does not have to depend on the teacher for explanations, however. There are grammar books (written for students) that she can use to get the explanations; she can also try to "stretch" and see if she can figure out at least some of the rules before turning to a rule book.

(2) She can talk to her teacher about her learning needs (in a mutually respectful way) and see what she can negotiate.

(3) She can seek assistance from classmates, who may have worked out the rules.

Figure 9.2

Depending on others

Allow yourself to depend on teachers, syllabus, textbooks, and other external guidance for as long as you need them. Not everyone can operate independently equally fast, and pushing yourself to autonomy before you are ready for it can be destructive to effective learning and to your self-confidence.

Being independent where you can

On the other hand, take over as much self-regulation as your knowledge and circumstances permit, as soon as you are ready. Some people may be ready to take a lot of control almost immediately, especially random learners (see chapter 3); others may need quite a lot more time before they are ready to manage most of their learning. Sooner or later, though, everyone can take some responsibility for learning even if it's only deciding what order to do your homework and when to take study breaks.

Affect in self-regulation

Although such cognitive activities as synthesizing, planning, and evaluation of your learning are the heart of self-regulation, you have probably experienced or observed how seriously feelings like stress, anxiety, or response to threat can disrupt these processes. On the other hand, cognition can also be greatly enhanced by positive feelings, such as motivation, well-being, and self-efficacy.

Motivation for independent learning

Much has been written about motivation and language learning, and an equal amount has been written about motivation and self-regulation in all forms of learning. Why is motivation important? First of all, learning is change, and change is difficult. Motivation underpins keeping up the emotional, intellectual, and physical effort needed to achieve change (Ehrman and Dörnyei, 1998).

Motivation promotes effort, i.e. time on task. This is the most basic condition for learning: the more time you spend on learning (and using effective strategies), the more you can take in, keep in, and retrieve when you need it. If you really want to achieve proficiency, you will expose yourself to the language as much as your circumstances permit. In a related vein, motivation leads to persistence when you are having difficulties. Persistence, together with well-targeted learning strategies, can often overcome limitations of ability and environment.

Anxiety and autonomy

Anxiety and stress are among the most powerful agents for derailing self-regulation. If you are overwhelmed by your feelings, your cognitive learning resources are diminished. Your abstract reasoning suffers, and you are likely to be taken over by your defense mechanisms, frequently immature ones. Such tactics for coping with anxiety and stress often attempt to protect self-esteem, but you pay a high price for your defensive position.

Self-regulation in the affective domain entails:

* Awareness of what you are feeling and what is bothering you;
* Reducing the intensity of negative feelings;
* Reframing and "choosing your battles;"
* Focusing on the positive and selecting helpful environments; and
* Attempting to use mature defenses (see chapter 4).

Self-awareness

Self-awareness is a great help in self-regulation. If you know you're feeling unhappy or anxious, rather than ignoring it, you can take some kind of action to keep it from hindering you (see some of the suggestions in chapter 4). It is surprising how much we can take our feelings for granted and assume that the way they are is how they have to be. Getting more information about what is bothering you can be very helpful. Is it something immediate in the classroom, such as making too many mistakes for your comfort, in the environment, e.g. style conflict, or something not related at all, such as a spat with a friend? Knowledge is a form of control, and it tells you where to look for solutions.

Reducing negative feelings

Attempt to turn down the "affective volume" when you are upset or anxious. If you are only hearing the bad feelings, there is little room for anything else, especially learning. Try distraction from what is bothering you or some of the other techniques mentioned in chapter 4 or this chapter.

Reframing

An extremely powerful technique is reframing your situation so that you see it in different terms. One of the authors illustrates reframing with a cartoon of a dog chained to a doghouse saying to a cat, "The reason they don't tie you up is because they want you to run away." The dog is turning a difficult circumstance (restriction) into a positive one (the owners care about him and want him to stay), and dealing with envy of the cat by turning the situation around in his favor. A related technique is choosing your "battles" – decide where you will expend your emotional resources, and find ways to avoid or sidestep the others. Reframing can help: after you have turned as much of the situation around in your mind as you can, you may know where the real problems are and be able to work on those.

Focusing on the positive

You may know that there are negative things going on, but do you have to keep thinking about them, to the detriment of your effectiveness? The only reason for ruminating about bad things is if it helps you solve problems.

Where possible, attempt to use relatively mature defense mechanisms, such as humor, altruism, or sublimation (cross-reference). These are likely to help you reclaim your cognitive resources. To the degree you can, select helpful environments where you feel work, study, or social success. Avoid to the degree possible situations that are toxic to you, or if you cannot avoid them, try using techniques like reframing, choosing your battles, and focus on what is good. Unless it's required, like a class, normally you don't have to spend a lot of time with people or in places where you don't feel good.

Interpersonal dimensions of learner autonomy

It may be that when you hear the terms *autonomous* or *independent*, you think of someone studying all alone. Actually, other people can play a number of important roles in autonomous, self-regulated learning. As we know, they can be sources of stress, but here we examine how they can help reduce tension and facilitate your independent learning.

We have seen that cognitive and metacognitive functions essential to self-regulation can be disrupted or enhanced by feelings. Frequently, such feelings arise from our relations with others: classmates, teachers, and family. These other

---

CASE STUDY

Problem

When Valerian began learning Greek, he was very excited and enthusiastic. He spent a lot of time on his homework and even did extra work. Now he has become more apathetic. He is tired of making so many mistakes and is beginning not to care about his language class; in fact, he is thinking of dropping it. What now?

Possible solutions

Valerian can use one or more of the following to deal with his "problem:"

(1) He can step back from the study for a while so he can get some perspective. A day or so doing something completely different could help.

(2) He can talk with someone, possibly his teacher or an experienced language learner, about what is causing him to feel this way.

(3) He can try some reframing. It is useful to keep in mind that if you're not making mistakes, you may not be learning much. He may have lost sight of this fact.

(4) He can decide whom he fears, i.e. whose opinion will make him feel bad. Then he can decide what to say to these people (silently) to get them off his emotional back. He should note that most likely he is his own worst critic.

Figure 9.3

people can have a profound effect on motivation, well-being, self-efficacy, and anxiety, because it matters to us how they feel about us (and how we feel about them). They have an influence not only on our sense of security with others but also on our self-concept.

The class

The atmosphere in the classroom or the nature of the group dynamics there raises or lowers anxiety and motivation. Coercion reduces motivation; personal investment in tasks increases it. To the degree that we build our self-image and our self-esteem from how others reflect us back to ourselves, we are likely to have greater or lesser self-efficacy as autonomous learners.

Other people

Finding social support is a key strategy to surviving an uncomfortable classroom situation. That means other people, like friends, advisors, teachers, relatives, and others you like and who like you. They can be among the best stress-reducers by listening (a truly powerful help) and providing sympathy and encouragement. Sometimes they provide useful advice, but of course it remains up to you to decide whether to take the advice or not. Of course, from others you get information, ranging from the next day's assignment if you missed it to knowledge they have that we do not.

Remember, too, that other people provide models for you to follow. For example, you can learn about self-regulation from models provided by other people, both in and outside of the classroom. Look at how they make plans and choices and how they manage their time. Ask the ones who seem especially successful about what they do. You can also pick up learning strategies from others, either directly or by observation. If it's working for someone else, it might work for you, too, some of the time. Try it out and see.

In addition to serving as models, other people play an important role in helping you define your goals and values, because you pick up social norms from the people in your life who matter to you. For example, you may have learned that it is important to be honest because your family and friends value it highly. Other people also provide reference points for us to aspire and measure ourselves against. Many students like being with classmates who learn faster or are more advanced, because not only do they learn things from the classmates, they also have something realistic to aim for.

Fellow learners can share the workload. It does not mean less autonomy for you to participate in study or project groups, especially if you have built that kind of activity into your planning. They can also help you when you get "stuck" with something. It's part of self-regulation to know when to call for help. It can also be enormously encouraging to you to provide help to others; it validates your skill and makes you a part of the social network that is essential to "the human animal." Social support can bring about a sense that you are valued: just the fact that others find you worth the investment of their time can be a boost to fraying self-esteem, and you can give the same to others.

Finally, Ehrman and Dörnyei (1998) indicate how other people are very much involved in our defensive maneuvers. For example, at the constructive end, joking and humor are normally very social activities, as are projection and blaming in the less constructive area. It's hard to blame without someone else as the target, and humor is much more effective when there's someone else to share it. (Blaming isn't usually a very good way to deal with perceived failure, though. It is better to be sure that you aren't trying to shift responsibility that is yours before you cast blame.)

Teacher's roles in promoting learner autonomy

Among the most important figures in the growth of learning autonomy is your teacher. Just as good parenting allows dependence when it is appropriate for a child but encourages independence when the child is ready, so a good teacher provides support as it is needed and lets go when the student is ready to "fly solo." (In education-speak, this is called "scaffolding," as when a building is supported until it can stand on its own.)

CASE STUDY

Problem

Patti and Paula are classmates and friends. Patti is having no particular trouble with her learning and is even taking on a lot of planning, monitoring of her work, and changing course where necessary. Her classmate, Paula, is not having as easy a time. She is becoming dependent on Patti and beginning to take up a lot of her time. What can Patti do without rejecting Paula or destroying her friendship?

Possible solutions

It may be gratifying to have the admiration and interest of a classmate, but it also can become confining. Patti should consider carefully how much she wants to have Paula depend on her. There are some ways that she can both help Paula and maintain her sanity and "space."

(1) She can think about some things to suggest to Paula that will help her work on her own more.

(2) She should decide on the role she can best take on: e.g. mentor, cheerleader, sympathetic ear. Then, she should try to set some limits on that role and perhaps suggest other people who could fill some of the other roles.

(3) She could also share strategies that have helped her become more autonomous.

Figure 9.4

Teachers play a multitude of roles in your learning, far too many to address here. But here are a few that they play in enhancing your independence:

- guide;
- cheerleader;
- role model; and
- motivator.

Guide

As a guide, teachers provide initial goals and guidelines to learners without enough information to make those decisions for themselves. This applies to most novices, who usually need guidance until they build up some expertise and knowledge. If the teacher provides too much or too little guidance, you need to be aware of this and find ways to cope. In the former case, which is likely to affect random and inductive learners in particular, you can find ways to meet the teacher's goals for your learning, but do it your way if that works better for you. (You could try the teacher's way first, just to see if you can pick up any new strategies.) In the latter case, sequential and deductive learners are likely to be most affected, and in that case, you can seek to make your own sequences and logical outlines, find organized references, and if necessary let the teacher know that you are getting lost and could use more guidance.

Table 9.1

Person or group	Help or hinder?	How	Comment
Anne	Hinders	Keeps talking when I want a chance to talk	I need to be more assertive to get my turn
The neighbor's dog	Hinders	Too noisy	Bring this up with the neighbor; try to have a constructive solution to offer
Jonathan	Helps	Is always encouraging	Am I giving him the same thing back?

Cheerleader

As cheerleader, the teacher encourages (and may discourage) you. This can be an important part of developing the "learning alliance" (see chapter 4) that has you and your teacher as teammates working toward the same goal. A teacher whose interest in your success is obvious will help you want to have more success. Of course the teacher also has the power to reward and punish by providing or withholding approval; if you need the rewards of good grades (and most of us want them), it will help to be aware of this fact and distinguish between adaptation to a temporary situation and what you really prefer.

Role model

Having a role model is especially important in language learning, where you may be building a foreign language identity. If the teacher is a native speaker, this is much easier than if she or he is not, but even in the latter case the teacher can represent the foreign culture and language to some degree. The teacher can be someone to internalize and model yourself on, someone whose speech and behavior can be imitated.

Motivator

Most of us are motivated by another person's interest in our worlds, both in and outside of the classroom. A teacher's interest in you and in your success can increase your desire for that success. Furthermore, a teacher who finds out your interests and helps you explore them is likely to enhance your interest in the language. For example, if you are interested in science more than literature, such a teacher will bring some recent scientific discoveries into the discussion from time to time and will help you find reading matter that is both interesting and at an appropriate level of difficulty for you.

Practice what you have learned!

1.   List some ways that you are already regulating yourself. Here's a starter checklist (but far from complete):
   a. Plan how to use homework time
   b. Use references without prompting
   c. Ask questions when I can't figure it out for myself
   d. Manage how much I expect myself to be able to do in a given period of time, such as a week, a month, or a semester
   e. Understand my learning style (and something of that of others) so that I can negotiate with my teacher or seek compatible learning opportunities outside the classroom
   f. Track my list of things to do
   g. Take opportunities to review on my own
   h. Evaluate my progress and review the strategies I'm using.

2.   Find a small task that doesn't take a lot of thinking, such as washing the dishes. Break it down into steps as you do it (you will need to observe yourself). Here is a starter list for dishwashing:
   a. notice dirty dishes in sink
   b. think about washing them
   c. think about whether it can be postponed
   d. if not, think about what you will need to do the job
   e. check to make sure that soap and scrubbers are there
   f. clear the sink if necessary to make room to work (entails making a judgement about the amount of space in the sink and where to put the dirty dishes)
   g. etc.

3.   Now try to do the same thing with a language-learning task. Make it one that is low pressure and where you are alone and undistracted, since you will have to do two things at once: the task itself, and observing and taking notes as you do it.

   How parallel were the routine and the learning tasks?
   Do you need to change the way you work in language? How?

4.   List all the people and groups who are involved in your learning. Indicate if they help, hinder, do both, and how. Table 9.1 on p. 212 is a starter sample.

Review

In this chapter, you considered these themes:

- Some myths and misunderstandings about learner autonomy
- Different levels of interaction
- Self-regulation leading to autonomy

- Cognition in self-regulation
- Affect in self-regulation
- Interpersonal dimensions of self-regulation
- Teachers' roles

Myths about autonomous learning

(1) Autonomous learning is done by people of all ages.
(2) It's not all or nothing.
(3) Self-directed doesn't mean isolated: other people are important to self-directed learning.

Cognition in self-regulation

(1) Most of the processes we use to think, such as planning, making hypotheses, and setting priorities, apply to self-directed language learning as well as to instructed learning.
(2) Coping strategies include planning, breaking big tasks down into little ones ("chunking"), looking for ways to work around difficulties, keeping aware of options, setting priorities so you do not try to do everything at once, accepting help and using instructional resources.

Affect in self-regulation

(1) Motivation helps you work through frustration and difficulty and keeps you on task.
(2) Anxiety can diminish your ability to self-regulate, because it takes away cognitive and affective resources you need to manage yourself and your learning.
(3) Tips for coping include being aware of your feelings, finding ways like distracting yourself to lower the "volume," reframing to see a bad-seeming situation in other terms, and using more mature defenses as much as you can.

Interpersonal dimensions

(1) The positive roles others play for you and that you play for them include listening and giving emotional support, serving as models and resources for autonomous strategies, sharing the workload (e.g. in study groups), and participating in our defensive maneuvers.
(2) Teachers can contribute a lot to your growing autonomy by modeling for you, encouraging you, and by giving you the support you need but no more (or they can get in its way). Among their most important roles in supporting your autonomy are guide, cheerleader, role model, and motivator.

If you want to learn more about the topics in this chapter, you will find the following references useful: Aoki (1999); Dickinson (1995); Dickinson and Wenden, eds. (1995); Ehrman (1998b); Ehrman (2000); Ehrman and Dörnyei (1998); Vygotsky (1962).

10 Controlling spoken and written communication

Preview

This chapter will introduce you to working at the full-text level of language (i.e. the level beyond single sentences and single paragraphs). It contains suggestions for dealing with full-blown communication in oral and written form. Topics that this chapter will address include:

- Managing oral communication
- Managing written communication

Managing oral communication

One can conceive of two kinds of communication, when it comes to linguistic interrelations among interlocutors. These are (1) speaking among native speakers, and (2) speaking among native speakers and non-native speakers. In the first case, language does not create problems in communication, although, of course, non-language problems may interfere. In the second kind of communication, language difficulties interfere with communication. In native speaker–non-native speaker interaction, the non-native speaker constantly performs dual activity in real time: keeping track of the ideas of both (or all) speakers as they evolve during the conversation and understanding and generating speech consciously through the manipulation of foreign forms, sounds, and word order. Moreover, sometimes (and perhaps, even, often) the content of the conversation depends not on what the non-native speaker *wishes* to express but rather what he or she is *able* to express in the foreign language – a situation that is diametrically opposite to that of the native speaker.

Beginning student speech is characterized by uncomfortable pauses, tedious searching for words, and annoying self-corrections. For advanced-level, and especially superior-level, students, the gap between the proficiency of the student and that of the native speaker narrows but rarely disappears completely. Even superior-level students can create a slower tempo in speaking, experience an occasional search for words, be occasionally imprecise, use grammar structures that reflect native-language linguistic patterns, and lack a complete understanding of native-speaker speech, especially in the case of dialects, substandard forms, jargon, double entendres, idioms, literary allusions, cultural biases, and the like. For this reason, it is good for all students, beginners and those who are significantly more advanced, to learn to manage oral communication.

Communication as a generic phenomenon (i.e. the making of meaning and the transferring of meaning) comprises a set of linguistic behaviors. These linguistic behaviors are subordinate to individual languages and cultures but superordinate to them. So are the communication strategies that influence, control, and make manageable communication between native and non-native speakers of any given language. Knowing these strategies (Shekhtman, 1990 and 2003a, calls them "Rules of Communication") allows non-native speakers at any level of language proficiency to communicate effectively with native speakers. How do they do that? By allowing you to take control of a communication, to eliminate pauses that destroy communication, and to gain confidence in your ability to communicate. How these rules are applied depends on the nature of the interaction.

Although there are a number of types of communication, we will consider only four of the most common here: functional transactions, informal conversations, interviews (one kind of formal conversation), and formal presentations; these are the ones that you are most likely to find yourself involved in, and if you know how to manage these communicative situations, you will most likely be able to manage any other kinds, as well. For each of these types of communications, there are communication strategies that will help you to be an equal partner with native speakers.

Functional transactions

Functional transactions are the most predictable form of communication. Functions are the linguistic behaviors associated with regularly occurring tasks in one's daily personal and professional life (Wilkins, 1976). Some typical functions are meetings and greetings, making purchases, using public and private transportation, making telephone calls, and the like. Every function has a "script" – a standard set of phrases that people use to transact that function. A script for meeting and greeting would include the greeting itself, asking after someone's health or affairs, and replying to such questions. There is a limited range of formulistic expressions that are generally used – at least, until the communication enters into the truly personal sphere or into another type of communication. For this reason, even someone who has no knowledge of the language can more or less successfully get through a specific transaction by memorizing a few of the key phrases it requires.

Let's take an example. Let's say that an immigrant to the United States goes to the supermarket for the first time. He makes his selection and heads for the checkout line, where the cashier asks, "Paper or plastic?" The foreigner stands there in uncomprehending silence, frantically racking his brain to figure out what this means: does he have to show some documents? The cashier, seeing the shopper's confusion, picks up one of each kind of bag and repeats the question, pointing at each one in turn. The foreigner experienced difficulty in this situation only because he did not know the script for making purchases in American grocery stores.

Most textbooks will teach you the scripts that go with functions. This is pretty standard fare, regardless of the teaching methodology underlying the textbook. By the time you reach intermediate levels of proficiency, you will probably be able to handle most daily living functions and you will not need the strategies which are described below. However, if you do encounter a situation where you find yourself out of control, here are three strategies that you can use to get back in control of this type of communication and complete your transaction.

*   Prepare ahead of time.
*   Wait it out.
*   Repeat the question.

Prepare ahead of time

Learn by heart the typical expressions for the situations in which you think you will find yourself. You will be able to find many of these in textbooks, especially those that provide dialogues on various functions. During your preparations, make sure that you have the right expressions for the social level and/or dialectal region the people you will be dealing with come from. For example, the Arab culture differs from one country to another. Thus, Arabs in most countries may say in greeting or parting "Allah yeatik al-afia" (may God give you health). The word *afia* means *health* in the whole Arab world, except in Morocco where it means *hell*. Clearly, proper preparation will keep you out of trouble in this case.

Wait it out

If you try to clarify what you do not understand, you are likely just to pull yourself deeper into the quagmire. Instead, give a short, non-committal response to whatever remark has been made, to the extent that you *have* understood it or the situation. If the person with whom you are conducting your transaction wants or expects a more detailed one, he or she will continue with the same theme, and there may be additional information that will help you understand where the interaction is going. Fortunately, with functions, there are only so many ways of doing things, and the person with whom you are speaking usually wants to get the transaction with you over and done with, in order to deal with the next person.

Repeat the question

If you ask a question but do not understand the answer, an effective strategy can be to repeat the question and continue doing so until something is said that you can interpret. Of course, it will help if you can repeat the question in a variety of ways.

Informal conversation

By informal conversation, we mean any two-way or multi-party inter-actions on any social or professional topic. Informal conversation is a complex form of communication that can have many registers. In conversation, people exchange information, solve problems, express their attitude towards what has been said, and reveal their emotions. Conversation goes beyond the more easily managed scripts associated with specific functions. There is much unpredictabil-ity in informal conversation. This makes it difficult for a foreign-language student to hold up his or her end of the conversation. Nonetheless, there are a number of strategies that will help you succeed at informal conversation. Here are eight of them:

*   When a native speaker asks you a question, give the most verbose answer possible.
*   Memorize short (and even long) discourses ("islands").
*   Change the topic when you are in trouble.
*   Simplify what you are trying to say.
*   Ask questions.
*   Use what you know.
*   Embellish your speech.
*   Ignore mistakes and keep on going.

Verbose answers

Every sentence usually contains a number of subordinate elements, each of which can be further developed. For example, *I like to read books* can be expanded by giving more information about *yourself*, more information about what you *like*, and more information about the kinds of *books* you like to read. Giving a verbose answer keeps you in control of the conversation for a longer period of time and lets you talk about the things you can talk about, rather than forcing you to try to answer questions from native speakers on topics that you cannot talk about.

Memorized discourse (islands)

"Islands" are memorized, much practiced, frequently used mono-logues. We call them islands because we compare speaking a foreign language with swimming. Every swimmer needs a small island upon which he/she can rest from time to time. Islands are developed naturally, including in your own language, by talking about the same thing over and over; you probably have a number of islands in your native speech. Islands can be developed in the same way in your foreign language. You can also deliberately increase the numbers and size of your islands through rote memory – writing up and learning whole pieces of discourse for topics that you know you will be required to talk about.

Change the topic

If you run into trouble in a conversation, change the topic from the one that is difficult for you to one that is related but which you can easily talk about. It is better to move on and talk about something else than try to express something that you cannot, creating frustration for both you and your interlocutor. You can make the change either directly or indirectly. If you make it directly, you will need to have phrases to use for this purpose; some such phrases are "Let's talk about something else." This can be awkward unless you can give a good reason for making the change. Alternatively, you can approach changing the topic in an indirect way, saying something like, "Gee, I really don't know much about that, but you know I heard X about Y," where X and Y refer to the new, probably related, topic. Again, you will need to have a number of foreign-language phrases at your command to make this shift.

Simplify

If you are having trouble expressing an idea, put it in as simple a form as possible, even if that means using a series of very short sentences. Let's say you want to express your negative opinion about a specific political issue and you want to do it in a sophisticated way showing how good you are at that problem and how deeply you understand it. You wish you could! Well, you can by using a few substitutions: (1) a lay word for a sophisticated or technical term, (2) a simple sentence for a compound, complex, or compound-complex sentence, and/or (3) a basic grammatical structure for a more complex one. All of these substitutions, while dealing with a larger or different kind of text, are manifestations of one strategy – simplify; you can probably think of other manifestations, as well.

The reason most learners need to apply the strategy of simplifying is that they try to speak at the same level of precision in their new language as they do in their native language. This is simply unrealistic at early levels of language learning. In your native language you probably know many synonyms for the word *put*: *lay, pile, heap, stack, pack up, compose*, but you know only one of these words in the foreign language. Use that word, then. After much language study and in-country experience, you will begin collecting synonyms in your new language, too, and ultimately, you will have the same choice of words and the same ability to be precise in speaking in your foreign language as you did in your native language. This is an important part of high-level language proficiency, and when you approach that level, your learning strategies and communication strategies will and must change (Leaver and Shekhtman, 2002). (Read the epilogue to this book for a sense of what happens at the highest levels of proficiency and how one moves from being very advanced to being near-native.)

For similar reasons and in similar ways, you can substitute whole sentence structure, not just individual words. If you can't say, "Since the body position in swimming is controlled by the position of the head and has a direct impact on the quality of swimming, most frequently the cause of inefficient swimming can be attributed to an improper head position," find a simple sentence to substitute. One example would be: "The way you hold your head can affect how well you swim."

Likewise, you can escape from having to use sophisticated grammar points that you do not know or have not yet internalized. In your native language, for example, it may be very easy for you to use the subjunctive mood, but you may not know it yet in the foreign language. So, for it substitute other patterns that you do know. Instead of saying "Had I been in the library, I would have taken the book out for you," say, "I wasn't in the library, so I was not able to take the book out."

Ask questions

Complete your answer to any question with a question to your interlocutor. In this way, you can gain or maintain control of the communication, eliminate an awkward pause should you not know what to say, and even get your interlocutor to change the topic of the conversation to one of your choice.

Use what you know

Many times you may be tempted to try to translate from your own language into the foreign language. Usually, this is a very easy way to get into very deep trouble very quickly. Rather than resorting to translation, think about what you *can* say and use those words and structures.

Embellish your speech

You can make your speech, no matter how limited your foreign-language skills, more natural by embellishing it in a number of ways. Here are some of those ways:

- Add some exclamations, such as "cool!" or "you bet!"
- Use parenthetical expressions, such as "you know," "in my opinion," and the like.
- Use guidance questions, such as "I forgot, what did you ask me?"
- Embellish your speech with idiomatic and slang expressions (of course, for any kind of speech embellishment, you will need to learn the appropriate expressions and practice using them).
- Learn how to say "um" in culturally appropriate ways; it can make you sound more fluent, as well as buying you some time.

Ignore mistakes

Being worried about mistakes can make you tongue-tied. Even if you hear yourself make one, keep on going. Stopping and correcting your mistake will make you and your interlocutor painfully aware of your linguistic deficiencies. (Do, of course, correct a content or factual error.) If a native speaker continues the conversation and does not ask you to repeat or clarify what you said, it means that your mistakes did not interfere with the communication.

The interview

An interview is no less unpredictable than a conversation unless you know the interviewee very well. The goal of an interview, however, differs dramatically from that of informal conversation, where often there is no goal at all. An interview is very goal-oriented and attaining that goal – obtaining specific information from the interviewee – is dependent on your ability to control the interview.

The interviewee may be overly talkative and may give more detail than the interviewer wants, or he may tend to stray from the topic. On the other hand, the interviewee may not enjoy talking at all or for various reasons may not wish to answer the questions put to him. A good interviewer must know how to keep the former type on track, and open up the latter.

It is very important in an interview to address issues related to cultural differences. Take, for example, an interview with a Russian banker in which he is asked to describe the current business climate in Russia. Suppose that in his response the banker says the following: "Since MMM, people no longer trust banks and publicly held companies." If you give a literal translation of this answer, it will make no sense at all. To understand this sentence you need to know that MMM was the largest and wealthiest company in Russia which collapsed and caused thousands of shareholders to lose their money. If you know this information, then it's good; but if not, you will need to make a detour and ask for clarification to make sense of what was said.

To do that, you will need some very specific speaking strategies beyond those that you used for informal conversation, as well as a number of good listening strategies, some of which you already learned.

- Ignore what you don't understand, stick to everything you do understand
- Verify and clarify
- Have a command of all types of questions of a target language
- Memorize the expressions for controlling interview
- Do your homework

Ignore what you don't understand, stick to what you do understand

In situations in which you are not able to interrupt the native speaker or you don't want to interrupt him/her for any reason, you need to follow these two rules:

- Pay no attention to unknown elements of a native speaker's speech
- Do not miss any familiar element of a native speaker's speech

These two rules will form your ability to get the gist of what is being said; they will allow you to keep up the main idea despite missing the details. By using these rules you will get much more information out of what is being said than if you attempt to understand every word and phrase, which makes you lose track of the whole. The advantage of using these two rules lies in the fact that they allow you to get a maximum of information without disrupting the flow of communication, that is, without interrupting communication. There is a disadvantage in using these rules. They do not allow you to verify the information you receive.

Verify and clarify

This strategy consists of a set of questions and statements which will help you to understand the details of what is being said. They come in two types: overt and covert.

Overt clarification strategies include questions and statements which show that you do not understand the target information and by which you openly ask for help. They consist of such expressions as: "Sorry, I don't understand you." "Repeat, please." "Say it again." "Repeat the last sentence/word." "Say what you just said but differently." "What is the English for this word?" "Give me the synonym for this word." "Speak slowly, please." "Write it down for me." "Try to explain it for me," and so forth and so on.

Covert clarification strategies include questions and statements which do not show that you don't understand a native speaker though in reality you need clarification of the target information. They are such expressions as: "What do you mean, when you are saying it?" "It's extremely interesting what you said. Let me write it down. Say it again slowly." "Your last statement is extremely important for me, may I listen to it again?" "Why are you saying (asking) it?" Or, if you didn't understand a certain word, don't speak about it directly but begin to ask questions about this word until it becomes clear for you. Let us say you did not understand the word *pliers* in the sentence *The pliers are on the bed*. Then you will say "What pliers?" "Why are they on the bed?" "Where did you get them from?" etc. The covert clarification strategies are very important when you do not want to jeopardize the normal flow of communication and you do not want your interlocutor to lose trust in your ability to communicate with him or her.

The main thing for you now is to know what strategies to use and when to use them, and they will not only help you to keep up with the unfettered native speaker's monologues and shorter utterances but also allow you to increase your effective level of listening comprehension significantly.

Have a command of all possible types of questions of the target language

The non-native speaker, just like a native speaker, must have an automatic command of the rules for forming various types of questions in the foreign language. These types may include simple questions with or without question words as well as more complex question forms: question-assertions, follow-up questions, and so on. The ability to manipulate the various types of questions during an interview as it evolves helps the interviewer be more at ease and less dependent on linguistic forms. When you experience difficulties in constructing your questions apply strategies from "Simplification" and "Use what you know."

Memorize expressions for controlling an interview

The expressions for controlling an interview may be divided into two groups. The first controls the contents of the interview and the second group the behavior of the interviewee. Let's consider both of them.

- The first group consists of phrases which do not allow the native speaker to turn the interview into undesirable directions. These directions are: (1) the informant strays from the subject of the interview or (2) the informant for some reason fails to address the issues raised in the interview. These phrases may be as follows: "Will you be so kind as to continue to stay on the topic I am interested in?" "It's quite interesting what you are saying but I prefer to get more information on my previous question." "Please, I really need your answer to the question I posed," etc.
- The second group consists of phrases that could be used to manage the reluctant communicator or the "hog." To the passive communicator you may say: "What do you think about it?" "Do you agree with me?" "Is there anything you want to add?" "How do you feel about this issue?" "What are your feelings on this subject?" To a conversation hog you may say: "Allow me to add . . . Speaking of that . . . You are absolutely right, however . . . May I interrupt . . . Let me say this . . ."

You can keep from being interrupted if you learn to pause in places where the language doesn't usually pause. In English, for example, if you stop after the words "and," "they," or "in," everyone will wait for you to finish because sentences do not end in conjunctions, pronouns or prepositions in English.

Prepare in advance; be ready

The difficulties in conducting the interview are often connected with factors indirectly related to language. These may include:

- Cultural factors and factors related to professional jargon, when a person uses words from his local dialect or complex professional jargon.
- Social factors, when native speakers use vocabulary or syntax that is too complex or too primitive.
- Physiological factors, when a native speaker has hearing or articulation problems.

- Psychological factors, when a person is extremely depressed or agitated and cannot express himself/herself clearly.
- Acoustic factors, when comprehension is diminished by different kinds of noise.

In all these cases you need to be prepared, assuming, of course, that you know about these specifics before the interview. You can prepare yourself psychologically and linguistically and should attend to doing both.

Formal oral presentation

A formal oral presentation is monologic (at least, in the presentation portion, although almost always there are questions that follow and, in some cases, questions that interrupt). A formal presentation almost always requires serious preparation both for content (except in the case in which you are sharing something that you do or have done) and for language. Because of its monologic nature, a presentation is an unusual mode of interaction, especially for non-native speakers, since the audience cannot react to any language mistakes that are made, only to errors or confusion. This places the need on you to make sure that your language is clear and free of errors. The task is somewhat simplified by the fact that you can and should prepare a presentation in advance – and rehearse it with a native speaker or your teacher.

Another significant feature of a presentation is that it is, as a rule, complex in content and, therefore, complex in form. For this reason, the presentation is very often more linguistically complex than informal conversation. Depending on how presentations are made in the culture you are studying, you may need to use language that is considerably more formal than conversation (i.e. that resembles written vocabulary, grammatical expression, and syntax). A formal presentation will be effective only if it offers a clear, logical exposition of a subject or a concept, organized using culturally appropriate discourse structure. What kind of opening is appropriate? What kind of internal organization? What kind of conclusion? The use of these structures must be automatic because of all the other cognitive activity that is taking place concurrently.

In addition, handouts or power-point slides may be required. In these cases, there is usually a culturally appropriate way to organize these, too. If you are delivering the presentation in-country, there may be other requirements to be concerned about – things that are not part of your western experience. Sometimes, you will not have access to modern technology, and you should be prepared to use flip charts and blackboards. Writing on flip-charts can be prepared in advance; writing on blackboards cannot be unless you simply copy from a piece of paper – which usually makes a presentation sound very stilted. If you will be using a blackboard, you may need even more rehearsal, and automaticity of linguistic expression is absolutely essential because you will be talking and writing at the same time, which is a heavy cognitive load even in your native language.

In preparing the presentation, you will need to keep your audience in mind. What do they know about the topic? What level of erudition will they expect? There are strategies that you can use to help you succeed in making a presentation, whether in the classroom or to a group of native speakers. The strategies below are based on making a presentation to native speakers; *if you are doing a presentation only for your class* then . . .?

• Identify your audience and determine what degree of complexity you will provide about the content and what level of erudition you will use in your presentational language.
• Analyze authentic writings on the same topic.
• Find the appropriate grammatical constructions, preferably among those you already know.
• At lower levels of proficiency, write out the entire presentation.
• Learn text organizing expressions and critical content terminology,
• Check the content and organization of your presentation with a native speaker.
• Over-practice.
• Do a trial run with a native speaker.
• Anticipate as many questions as you can and prepare for answering them in the same way that you prepare for the presentation itself.
• Use those informal conversation strategies that are also appropriate for a presentation.

Identify the audience

Obviously, if you are going to be talking about brain physiology to a group of school children, you will structure your presentation quite differently than you would if you were going to be talking to a group of cognitive neuroscientists. For the former, you will use simplified content concepts and everyday language. For the latter, you will use scientific terminology and considerable detail, along with scholarly grammatical constructions and more complex forms of sentence structure. Without knowing something about your audience, you cannot properly prepare a presentation. Therefore, when you do not know who your audience will be, you will need to contact someone who does and find out as much as you possibly can about these people.

Analyze authentic writings

Find some articles on the topic that you will be presenting. These will show you the discourse structure: opening, topical treatment and organization, ending. You will need to use the same approach in your presentation if you want the audience to understand you. These authentic writings will also give you the vocabulary and grammar that is typically used when discussing your topic.

Find appropriate grammatical constructions

If you are going to be speaking in front of a professional group, you will need to speak at their level, as much as possible. In the articles you have chosen for analysis, look at the grammatical constructions that are used. How many of these do you know? Pick them! Use them often and well. How many do you not know? Are they essential? Can you replace them with structures that you do know that will sound more or less as scholarly? If yes, do that. If not, you may need some additional time for preparation so that you can learn and automate the constructions that you will need. If you find that you are having to include more than 10 per cent new constructions in your presentation, you may be in over your head, and the best thing to do might be not to make the presentation but find an alternative. Making a presentation that is inappropriately simplified or in which you will stumble because you are handling too many constructions that are new to you is a situation to be avoided.

Write out the presentation

If your language proficiency is near-native, you can get by with note-cards or an outline to keep you on task. Power point slides can also serve that same purpose. However, if you are not a near-native speaker, even if you consider yourself very competent and secure, writing out the presentation in advance has many advantages. It gives you a set structure that you can memorize. It makes terminology use and choice of grammar and vocabulary constant. This will help you very much when you start to make your presentation for real. (Many native speakers write out presentations in their own language before presenting them publicly; this is also a matter of personal style and preference.)

Learn text organizing devices

There are many text organizing devices in a formal presentation. Formal presentation is like a game with its own set of rules and regulations. If you want to play, you need to know the rules. Text organizers are a very important part of these rules. There are text organizers for the introduction, for the main part and for the conclusion. You need to know how to present yourself, how to develop discourse, how to work with the audience; and it all requires special expressions, which are not changeable, being like mathematical formulas. You simply need to know them automatically. Here are some of them: "In the beginning of my presentation I would like to . . . the main idea of . . . the thing is that . . . I would disagree . . . in conclusion I would like to underline." To have a command of the text, organizers will help you to present ideas clearly for an audience, facilitate the perception of a complex content and make the language level of your presentation approximate closely to the native speaker performance.

Check with a native speaker

Checking with a native speaker is always a good idea. Even highly proficient speakers of foreign languages – those with near-native proficiency – routinely check with native speakers before they make a presentation. Sometimes, they will even give the presentation to the native speaker, who can give them pointers on delivery.

Over-practice

This is not just a technique for delivering a speech in a foreign language. It is a technique for delivering a good presentation in your own language, as well. If the speech is more than memorized, if every bit of it is as familiar to you as your own name, you will make a very good presentation.

Do a trial run

Trial runs rank right up there with checking with a native speaker. It is always a good idea to practice in front of a friendly audience, if you can, before you present in front of a group of strangers. After all, actors do not present a play until it has been well rehearsed.

Anticipate questions

A well-delivered presentation can be marred by the inability to answer questions well. Although you cannot prepare fully for any and every question that might be asked, you can certainly anticipate some questions – and prepare answers for them – in advance. If you do a trial run, you will find out some unexpected questions – and you can prepare answers for these, too, in the event that someone in your audience should ask them.

Use appropriate informal conversation strategies

It is important for the person delivering a briefing to be prepared to answer questions afterwards. Only a person who is extremely well-prepared on the subject of the presentation will be able to handle with ease the kinds of questions that are often asked following the lengthy monologue portion of presentation, since they are often unpredictable and may be quite complex. This poses an extremely difficult challenge for the person wishing to deliver a presentation in a foreign language. To prepare oneself for this it is absolutely essential to go through a series of practice rehearsals in which one is made to use the entire arsenal of all the strategies to field complex, unexpected and even provocative questions either by answering them or avoiding answering them, all without revealing linguistic weak spots. The question part of the presentation covers all the types of oral communication discussed in this chapter. This is the time to make your presentation even more interesting to the audience, that is, to embellish it, to mix the complicated linguistic material of your presentation with elements that stand out and are easily understood. It is important now to put into your language some

---

CASE STUDY

Problem
Richard was in Finland and talking to a taxi driver in Finnish. He asked him how much it would cost to go to the Continental Hotel.

The taxi driver answered: "It will not be cheap; life is becoming more and more expensive in this town. I wish I could offer you a lower fare, but I can't. What do you have in mind?"

Richard did not understand a word and simply held out a wad of money, indicating with a gesture that the cab driver should take what he needed. What could he have done differently that would have been more communicative?

Possible solutions
Richard is not alone. Everyone gets "stuck" sometimes. Here are some things Richard could have done.

(1) He could have told the driver that he was a foreigner and did not understand what had been said; asking the driver to speak slowly or to write what he had just said on paper.

(2) He could have asked the driver to repeat what he had said.

(3) He could have asked the driver to clarify what he said by questioning him in various ways.

(4) He could have repeated the original question to the driver and, hopefully, the driver would have understood the second time that all Richard wanted to hear was the price.

Figure 10.1

light and therefore easily delivered fragments or short anecdotes (and the like) that are interesting and catch the audience's attention. If you do run into a question for which you have not prepared, there are still some things you can do. One example – also useful in your native language – is to say, "That's an interesting question, but I'm afraid it's a bit too involved to give you an answer here. Why don't you come up and talk with me afterwards?" Then you get another chance to understand the question, and if you still can't answer it, at least the audience is small.

Managing written communication

As with oral communication, written communication comes in a variety of forms. There are clear differences, for example, among informal written communication, such as personal letters and illocutionary or informative notes, and formal written communication, such as business correspondence, legal briefs, literary epics, newspaper articles, and the writing of informational books and articles. We will discuss here the three major categories – informal communications, specialized formal communications, and publications – from the point of view of managing the communication in effective ways.

Informal written communications

Informal written communication typically consists of colloquial language, ellipsis, incomplete sentences, illocutions, and implicitly shared information. There are a number of strategies you can use to learn to manage informal written communication, including:

- comparing the handwriting style of several native speakers and adopting the kind of penmanship that works for you;
- find a pen-pal in a country where your language is spoken;
- analyze the various genres (notes, letters, etc.) and compare them with each other and with the same genres in English;
- use native-speaker prepared, preferably authentic, materials as guides.

Penmanship

Penmanship is one area that is paid nearly no attention in foreign-language classrooms. Yet, this is one of the first things that gives away someone as a foreigner and, moreover, makes it hard to understand what has been written even if all the language is correct. It takes only a little practice to develop handwriting that looks close to that of a native speaker, given all the idiosyncratic versions of handwriting that are acceptable for any alphabet.

Pen-pals

Pen-pals are a great source for feedback on informal writing. If you have a pen-pal, ask him or her to return your letters with errors marked. Moreover, when you get a letter from your pen-pal, pay attention to how he or she responds to your letter. You will see many automatic corrections. Look beyond grammar to text organization. See how your pen-pal organizes his or her thoughts. Try to organize yours similarly when you write back.

Genre analysis

There are several genres of information writing. In other words, one writes differently in a narrative letter, relaying information about one's country to a pen-pal, than one writes to one's parents, asking for money. Description, narration, explanation, argumentation, and other genres all require the use of different expressions, text organizations, and grammatical structures. Pay careful attention to these when you read them and try to emulate them in your writing.

Authentic guides

Read notes that native speakers have jotted down and letters that they have written to each other. Buy a novel that is written in the form of a diary. Watch for the communicative devices used and try to emulate them in your writing. Keep a diary and try to match some of the styles you read in works of native speakers.

Formal, specialized communications

The ability to manage successfully formal communications is one attribute that distinguished-level speakers have that superior-level speakers usually do not. Formal communications take the form of business letters, communiqués, policy statements, orders, letters to the editor, public announcements, and the like. It is not very likely that you will be writing these kinds of communications in your foreign-language classroom unless you are in a very advanced class. However, if you intern somewhere, there may be a need to prepare business communications, or, perhaps you have a strong interest in political issues and want to write a letter to the editor (or the mayor or president) – and for that you will need strong literacy skills. To develop these, you will need to do some or all of the following:

* follow authentic guides;
* revise; and/or
* check with a native speaker.

Authentic guides

Authentic materials are a better guide than are dictionaries, textbooks, and references because they show how a native-speaker author treats the same topic that you will be writing about. They will give you examples of mindset, and they will provide the typical expressions and constructions used in writing about these topics.

Revision

No wise writer expects to produce a final draft on the first try. Just as you probably use "process writing" (writing and re-writing) in your English classes, you can use it to acquire good literacy skills in your foreign language. If you have to revise two or three times in English, assume that you will have to revise double that amount in your foreign language.

Check with a native speaker

Just as it is important to check oral presentations with a native speaker, so it is important to check written work in advance with a native speaker.

CASE STUDY

Problem

Jason worked as an intern in a French–American international company, where his boss asked him to prepare the draft of a very important business letter. Jason has never written a business letter before in French, but he did have a fairly high level of foreign language proficiency in general. How could he take advantage of what he does know and can do and fill in the gaps of what he does not yet know in order to prepare an acceptable letter for his boss?

Possible solutions

There are a few places that Jason can look for help. Here are some:

(1) Check the files for previous correspondence on this and related topics. If he finds some letters, he can use them as models. This is probably his best bet.

(2) A second best would be to find a book on letter writing for native speakers.

(3) Of course, whichever way he finds out how to write the letter, he should ask a colleague who is a native speaker to proofread it for him.

Figure 10.2

Publications

Writing for publication is another skill that is associated nearly exclusively with the distinguished level. Individuals with proficiency at levels lower than that are generally incapable of publishing in the foreign languages.

Publication can take many forms. Articles, monographs, books, and poetry have all seen non-native writers succeed in another culture. However, such work requires the development of very high-level skills, borne of much in-country experience and the reading of much literature of all genres. Even with this kind of writing – and perhaps especially with this kind of writing – the help of a native speaker is usually needed, no matter how fluent the non-native (with rare exceptions).

Practice what you have learned!

1. Prepare a short speech on a topic of your choosing. Using the advice presented in this chapter, get ready to present the speech to a group of native speakers. If you do not have access to such a group, present the speech to your class. If you do have access to a group of native speakers, ask to present your speech to them. When you are done with your speech and with their questions, ask them to critique how well you did and give you some suggestions for improvement.

2.   Try writing something for publication in your foreign language. It might be a letter to the editor of a newspaper or magazine in the target country. Find some sample letters to use as a guide. Analyze the text organization and rhetorical devices used in those sample letters. Then, present your opinion on an issue important to the publication (for that, you will need to read several back issues of the publication). Then, draft your letter, let it sit for a couple of days, then revise it. Repeat this process a few times until you are happy with the letter. Then, ask a native speaker (or your teacher) to review it. Make a final revision – and send it!

Review

In this chapter, you considered two themes. The content of these themes can be summarized as follows:

- Managing oral communication
- Managing written communication

Oral communication

Oral communication consists of transactions, informal presentations, and formal presentations.

(1) **Transactions** are everyday activities in which you communicate immediate needs or desires (such as making a purchase). Effective strategies for functional transactions are preparing ahead of time, waiting it out, and repeating questions.

(2) **Informal conversations** are those between you and colleagues, friends, and relatives. Effective strategies for informal conversations include verbose answers, memorized discourse, changing the topic, simplification, asking questions, using what you know, embellishment, and ignoring your mistakes.

(3) **Interviews** are formal conversations in which you elicit information from someone else. Effective strategies for interviews include ignoring what you don't understand while using what you do know, verifying and clarifying, having a command of all the possible question types in your foreign language, memorizing the kinds of questions that are useful for controlling an interview, and preparing in advance in order to be ready for nearly anything.

(4) **Formal presentations** are events at which you share information with a group of people and entertain their questions. Effective strategies for formal presentations include: identify the target audience, analyze authentic presentations, find appropriate grammatical constructions, write out the presentation, learn text organization devices, check with a native speaker, over-practice, do a trial run, anticipate questions, and, where appropriate, use informal conversation strategies.

Written communication

Written communication consists of informal writing, formal-specialized writing, and writing for publication.

(1) Informal writing is the preparation of materials for personal, not public, audiences. Effective strategies for informal writing include developing native-like handwriting, finding pen-pals, analyzing genres, and checking with native speakers.

(2) Formal-specialized writing is the preparation of materials for a particular group of people, such as interoffice communications. Effective strategies for specialized-formal writing include using authentic materials as a guide, revising frequently, and checking with a native speaker.

(3) Writing for publication includes such things as letters to the editor as well as belletristic works. Effective strategies for writing for publication include extensive reading and checking with a native speaker.

If you want to learn more about the topics in this chapter, consult the following: Belcher and Connor (2001); Boping and Quian (2003); Gaudiani (1981); Haas (1979); Hyland (2004); Hyland and Richards (2003); Kozyrev (2002); Kroll, Long, and Richards (2003); Mazraani (1997); Musumeci (1998); Okada (1977); Scott (1996); Segal-Cook (1995); Shekhtman (2003a); Shekhtman (2003b); Wennerstrom (2003); Wing ed. (1986).

Epilogue
From here to there: attaining near-native proficiency

You may be taking a language for university requirements or general casual interest. Perhaps you do not plan a career based on language skill. In that case, this epilogue is not for you.

If, however, you do plan a career in which you will need to use foreign language professionally or wish to become very, very proficient in the language you are learning, you should be aware that the level of language proficiency attained in a typical university foreign-language program is insufficient for professional use of the foreign language. You will need to develop a lifelong-learning approach to foreign-language acquisition to acquire professional and advanced professional (near-native) levels of foreign language proficiency. To date, there is not a lot known about how to do this. Among the authors of this book are those who have achieved near-native proficiency in one or more languages, those who have taught or supervised foreign-language programs for highly advanced students, and those who have conducted research on the attributes of high-level proficiency and what it takes to reach it. This chapter, then, reports on what we do know to date from personal experience in learning and teaching at high levels and in early research results from surveys of individuals who have reached these levels.

Attributes and experiences of successful high-level learners

You may have heard a lot about what a good language learner is. You may have been told that one learning style or another is better. You may have heard that a high language aptitude test score is necessary if you want to reach high levels of foreign-language proficiency. You may think that one teaching method is better than another. You may think that study abroad is essential. If you think any or all of these things, you will be surprised to learn that the current research shows that there are multiple paths to high levels of proficiency and that all kinds of people from all walks of life reach near-native levels. Here, specifically, are some of the findings:

- Students of all learning styles (synoptic and ectenic; visual, auditory, and kinesthetic; any personality type) have successfully reached near-native proficiency – although some types may have more success at earlier stages and others at later stages in the typically long process of reaching near-native levels (5–17 years is the norm).

- Individuals with high scores on language aptitude tests reach high levels of proficiency; so can students with low scores on language aptitude tests.
- Students who were slow starters are often the tortoises that win the proficiency race.
- Students have reached high levels of proficiency regardless of the method by which they were taught: grammar-based, audiolingual, communicative, or even individual mixes.
- Some individuals have reached high levels of proficiency without having spent more than a few weeks abroad.
- Students have reached high levels of proficiency whether or not they received formal instruction at high levels.

Learning styles

The information on learning styles is mixed. However, in all samples of students at high levels of proficiency, there have been individuals of all learning styles possible.

In the 1980s, a study of 102 diplomats in training indicated that students who were left-brain dominant (or better, whole-brain dominant with some left leanings) – a style that is quite similar to what we have been referring to as ectenic learners in this book – reached near-native proficiency in a language course three times more often than students who were right-brain dominant (i.e. exhibited more synoptic traits). A number of these successful students started out slowly and did not keep pace initially with their more synoptic peers, but once they had reached advanced levels, they began to outstrip them in what looked like the traditional tortoise vs. hare race (Leaver, 1986).

On the other hand, in a recent study of 20+ diplomats currently or previously in training, synoptic learners were substantially overrepresented relative to ectenic learners. Nonetheless, ectenic learners were, indeed, in the mix, and among the synoptic learners, the majority reported a preference for the ectenic trait of sharpening (Ehrman and Lord, 2004).

Another recent and ongoing study of nearly sixty high-level language users from a variety of professions – legal, teaching, political science, translation & interpretation, and journalism, among others – was closer to the Leaver 1986 study of diplomats in its findings. While there were both synoptic and ectenic learners in this recent group, a slight majority reported themselves to be ectenic in their approaches (Leaver, 2003a).

What does all of this mean? Frankly, we are still investigating the situation, but these early results of information gathering would seem to indicate that it really does not matter what your learning style is. You can make it to near-native levels if you take advantage of your strengths and find strategies to compensate for your weaknesses.

Language aptitude

The Defense Language Institute uses scores on these tests to indicate whether or not students should be enrolled in specific languages, and they are influential in assignment to language study at the Foreign Service Institute. Nonetheless, among successful high-level language users have been a number of students who performed poorly on these tests and there are, in the collective experience of the authors, students with high language aptitude scores who have failed to achieve high levels of proficiency.

The reasons for this are unclear as yet, but there are several possibilities. One is that when students do poorly on a test, there may be many reasons other than what the test is assessing. For example, they might be very fatigued when they take the test. That is an individual difference rather than a systematic one. Another explanation could be that different factors come into play at higher levels than at lower levels, which in turn raises the question of whether the variables considered to indicate strong potential for successful language learning on the extant tests might give less useful information about eventual attainment of near-native language proficiency (John B. Carroll, personal communication, September 1988). Stansfield (1989), too, noted that current language aptitude tests (and they have not changed to this day) did not take into account the attributes needed for attainment of high-level proficiency. If this is the case, the possible dichotomy in attributes needed for initial language learning and those needed at higher levels might also explain the prevalent tortoise–hare phenomenon.

Teaching method

Often, one hears contemporary educators say that if someone is not taught via a communicative method, he or she will not be able to learn a language well. In stark contrast to this statement, the majority of individuals in the recent study of students from various walks of life learned from either grammar-based or audiolingual methods (Leaver and Atwell, 2002). Only one of them mentioned teaching method at all as something important in how he acquired language, and that individual lambasted current teaching methods (Cole, 2004). That does not mean, though, that your teachers are wrong to use communicative methods. We all hope that communicative methods will produce even better results, and in a shorter time, than the older methods. The problem is that reaching high levels of proficiency simply takes a long time (what we call "time on task"), and newer teaching methods have not been in use long enough to know whether or not they will have better results than the older methods (Leaver, 2001). Furthermore, we need to keep the issue of style match in mind. One method may be better for a given student, and another more helpful to a different one.

Study abroad

The results on study abroad were a little surprising because every-one agreed – and it is commonsense – that one needs to be thoroughly familiar with the foreign culture in order to reach near-native levels of proficiency. How-ever, many of the nearly sixty respondents in the Leaver–Atwell study (2002) stated that study abroad helped them at intermediate levels, but not at high levels (Leaver, 2001). This is in keeping with Bernhardt's finding (cited in Ehrman, 2002) that two weeks in an émigré community is usually sufficient for anything needed at the highest levels of proficiency (the situation being that none of these students would be at those levels had they not had study abroad experience or the equivalent at earlier levels of instruction). Similarly, Shekhtman (2003b) reported no differences in high-level journalists who went abroad without accompanying classroom instruction, either in-country or prior to departure; it was the combina-tion of in-country experience and classroom instruction that made a difference – and if only one or the other learning experience was possible, the classroom instruction experience was the most powerful at helping students attain higher levels. (Another kind of classroom experience was as highly powerful as the lan-guage classroom – attending classes in subject matter courses or advanced degree programs in the foreign country with foreign peers and without access to other speakers of English.)

There were, in fact, a number of individuals in the Leaver–Atwell study who had either never been to a country where their foreign language was spoken or had been there for a very short period of time (such as two weeks). Either per-sonal reasons or the international political climate kept them from soaking up the culture onsite. That does not mean that they had no cultural input or experiences. Quite the reverse: they sought out émigrés and spent much time in the émigré community. In essence, they made a living-abroad experience for themselves at home.

Formal instruction

Some individuals who have reached near-native levels have had class-room instruction at high levels; others have not. Those who had it have stated that it was essential for their reaching the levels that they did. Those who did not have it wished that they had had it, although there was a small minority who had achieved a high level without classroom instruction, had done it quite quickly, and considered that classroom instruction would have been a waste of their time. The statistics, though, suggest an advantage for instruction for most learners. Those who received outcomes-based (i.e. the goal had to be met) instruction at a professional level of proficiency, with the goal being to reach near-native pro-ficiency, achieved that level at a saving of ten years or more, compared to those who just tried to get it on their own through personal experience in using the language.

Ways to reach high levels of proficiency

Although students of all types reach high levels of proficiency, they do have a number of learning approaches in common. The kinds of activities that typical successful high-level language learners have practiced include:

*   assessments
*   individualized study plans
*   high-level courses
*   cross-cultural observations
*   contact with native speakers
*   time on task
*   foreign-degree work
*   formal language use

Assessment

Many successful high-level language users have found it useful to have their proficiency level and proficiency gain checked periodically. It helps them plan their activities better. There are several mechanisms for doing this. Introduced in chapter 1, these include: (1) proficiency test; (2) can-do assessment; (3) diagnostic assessment.

If you choose to do periodic assessments to help you stay on track and to measure your progress, keep in mind that the higher your proficiency, the slower will be your overt progress, i.e. the next-higher proficiency level will take longer to reach. There is a learning curve that flattens out at the higher levels because there is so much to know by the time you start approaching near-native levels of speech. For this reason, it is unlikely that you would need an assessment more often than twice a year, even if you are working intensively on language improvement.

Proficiency test

You might take a proficiency test whenever you feel that you have made significant progress. A proficiency test can give you information about the progress you have made (or not made), the various aspects of proficiency that you need to work on, and the level at which you are speaking, reading, writing, and listening. As noted in chapter 1, there are two extant proficiency tests. One is given by the US government; it can include all four skills, but it is given only to government employees and only in those skills that are work-pertinent. If you work for the government, this test is, indeed, an option for you. If you do not work for the US government, you can take a test from the American Council on Teaching Foreign Languages (ACTFL), the Association of Language Testers Europe (ALTE), or the Center for Applied Linguistics (CAL) in Washington (all these organizations can be found on the Internet). The ACTFL test is most typically given for speaking skills; however, scales are available for all four language skills, and ACTFL is now giving a writing test in some languages with more to come. We would note that the ACTFL proficiency test, as it currently exists, is useful only up to and including Superior-level proficiency, which is short of the high levels we are discussing here (higher level tests are in the planning and may soon be available). In any event, the ACTFL test can serve as a baseline for you. We would also note that for purposes of tracking your progress you do not need to take a formal proficiency test. Rather, you can have a certified tester (or a former certified tester) give you an informal approximation of your current level.

Can-do statements

Another mechanism for checking your progress is the use of can-do statements. The organizations mentioned in chapter 1 – the National Foreign Language Center, the Defense Language Institute, and the Association of Language Testers Europe – all have can-do statements online that cover high levels, as well as lower ones. (The URLs for these sites can be found in chapter 1.)

Diagnostic assessment

If you take a formal course at this level, you may find yourself at an institution that uses diagnostic assessments. There are both government programs and private ones that use diagnostic assessments to guide their teaching practices. Typically, a diagnostic assessment includes a test that indicates linguistic specifics that a student possesses well, a little, or poorly (found through a diagnostic test, proficiency test, or can-do statements), learning styles and strategies information, and a learning plan for self-study situations or teaching plan for classroom situations (Ehrman, 2001; Cohen, 2003; Shekhtman, 2003b).

Individualized study plan

Just as, at lower levels, you made an ISP to help you organize your language learning, so, too, can you make an ISP at higher levels (Leaver, 2003b). The contents, however, will probably look quite different. Actual classroom work may well be a very small part of your learning plan, partly because courses are rarely available at this level. Opportunities for making presentations or writing for publication, as well as for working in jobs that require language use, on the other hand, may figure prominently in your plan.

High-level course

If you find yourself in a high-level course or able to take one, there are at least five things that you might want to have included in your program. These are:

- the development of automaticity
- replacement of fossilized, incorrect forms with accurate ones;
- the development of sociolinguistic sophistication
- the development of sociocultural observation
- practice in making very fine distinctions among similar language elements.

Automaticity

Level 4 speech is characterized by large amounts of automatic, correct speech. The more you can automate the expressions that are not yet automatic, the more your speech will sound distinguished.

Fossilization

While acquiring a foreign language, most people learn some things wrong. These then become "stuck" or "fossilized" in their speech habits, and it takes much effort to break these incorrect habits. Ehrman (2002) posits five kinds of fossilization at high levels of foreign language proficiency:

- functional fossilization ("the continued use of incorrect or limited linguistic forms, structures, or semantic domains," p. 249);
- instruction-fostered fossilization ("the result of overly compliant interlocutors, teachers, and non-teachers who adapt to the learner's errors," p. 249);
- domain fossilization (the use of routinized, stereotyped language that accompanies narrow work tasks);
- affective fossilization (protection of self-esteem and self-image to the point of avoiding increased sophistication in language use for fear of errors); and
- strategic fossilization (overuse of strategies that are more appropriate at lower levels of proficiency, e.g. compensation strategies, and underuse of those that are more appropriate at higher levels, e.g. planning and evaluation strategies; can also refer to becoming fixated on the particular teaching method used at lower levels).

To reach very high levels of proficiency, any morphology (word forms) that has been fossilized in incorrect form needs to be replaced not only with accurate forms but with ones that are used automatically, as well as correctly. Further, if you have been using simplified grammar (even if accurately and automatically), this, too, can be a kind of fossilization (we call it "level fossilization" [Shekhtman, Lord, and Kuznetsova, 2003]), and you will need to work on replacing those constructions with more sophisticated ones. For example, the constructions "I could do it, if I had the means" or "I will do it if I have the means," in your linguistic repertoire need to be joined by other, more sophisticated constructions that are synonymous in meaning, such as "Were I to have the means, I could do it," as well as colloquial forms for use in tailoring, e.g. "Give me the stuff I need, and I could pull it off."

Sociolinguistic sophistication

At higher levels of proficiency, speakers are expected to tailor their language to their audiences (see chapter 7). Coursework that teaches register and genre differences can be very helpful at this level.

Sociocultural observation

Understanding the culture, its unwritten words, and its icons is very important at high levels of proficiency. Such advanced speakers are expected not only to understand references to history, films, literary quotations, political and social humor, and everyday reality from pets to potty training but also to use references, humor, and household vocabulary (not typically taught in the class-room or textbook) appropriately. A course that explains sociocultural differences and teaches you to observe these phenomena can help you reach high levels of proficiency faster.

Fine distinctions

One of the main hallmarks of very high-level language is its precision. The speaker uses just the right synonym, construction, or idiom, rather than relying on circumlocutions or the ability of the interlocutor to understand from context what is really meant by a less precise term. A tendency to notice and make such fine distinctions may help explain why sharpening was so important for the synoptic learners in the Ehrman and Lord (2004) study, and why ectenics do very well in the Leaver studies. Precision is the sharpener's stock in trade. If you do not tend to sharpen, this is a skill that needs developing for most who aspire to the highest proficiency levels.

Cross-cultural observation

High-level language users are not dependent on a teacher, native speaker, or book, to point out cross-cultural differences. They notice the differences between their own culture and the foreign culture on their own. Several respondents in the Leaver–Atwell (2002) study observed that developing good observational skills was a must for them in reaching distinguished levels of proficiency (Leaver, 2003a).

Extensive and intensive contact with native speakers

It goes without saying that one cannot reach high levels of foreign-language proficiency without contact with native speakers. The more extensive, the better. The more intensive, the better. Extensive contact with native speakers will introduce you to many dialects, a variety of social styles, and a wide range of language domains. Intensive contact will require you to develop a large vocabulary reserve in one or more narrow domains. Both are important. To make the most of your contact time with native speakers, you might consider keeping a notebook of questions that you would like to ask a native speaker; in the notebook might be linguistic items you heard or read and did not understand, inexplicable cultural behaviors, or instances of *faux pas* that you have made.

Time on task

If anything is crystal clear from the research to date of high-end language users, it is that time on task is inescapable. The more time you spend reading, writing, listening to, and speaking your foreign language, the better you will be at it, regardless of whether you learn quickly or with difficulty. Every learner who has reached high levels of proficiency has done so through a lengthy period of study – sometimes intentional and sometimes a result of circumstances. A high-level program of study can significantly reduce the overall amount of study, but no matter what, language proficiency takes time to take hold (Leaver, 2003a).

Foreign degree work

Next to language programs at the superior level of proficiency, foreign-degree work has been reported by language learners as an effective mechanism to improve foreign-language skills rapidly. Many more high-level language users in the Leaver–Atwell study had experienced foreign-degree work than had experienced study abroad and of those with both kinds of experience, all indicated that the foreign-degree work was the most significant in moving them from the superior level to the distinguished level (Leaver, 2003a).

Formal language use

Finally, finding every possible opportunity to develop and use formal language can be critical to the development of high-level skills. A major distinction between the superior and distinguished level of proficiency is the ability to use formal language structures and lexis (vocabulary and idioms), of the sort that are used in speeches, lectures, and academic discourse. In this case, the guidelines are not talking about just understanding and using formal *communication*, but rather, the subtleties of formal language that are needed for writing for *publication*, *editing*, *negotiating* effectively, truly *controlling* the conversational partner when that is desirable, *adapting* speech and writing to the audience. These are often skills that not even every native speaker has; they are the skills that are generally developed by native speakers (and foreign-language learners) as a result of experience and meeting the linguistic requirements of higher education.

Conclusion

Here we end our epilogue to this volume. If you make it all the way to the near-native level of proficiency, you are to be commended, for you will belong to an elite group. We hope that the suggestions in this chapter, based on the practices and experiences of successful high-level language users, will help you join that crowd. We know it can be done – with time, diligence, and the appropriate strategies.

Appendix A
Answers to "practicing what you have learned"

Most of the exercises you have encountered in this book have open answers; that is, there are many possible answers, quite a few of them highly personalized. The answer below is to the exercise that does have one right answer.

Answer to chapter 6, exercise 5

Steps to the solution:

To figure out what he needs to say, John will need to do a little more sleuthing, but he has almost everything he needs right now, thanks to these sentences that look like boring examples. (Any collection of examples, whether from a textbook or from authentic materials, can be used in a case like this for analysis.). So, here is what John can now do to be able to create the sentence that he needs.:

(1) He can start his sentence with *wawo*.
(2) From (3), it is clear that word order in Puyon is SOV. Second, he knows that the word for "homework," once he figures it out, will have to come second and have an -*u* ending because all the direct objects in the sentences he has seen, e.g. in (3), have the -*u* ending.
(3) "At home" will be *craipinpon* since *pon* is being used as a postposition (i.e. follows the noun instead of preceding), according to the sample sentences, and the location will be the third element in the sentence since the verb in all the sample sentences is at the end of the sentence.
(4) The verb will be either *tropirtropir* or *afpirpir*; John does not have enough information yet to know which; however, he might be able to figure out that he will have to double the stem for the past tense and will need no ending on the verb because he is male.
  So far, from analysis and comparison alone, he has almost everything he needs, except for how to say "my," how to combine "home" and "work," and which verb to use. For all of these, he will have to make some assumptions, which he may or not be able to test out.
(5) Since an -*i*- was used to combine "man" and "book" to form "man's book," John can try the same for "my book" and for "homework." It could be that "homework" is not treated the same as a possessive, "man's book," and John will be wrong, but he will be close enough for any speaker of the language to understand.

(6) He can do one of two things with "*my* homework." He can try changing *wawo* to *wawi* or adding the *-i-* to *wawo*, giving *wawoi*. He might be wiser, though, just to omit that word. Who else's homework would he be talking about anyway? (Some languages do not use possessives in such cases, and perhaps Puyon is like that.)

(7) For the verb, he needs to find out where each of the verbs is used. He can find that out in the dictionary. If he looks at the dictionary again, he will see that *tropir* is marked "vt" and *afpir* "vi." "Vt" means "transitive verb," one that takes a direct object. This is the one he needs because "homework" is the direct object in the sentence. "Vi," intransitive verbs, do not take objects, and in the case of this verb probably means "leave" in the sense of "to depart." John could also look up the two verbs in the Puyon–English dictionary and perhaps get more information that would help him decide.

Now, John has a usable sentence, which even if it has a few imperfections will be fully understood by a Puyon speaker: *Wawo craipinitrapinu craipinpon troptrop.*

If you want to tell the teacher you left your homework at home, and you are male, the answer will be the same. If you are female, the answer will be *Wawo craipinitrapinu craipinpon troptropa.*

If you want to tell the teacher that John left his geography homework at home, assuming that *ano* ("he") works like *wawo* ("I"), you would say *John anirabui-craipinitrapinu craipinpon troptrop.*

Appendix B
Learning strategies taxonomies

Nanda Poulisse (1990) suggested a taxonomy for compensation strategies in French as a foreign language. These were used by Poulisse and her colleagues to research how students compensate when they find themselves in conversations that are above their heads. The result was that four kinds of compensation strategies are used:

- holistic (using words that share the concept);
- analytic (e.g. describing features of the concept);
- transfer; and
- appeal for assistance.

Tarone taxonomy

Elaine Tarone (1980) has suggested five categories in her taxonomy:

- avoidance (topic avoidance and memory abandonment);
- paraphrase (approximation, word coinage, and circumlocution);
- conscious transfer (literal translation and language switch – this one might get you into more trouble than it gets you out of);
- appeal for assistance, and
- mime (use of nonverbal language).

For the most part, she is referring to speaking strategies used for communication. See chapter 10 for a detailed description of managing communication situations.

Oxford taxonomy

One of the most widely used taxonomies was suggested by Oxford (1990). In this taxonomy, she breaks learning strategies into six kinds:

- cognitive, such as analysis, applying background knowledge, and prediction, among others;
- metacognitive, such as self-evaluation of progress, planning language study, and reviewing, among others;
- affective, such as keeping diaries and positive self-talk, among others;
- social, such as joining a language table or asking questions, among others;
- compensation, such as paraphrasing, guessing from context, and circumlocution, among others; and
- memory, such as using mnemonics and keywords, among others.

The Strategy Inventory for Language Learning (SILL) is available in a number of languages for determining your strategy usage. It conforms to Oxford's categories and can be found online at www.syjy.com.cn/english/ xingkc/05.doc.

Chamot & O'Malley taxonomy (CALLA)

Chamot and O'Malley (1994) developed the Cognitive Academic Language Learning Approach (CALLA), which comprises academic content, language skills, and learning strategies. The language learning strategies that they use in this framework include the following categories:

- metacognitive strategies (planning, monitoring one's progress, and evaluating success);
- metacognitive knowledge (understanding how learning happens, understanding what learning is about, knowing what strategies to select for effective learning);
- cognitive strategies (rehearsal, organizing, elaborating, etc.); and
- social/affective strategies (interacting with others/managing one's emotional response).

References

AATSEEL Publications Committee (2001) *Why study Russian? www.russnet.org/why/ index.html* and www.aatseel.org.

Adorni, S. and K. Primorac (1995) *English grammar for students of Italian.* Ann Arbor, MI: Olivia and Hill Press.

Ager, D. E. (1999) *Sociolinguistics and contemporary French.* Cambridge: Cambridge University Press.

Aoki, N. (1999) The role of affect in the development of learner autonomy. In J. Arnold (ed.), *Affect in language learning* (pp. 142–154). Cambridge: Cambridge University Press.

American Psychological Association (2001) *Publication manual of the American Psychological Association.* Washington, DC: APA.

Ausubel, D. P. (1960) The use of advance organizers in the learning and retention of meaningful verbal material. *Journal of Educational Psychology 51,* 267–272.

Axtell, R. E. (1990) *Do's and taboos of hosting international visitors.* NY: John Wiley and Sons.

(1993) *Gestures: the do's and taboos of body language around the world.* NY: John Wiley and Sons.

Badawi, E. (2002) In the quest for the level 4+ in Arabic: training level 2–3 learners in independent reading. In B. L. Leaver and B. Shekhtman (eds.), *Developing professional-level language proficiency* (pp. 156–176). Cambridge: Cambridge University Press.

Bandler, R. (1985) *Using your brain – for a change: neurolinguistic programming.* Moab, UT: Real People Press.

Bandura, A. (1993) Perceived self-efficacy in cognitive development and functioning. *Educational Psychologist, 28* (2), 117–148.

Belcher, D. and U. Connor (2001) *Reflections on multiliterate lives.* Clevedon, UK: Multilingual Matters.

Bergen, J. J. (1990) *Spanish in the United States: sociolinguistic issues.* Washington, DC: Georgetown University Press.

Birdsong, D., ed. (1999) *Second language acquisition and the critical period hypothesis.* Mahwah, NJ: Lawrence Erlbaum.

Boping, Y. and K. Quian (2003) *Developing writing skills in Chinese.* London: Routledge.

Brecht, R. D., D. Davidson, and R. B. Ginsburg (1993) *Predictors of foreign language gain during study abroad.* Washington, DC: National Foreign Language Center.

Broadbent, D. E. (1982) Task combination and the selective intake of information. *Acta Psychologica 50:* 253–290.

(1952) Failures of attention in selective listening. *Journal of Experimental Psychology 44:* 428–433.

(1958) Perception and communication. NY: Pergamon Press.

Brown, S. and S. Attardo (2000) *Understanding language structure, interaction, and variation: an introduction to applied linguistics and sociolinguistics for nonspecialists.* Ann Arbor, MI: University of Michigan Press.

Busato, V., F. J. Prins, J. J. Elshout, and C. Hamaker (1999) The relation between learning style, the Big Five personality traits, and achievement motivation in higher education. *Personality and Individual Differences 26* (1), 129–140.

Bybee, J., R. Perkins, and W. Pagliuca (1994) *The evolution of grammar: tense, aspect, and modality in the languages of the world.* Chicago: University of Chicago Press.

Calbris, G., O. Doyle, and I. Fonagy (1999) *The semiotics of French gestures.* Bloomington, IN: Indiana University Press.

Campbell, A. (2000) *Passport Argentina.* Novato, CA: World Trade Press.

Canale, M. and M. Swain (1980) Theoretical bases of communicative approaches to second language teaching and testing. *Applied Linguistics 1* (1): 8–24.

Carroll, J. B., and S. M. Sapon (1959) *Modern language aptitude test (Form A).* NY: Psychological Corporation.

Chamot, A. U. and J. M. O'Malley (1994) The CALLA handbook: implementing the cognitive academic language learning approach. New York: Addison Wesley.

Champine, M. (1999) A word to the student. In B. L. Leaver, I. Dubinsky, and M. Champine (eds.), *Passport to the world: learning to communicate in a foreign language* (pp. ix–x). San Diego, CA: LARC Press.

Chavarriaga-Doak, R. (1999) Language learning strategies – instruments for successful language study. In B. L. Leaver, I. Dubinsky, and M. Champine (eds.), *Passport to the world: learning to communicate in a foreign language* (pp. 17–33). San Diego, CA: LARC Press.

Chomsky, N. (1998) *On language.* NY: New Press.

Claxton, C. S. and P. Murrell (1987) *Learning styles: implications for improving educational practices.* College Station, TX: Association for the Study of Higher Education.

Cohen, B. (2003) *Diagnostic assessment at the superior-distinguished threshold.* Salinas, CA: MSI Press.

Cole, C. (2004) My journey through "learn-Russian-land." *Journal for Distinguished Language Studies 2*: 5–8.

Cole, G. (1997) *Passport Indonesia.* Novato, CA: World Trade Press.

Comrie, B. (1989) *Language universals and linguistic typology: syntax and morphology.* Chicago: University of Chicago Press.

Costantino, M. and L. R. Gambella (1996) *The Italian way.* NY: McGraw-Hill.

Council on International Educational Exchange (1994–1995) *Work, travel, study abroad: the whole world handbook.* NY: St. Martin's Press.

Cowan, N. (1997) *Attention and memory.* Oxford: Oxford University Press.

Cruise, E. J. (1993) *English grammar for students of Russian.* Ann Arbor, MI: Olivia and Hill Press.

Crystal, D. (1985) *A dictionary of linguistics and phonetics.* Oxford: Blackwell.

(1997) *The Cambridge encyclopedia of the English language.* Cambridge: Cambridge University Press.

Curry, J. (1998) *Passport Taiwan.* Novato, CA: World Trade Press.

Curry, J. and J. C. Nguyen (1997) *Passport Vietnam*. Novato, CA: World Trade Press.

Dabars, Z. and L. L. Vokhmina (2002) *The Russian way, second edition: aspects of behavior, attitudes, and customs of the Russians*. NY: McGraw-Hill.

Daun, A. and D. Cooperman (1996) *Swedish mentality*. University Park, PA: The Pennsylvania State University.

Dickinson, L. (1995) Autonomy and motivation: a literature review. *System 23*, 165–174.

Dickinson, L. and A. Wenden, eds. (1995) Special issue on autonomy. *System 23* (2).

Dilts, R. B. (1979) *Neuro-linguistic programming I*. Cupertino, CA: Meta Publications.

Dörnyei, Z. (2001) *Motivation strategies in the language classroom*. Cambridge: Cambridge University Press.

Dörnyei, Z. and A. Malderez (1997) Group dynamics and foreign language teaching. *System 25*, 65–81.

Dunn, R. S. and K. Dunn (1978) *Teaching students through their individual learning styles*. Englewood Cliffs, NJ: Prentice Hall.

Ehrman, M. E. (1993) Ego boundaries revisited: toward a model of personality and learning. In J. Alaitis (ed.), *Research* (pp. 331–362). Washington, DC: Georgetown University.

(1996) *Understanding second language learning difficulties: looking beneath the surface*. Thousand Oaks, CA: Sage.

(1997) Field independence, field dependence, and field sensitivity. In J. Reid (ed.), *Understanding learning styles in the second language classroom* (pp. 62–70). Englewood Cliffs, NJ: Regents Prentice Hall.

(1998a) A study of the modern language aptitude test for predicting learning success and advising students. *Applied Language Learning 9* (1 and 2): 31–70.

(1998b) The learning alliance: conscious and unconscious aspects of the second language teacher's role. *System 26 (1)*, 93–106.

(1999) Ego boundaries and tolerance of ambiguity in second language learning. In J. Arnold (ed.), *Affect in language learning* (pp. 68–86). New York: Cambridge University Press.

(2000) Affect, cognition, and learner self-regulation in second language learning. In O. Kagan and B. Rifkin (eds.), *The learning and teaching of Slavic languages and cultures: toward the 21st century* (pp. 109–133). Bloomington, IN: Slavica.

(2002) Understanding the learner at the superior-distinguished threshold. In B. L. Leaver and B. Shekhtman (eds.), *Developing professional-level language proficiency* (pp. 245–259). Cambridge: Cambridge University Press.

Ehrman, M. E. and Z. Dörnyei (1998) *Interpersonal dynamics in second language education: the visible and invisible classroom*. Thousand Oaks, CA: Sage.

Ehrman, M. E. and B. L. Leaver (1997) Sorting out global and analytic functions. Orlando, FL: AAAL Annual Meeting.

(2002) *The Ehrman and Leaver Learning Styles Questionnaire v. 2*. Unpublished, copyrighted questionnaire.

(2003) Cognitive styles in the service of language learning. *System 31*, 393–415.

Ehrman, M. E. and N. Lord (2004) Counseling level 4 students. Unpublished manuscript.

Ehrman, M. E. and R. L. Oxford (1995) Cognition plus: correlates of language learning success. *Modern Language Journal 79* (1), 67–89.

El-Omari, J. (2003) *The Arab way: how to work more effectively with Arab cultures*. How To Books.

Ellis, D. (2002) *Becoming a master student*. Boston, MA: Houghton Mifflin.

Engel, D. and K. Murakami (2000) *Passport Japan*. Novato, CA: World Trade Press.

Eysenck, H. (1991) Dimensions of personality: the biosocial approach to personality. In J. Strelau and A. Angleitner (eds.), *Explorations in temperament: international perspectives on theory and measuremen*t (pp. 87–103). London: Plenum.

Flamini, R. and B. Szerlip (1997) *Passport Germany*. Novato, CA: World Trade Press.

Flippo, H. (1996) *The German way: Aspects of behavior, attitudes, and customs in the German-speaking world*. NY: McGraw-Hill.

Flyman, A. 1997. Communication strategies in French as a foreign language. *Working Papers 46*: 57–73. Lund, Sweden: Lund University.

Forsythe, J. (1970) *A grammar of aspect: usage and meaning in the Russian verb*. Cambridge: Cambridge University Press.

Foster, D. (2000) *The global etiquette guide to Asia*. John Wiley and Sons.

Francia, L. (1997) *Passport Philippines*. Novato, CA: World Trade Press.

Franke, E. with P. Rinere (1999) Shane and Jasmine read the map: they analyze the language "terrain." In Leaver, Dubinsky, and Champine, eds. (1999).

Frantz, A. C. (1996) Seventeen values of foreign language study. *ADFL Bulletin 28* (1), 44–49.

Gardner, H. (1983) *Frames of mind: the theory of Multiple Intelligences*. New York: Basic Books.

Gardner, R. and W. E. Lambert (1972) *Attitudes and motivation in second language learning*. Rowley, MA: Newbury House Publishers.

Gass, S. M. and L. Selinker (2001) *Second language acquisition: an introductory course*. Mahwah, NJ: Lawrence Erlbaum.

Gaudiani, C. (1981) *Teaching writing in the foreign language curriculum*. Washington, DC: Center for Applied Linguistics.

Gioseffi, C. (1996) *Passport Italy*. Novato, CA: World Trade Press.

Gliozzo, C. and K. Bishop, eds. (1994) *Directory of international internships: a guide to international internships sponsored by educational institutions*. East Lansing, MI: Michigan State University.

Goldman, N. and L. Szymanski (1993) *English grammar for students of Latin*. Ann Arbor, MI: Olivia and Hill Press.

Golinkoff, R. M. and K. Hirsh-Pasek, eds. (2000) *Becoming a word learner: a debate on lexical acquisition (counterpoints: cognition, memory, and language)*. Oxford: Oxford University Press.

Goodison, R. A. C. (1987) *Language training and language use – the uncertain connection*. Unpublished manuscript.

Greene, R. L. (1986) A common basis for recency effects in immediate and delayed recall. *Journal of Experimental Psychology: Learning, Memory, and Cognition 12*, 413–418.

Greene, R. L. and A. G. Samuel (1986) Recency and suffix effects in serial recall of musical stimuli. *Journal of Experimental Psychology: Learning, Memory, and Cognition 12*, 517–524.

Gregorc, A. (1982) Learning style/brain research: harbinger of an emerging psychology. In J. Keefe (ed.), *Student learning styles and brain behavior*. Reston, VA: National Association of High School Principals.

Haas, M. R. (1979) *Thai system of writing*. Denver, CO: Spoken Language Series.

Hartmann, E. (1991) *Boundaries in the mind: a new psychology of personality.* New York: Basic Books.

Herrington, E. A. (n.d.) *Passport Brazil.* Novato, CA: World Trade Press.

Holzman, P. S. and R. W. Gardner (1959) Leveling-sharpening and memory organization. *Journal of Abnormal and Social Psychology 61*, 176–180.

Horwitz, E. K. and D. J. Young (1991) *Language anxiety: from theory and research to classroom implications.* Englewood Cliffs, NJ: Prentice Hall.

Hudson, M. E. (1994) *English grammar for students of Japanese.* Ann Arbor, MI: Olivia and Hill Press.

Hyland, K. (2004) *Genre and second language writing.* Ann Arbor, MI: University of Michigan Press.

Hyland, K. and J. C. Richards (2003) *Second language writing.* Cambridge: Cambridge University Press.

Itsines, N. (1996) *The life and work of Hippocrates.* Unpublished manuscript.

Joseph, N. (1996) *Passport France.* Novato, CA: World Trade Press.

Joshi, M. (1997) *Passport India.* Novato, CA: World Trade Press.

Jung, C. G. (1971) *Psychological types* (H. G. Baynes trans., rev. R. F. Hull). Reprinted 1971. In Sir H. Read, M. Fordham, G. Adler, and W. McGuire (eds.), *Collected works of C. G. Jung Vol. 6*, Bollingen Series 20. Princeton, NJ: Princeton University (Original work published 1921).

Kant, I. (1781/1998) *The critique of pure reason*, trans. P. Guyer and A. W. Wood. Cambridge: Cambridge University Press.

Keating, K. (1998) *Passport Korea.* Novato, CA: World Trade Press.

Keefe, J. W. (1982) *Student learning styles.* Reston, VA: National Association of High School Principals.

Keirsey, D. (1998) *Please understand me II: temperament, character, intelligence.* Del Mar, CA: Prometheus Nemesis.

Keirsey, D. and M. Bates (1988) *Please understand me.* Del Mar, CA: Prometheus Nemesis.

Kevane, M. (2004) *Women and development in Africa: how gender works.* Ontario, Canada: Lynne Rienner Publishers.

Kissel, N. (2000) *Passport Poland.* Novato, CA: World Trade Press.

Kolb, D. A. (1984) *Experiential learning: experience as the source of learning and development.* New Jersey: Prentice Hall.

(1995) *Learning-style inventory.* Boston, MA: McBer and Company.

Kolb, D. A. and R. E. Boyatzis (1984) Goal setting and self-directed behavior change. In D. A. Kolb, I. M. Rubin, and J. M. McIntyre (eds.), *Organizational psychology: readings on human behavior in organizations* (4th edn.). Englewood Cliffs, NJ: Prentice Hall, 104–124.

Kozyrev, J. (2002) *Talk it up! Listening, speaking, and pronunciation.* Boston: Houghton Mifflin.

Krannich, R. and C. R. Krannich (1994). *Almanac of international jobs and careers: a guide to over 1001 employers and the complete guide to international jobs and careers.* Manassas Park, VA: Impact Publications.

Krashen, S. (1993) *The power of reading: insights from the research.* Littleton, CO: Libraries Unlimited.

Kroll, B., M. Long, and J. C. Richards (2003) *Exploring the dynamics of second language writing.* Cambridge: Cambridge University Press.

Leaver, B. L. (1986) Hemisphericity of the brain and foreign-language teaching. *Folia Slavica 8*, 76–90.

(1998) *Teaching the whole class: fifth edition.* Dubuque, IA: Kendall Hunt.

(2000) Doctoral dissertation, Pushkin Institute, Moscow.

(2001) Is teaching Russian really different from teaching other foreign languages? *ACTR Letter 28* (2), 1–5.

(2003a) *Achieving native-like second language proficiency: a catalogue of critical factors: Volume 1: Speaking.* Salinas, CA: MSI Press.

(2003b) *Individualized study plans for very advanced students of foreign language.* Salinas, CA: MSI Press.

Leaver, B. L. and S. Atwell (2002) Preliminary qualitative findings from a study of the processes leading to advanced professional proficiency level (ILR 4). In B. L. Leaver and B. Shekhtman (eds.), *Developing professional-level language proficiency* (pp. 260–279). Cambridge: Cambridge University Press.

Leaver, B. L. and M. Champine (1999) Beginning a journey: the choice to study a foreign language. In B. L. Leaver, I. Dubinsky, and M. Champine (ed.), *Passport to the world: learning to communicate in a foreign language* (pp. 1–15). San Diego, CA: LARC Press.

Leaver, B. L., I. Dubinsky, and M. Champine, eds. (1999) *Passport to the world: learning to communicate in a foreign language.* San Diego, CA: LARC Press.

Leaver, B. L. and B. Shekhtman (2002) Principles and practices in teaching superior-level language skills: not just more of the same. In B. L. Leaver and B. Shekhtman (eds.), *Developing professional-level language proficiency* (pp. 3–33). Cambridge: Cambridge University Press.

Leaver, E. (1999a) Making the most of memory. In B. L. Leaver, I. Dubinsky, and M. Champine (eds.), *Passport to the world: learning to communicate in a foreign language* (pp. 87–109). San Diego, CA: LARC Press.

(1999b) From knowledge perceived to knowledge controlled: applications of memory research to language learning. In B. L. Leaver (ed.), *Twelve years of dialogue on teaching Russian: from the front pages of the ACTR letter 1989–1999* (pp. 321–328). Washington, DC: ACTR/ACCELS Publications.

Levin, R. (1990) Ego boundary impairment and thought disorder in frequent nightmare sufferers. *Psychoanalytic Psychology 7* (4), 529–543.

Li, J. (2000) *Passport China.* Novato, CA: World Trade Press.

Lorayne, H. L. and J. Lucas (1996) *The memory book.* New York: Ballantine.

Lowery, R. (1982) *Letteri's information processing as related to cognitive structure.* Paper presented at Washington Junior High/Middle School Principals' Association. Seattle, WA.

Luus, C. A. E. and G. W. Wells (1991) Eyewitness identification and the selection of distractors for line-ups. *Law and Human Behavior 15*, 43–57.

McCarthy, B. (1980) *The 4Mat system: teaching to learning styles with right/left mode techniques.* Barrington, IL: Excel.

(1996) *About learning.* Barrington, IL: Excel.

McCauley, C., G. Kellas, J. Dugas, and R. F. DeVillis (1976) Effects of serial rehearsal training on memory search. *Journal of Educational Psychology 68*, 474–481.

Malat, R. (2003) *Passport Mexico.* Novato, CA: World Trade Press.

Massaro, D. (1972) Perceptual images, processing time, and perceptual units in auditory perception. *Psychological Review 79*, 124–145.

Mazraani, N. (1997) *Aspects of language variation in Arabic speech-making*. Curzon Press.

Meara, Paul, J. Milton, and N. Lorenzo-Dus (2000) *Language aptitude tests*. Newbury, UK: Express Publishing.

Mears, M. (1997) *Foreign languages and businesses in the future*. Paper presented at the Monterey Global Career Strategies Conference, Monterey, CA.

Messick, S. (1984) The nature of cognitive styles: problems and promise in educational practice. *Educational Psychologist 59*, 59–74.

Micheloud, F. (2001) *Passport Switzerland*. Novato, CA: World Trade Press.

Miller, G. (1956) The magic number seven, plus or minus two: some limits on our capacity for processing information. *Psychological Review 63*, 81–93.

Mishne, J. M. (1996) *The learning curve: elevating children's academic and social competence*. Northvale, NJ: Jason Aronson.

Mitchell, C. (1998a) *Passport Russia*. Novato, CA: World Trade Press.
  (1998b) *Passport South Africa*. Novato, CA: World Trade Press.

Modern Language Association (n.d.) *Knowing other languages brings you opportunity*. Online informational booklet: www.mla.org/resources/kol_brochure.

Monahan, B. (1984) *A dictionary of Russian gesture*. NY: Hermitage.

Morrison, T., W. A. Conaway, and G. A. Borden (1994) *Kiss, bow, or shake hands: how to do business in sixty countries*. Holbrook, MA: Adams Media Corporation.

Morton, J. (2002) *English grammar for students of French*. Ann Arbor, MI: Olivia and Hill Press.

Morton, J., R. G. Crowder, and H. A. Prussin (1971) Experiments with the stimulus suffix effect. *Journal of Experimental Psychology 60*, 329–346.

Musumeci, D. (1998) *Writing in the foreign language: soup and (fire) crackers*. Washington, DC: Center for Applied Linguistics.

Myers, I. B., M. H. McCaulley, N. L. Quenk, and A. L. Hammer (1998) *MBTI manual: a guide to the development and use of the Myers-Briggs Type Indicator®*, Third Edition. Palo Alto, CA: Consulting Psychologists.

Myers, I. B. with P. Myers (1980) *Gifts differing*. Palo Alto, CA: Consulting Psychologists.

Naiman, N., M. Fröhlich, H. H. Stern., and A. Todesco (1978) *The good language learner*. Clevedon: Multilingual Matters.

Novas, H. and R. E. Silva (1997) *Passport Spain*. Novato, CA: World Trade Press.

O'Grady, W., J. Archibald, M. Aronoff, and J. Rees-Miller (1997) *Contemporary linguistics: an introduction [fourth edition]*. New York: Bedford/St. Martin's.

O'Malley, M. and A. U. Chamot (1990) *Learning strategies in second language acquisition*. Cambridge: Cambridge University Press.

Okada, M. (1977) *The language of courtesy: honorific speech in Japanese*. Far Eastern Press.

Onishi, N. (2003) Japanese honorifics fading. *New York Times*, October 30.

Oxford, R. L. (1989) *Strategy inventory for language learning*. Alexandria, VA: Oxford Associates.
  (1990) *Language learning strategies: what every teacher should know*. New York: HarperCollins.

Parry, T. S. and J. R. Child (1989) Preliminary investigation of the relationship between VORD, MLAT, and language proficiency. In T. S. Parry and C. W. Stansfield (eds.), *Language aptitude reconsidered*. Englewood Cliffs, NJ: Prentice Hall.

Peirce, C. S. (1878) Deduction, induction, and hypothesis. *Popular Science Monthly, 13*: 470–482.

Peterson, C. R. and A. R. Al-Haik (1976) The development of the Defense Language Aptitude Battery (DLAB). *Educational and Psychological Measurement 36*, 369–380.

Pfeiffer, J. W. and J. E. Jones, eds. (1972) *The 1972 annual handbook for group facilitators.* San Diego, CA: University Associates.

Piaget, J. (1967) *Biologie et connaissance* [Biology and knowledge]. Paris: Gallimard.

Piaget, J. and B. Inhelder (1973) *Memory and intelligence.* New York: Basic Books.

Pimsleur, P. (1966) *Pimsleur language aptitude battery.* NY: Harcourt Brace Jovanovich.

Poulisse, N., T. Bongaerts, and E. Kellerman (1990) *The use of compensatory strategies by Dutch learners of English.* Dordrecht, Netherlands: Foris Publications.

Ramírez III, Manuel, and A. Castañeda (1974) *Cultural democracy, bicognitive development and education.* NY: Academic.

Redmond, M. (1998) *Wandering into Thai culture, or Thai why's and otherwise.* Bangkok: Redmondian Enterprises.

Reiser, M. (1991) *Memory in mind and brain.* New Haven, CT: Yale University Press.

Restak, R. (2002) *Mozart's brain and the fighter pilot: unleashing your brain's potential.* Pittsburgh, PA: Three Rivers Press.

(2003) *The new brain: how the modern age is rewiring your brain.* Emmaus, PA: Rodale Press.

Revelle, W., K. J. Anderson, and M. S. Humphreys (1987) Empirical tests and theoretical extensions of arousal based theories of personality. In J. Strelau and H. J. Eysenck (eds.), *Personality dimensions and arousal.* London: Plenum.

Robinson, P. (2002) Learning conditions, aptitude complexes and SLA: a framework for research and pedagogy. In P. Robinson, ed. (2002).

Robinson, P., ed. (2002) *Individual differences and instructed language learning.* Amsterdam/Philadelphia: Benjamins.

Rosenthal, D. (1997) *Passport Israel.* Novato, CA: World Trade Press.

Rubin, J. and I. Thompson (1994) *How to be a more successful language learner.* Boston: Heinle and Heinle.

Sapountzis, P. S. (n.d.) *Defense mechanisms.* Unpublished manuscript. Arlington, VA: Foreign Service Institute.

Schachter, D. (2002) *Seven sins of memory: how the mind forgets and remembers.* Boston: Mainer Books.

Schleppegrell, M. (1987) *The older language learner.* Washington, DC: ERIC Clearinghouse on Languages and Linguistics.

Schmeck, R. R. 1988. *Learning strategies and learning styles.* NY: Plenum.

Scott, V. M. (1996) *Rethinking foreign language writing.* Boston: Heinle and Heinle.

Scovel, T. (1988) *A time to speak: a psycholinguistic inquiry into the critical period for human speec*h. Florence, KY: Wadsworth Publishing.

Segal-Cook, B. E. (1995) *Teaching foreign language: speaking, reading, writing.* Berty-Segal Incorporated.

Seligman, S. D. (2003) *Chinese business etiquette: a guide to protocol, manners, and culture in the People's Republic of China.* Warner Books.

Shekhtman, B. (2003a) *How to improve your foreign language immediately.* Salinas, CA: MSI Press. Originally published by SLTC, Rockville, MD, 1990.

(2003b) *Working with advanced foreign language students.* Salinas, CA: MSI Press.

Shekhtman, B. and N. Lord (1986) *Mark Smith's diary.* Arlington, VA: Foreign Service Institute. Also available from ERIC Clearinghouse on Languages and Literatures.

Shekhtman, B., N. Lord, and E. Kuznetsova (2003) Complication exercises for raising the oral proficiency level of highly advanced language students. *Journal for Distinguished Language Studies 1* (1), 32–50.

Shryock, R. (n.d.) *French: the most practical foreign language.* www.flt.vt.edu/french/whyfrench/html.

Silver, H. F. and J. Robert Hanson (1996) *Learning styles and strategies.* Ho-ho-kus, NJ: Silver, Strong, and Associates.

Skehan, P. (1998) *A cognitive approach to language learning.* Oxford: Oxford University Press.

(2002) Theorising and updating aptitude. In P. Robinson (ed.), *Individual differences and instructed language learning* (pp. 69–94). Amsterdam/Philadelphia: Benjamins.

Spinelli, E. (2003) *English grammar for students of Spanish.* Ann Arbor, MI: Olivia and Hill Press.

Stansfield, C. W. (1989) *Language aptitude reconsidered.* ERIC Digest 318226. Washington, DC: ERIC Clearinghouse on Languages and Linguistics.

Stern, H. H. (1975) What can we learn from the good language learner? *Canadian Modern Language Review, 31,* 304–318.

Sternberg, R. J. (1994) Thinking styles: theory and assessment at the interface between intelligence and personality. In R. Sternberg and P. Ruzgis (eds.), *Intelligence and personality.* New York: Cambridge University Press.

(2002) The theory of successful intelligence and its implications for language aptitude testing. In P. Robinson (ed.), *Individual differences and instructed language learning* (pp. 13–44). Philadelphia: Benjamins.

(2003) Comments on the "Summary of the DLAB2 Workshop." Unpublished manuscript.

Stevick, E. W. (1980) *Teaching languages: a way and ways.* NY: Newbury House.

(1996) *Memory, meaning, and method.* Upper Saddle Back, NJ: Prentice Hall.

Strunk, W., Jr., E. B. White, and R. Angell (2000) *The elements of style: fifth edition.* London: Pearson.

Tada, M. (2003) *Japanese gestures: modern manifestations of a classic culture.* Three Forks Press.

Tannen, D. (1985) *Analyzing discourse: text and talk.* Washington, DC: Georgetown University Press.

(1987) *That's not what I meant!* NY: Ballantine Books.

(1996) *Gender and discourse.* Oxford, OH: Oxford Press.

(2001a) *Talking from 9 to 5: women and men at work.* Nottingham, UK: Quill.

(2001b) *You just don't understand: women and men in conversation.* Nottingham, UK: Quill.

Tarone, E. (1980) Communication strategies, foreigner talk, and repair in interlanguage. *Language Learning 30,* 417–431.

Terrell, T. (1986) Acquisition in the natural approach: the binding/access framework. *Modern Language Journal 70* (3), 63–76.

Torrance, E. P. (1980) *Your style of learning and thinking, forms B and C.* Athens, GA: University of Georgia.

Torrance, E. P., C. R. Reynolds, T. R. Riegel, and O. E. Ball (1977) Your style of learning and thinking (SOLAT), Forms A and B. *Gifted Child Quarterly 21*, 564–573.

Trudgill, P. (2001) *Sociolinguistics: an introduction to language and society*. NY: Penguin.

Turvey, M. T. (1973) On peripheral and central processes in vision: inferences from an information processing analysis of masking with patterned stimuli. *Psychological Review 80*: 1–52.

University of Chicago Press staff (2003) *Chicago manual of style*. Chicago, IL: University of Chicago Press.

US Air Force (n.d.) *FLPP (Foreign Language Proficiency Pay)*. www-pom.army.mil/pages/dpmsd/Satellite%20Personnel%20Activity%20Main%20Page_files/flpp.htm

US Marine Corps (1998) *Marine Corps Order 7220.52C: Foreign Language Proficiency Pay (FLPP) Program*. Washington, DC: USMC.

Vaillant, G. E. (1993) *The wisdom of the ego*. Cambridge, MA: Harvard University Press.

Vygotsky, L. S. (1962) *Thought and language*. Cambridge, MA: MIT Press.

Wardhaugh, R. (2001) *An introduction to sociolinguistics*. Oxford: Blackwell.

Wennerstrom, A. K. (2003) *Discourse analysis in the language classroom: genres of writing*. Ann Arbor, MI: University of Michigan Press.

Wilkins, D. A. (1976) *Notional-functional syllabuses*. Oxford: Oxford University Press.

Wilson Learning Corporation (1999) *The do's and don't's in Sweden*. The Wilson Learning Corporation.

Wing, B. H., ed. (1986) *Listening, reading, writing: analysis and application*. NY: Northeast Conference.

Winne, P. H. (1995) Inherent details in self-regulated learning. *Educational Psychologist 30* (4), 173–187.

Wise, N. and L. L. Whitney (1998) *Passport Thailand*. Novato, CA: World Trade Press.

Witkin, H. A. and D. R. Goodenough (1981) *Cognitive styles: essence and origins: Field dependence and field independence*. NY: International Universities.

Wolfe, D. M., and D. A. Kolb (1984) Career development, personal growth, and experiential learning. In D. A. Kolb, I. M. Rubin, and J. M. McIntyre (eds.), *Organizational psychology: readings on human behavior in organizations* (4th ed.) (pp. 124–152). Englewood Cliffs, NJ: Prentice Hall, 124–152.

Wool, G. (1989) Relational aspects of learning. In K. Field, B. J. Cohler, and G. Wool (eds.), *Learning and education: psychoanalytic perspectives* (pp. 747–769). Madison, CT: International Universities Press.

Yamada, H. (2002) *Different games, different rules: why Americans and Japanese misunderstand each other*. Oxford: Oxford University Press.

Zorach, C. and C. Melin (2001) *English grammar for students of German*. Ann Arbor, MI: Olivia and Hill Press.

Index